Millie Kuil:
To our Transplanted

Roelfi

Peter C. Tillema

THIS WAY
OF LIFE

THIS WAY OF LIFE

Reflections of 800 country
women who express a common
philosophy that comes from
down-to-earth living

Compiled and edited by
MAUDE LONGWELL

from a quarter century of
"Letters from Farm Women"

Book Design and Cover Photograph
AL J. REAGAN
Art Editor, Farm Journal

FOREWORD

"This Way of Life" is an anthology of letters and verse written by country women to FARM JOURNAL over the past quarter century of the magazine's nearly 100 years.

There is a strong bond of sisterhood among farm wives who share the unique experiences of bringing up a family close to the soil. They tell us that it is so—in the letters they write and across the kitchen table when we visit them. They say: "Reading *From the Countryside: Letters from Farm Women* gives me such a lift, a feeling of kinship." . . . "It's heartwarming to read that so many women feel as I do about the land we live on." . . . "That could have been me writing! Each letter contains some thought or experience with which I can identify."

We—the editors who have read millions of letters— present this book as a permanent record of this meeting ground. Another reason: We know from letters we receive that thousands of non-farmers in towns and cities share a wistful yearning for the land. Today "back to the land" has become a recognized trend, particularly among the young urban disenchanteds. If you are one of these home- sick ones the book is for you, too.

Putting the volume together hasn't been without com- plications—how to select *the* contributions from an irresist- ible variety, most of them published in FARM JOURNAL, but some too good to discard even though lack of space had eliminated them from the magazine. We have tried to include a representative collection on typical subjects recurring over the years.

You will discover that this book has many uses. How convenient when you need some thoughts for a club program, a quote for roll call or a bit of wry humor to introduce your speech—a multifaceted source.

We believe the topics about which FARM JOURNAL readers write have universal appeal for women of all ages, all walks of life; and also for sensitive men who want to better understand their women.

As our readers take pleasure in writing to us, so we take pleasure in sharing their observations. We hope you will find some useful and inspirational gems.

The final paragraph of this foreword gets down to a very personal "why" of this anthology. For the compiling editor, racing to complete it before her scheduled retirement, the book is a gesture of love—and farewell.

God bless FARM JOURNAL. And bless all its contributors—past, present and forevermore.

MAUDE LONGWELL
Farm Journal Family Living Editor, 1947-1971

CONTENTS

Good Idea

Try borrowing someone's pet adventure, project or discovery. You are welcome! You don't have to pay it back, but you may wish to pass it along

Neighbors

We love our neighbors; while with them, we have a feeling of kinship and assurance that everyone has a cherished place in the scheme of things

Yesterday and Today

Time brings some astonishing developments. Pausing to survey a stretch of the road we've traveled— and the mile we're on now—we view a kaleidoscope pattern: the expendable old, and often-controversial new—and now and then a value that doesn't change

Wider World

When I was a little girl, I wanted to grow up and be a mama. Now that I have accomplished that, I want to "grow up" and be a person—in ways that extend myself and my world— and my role in the world

Awareness

. . . whatsoever things are lovely
. . . think on these things.

Awareness

Whence Cometh My Help

UNLIKE the Psalmist, I do not lift up mine eyes unto the hills. I live in the heart of the High Plains of Texas, and in these parts about the nearest thing to a hill are the little heaps of dirt excavated by home-building prairie dogs.

Being an early riser, I often go at dawn to our front door and look out across the spread of fields. The land lies table-level as far as eye can see, stretching its flatness to reach a blue down-curve of sky.

At times the field before me suggests a broad piece of fabric cut to the pattern of a particular season. The serenity remains constant, yet the field itself is forever changing. During winter its dull brownness may lie under snow, with nothing more than an occasional jackrabbit train adorning that white blanket. The sun lifts itself to cast a dazzling illumination over this expanse of emptiness.

The snow melts, and after that tractors wend up and down pulling plows that stir the soil to a rich new brownness. The smell of moist earth drifts across the road. . . .

The men plow, the spring rain falls on each straight-as-an-arrow row. The men plant, and in a little while green shoots begin to peek through the earth. They grow without a sound.

Spring green becomes the deeper green of summer as the stalks reach skyward. Workers still come occasionally, to set the aluminum tubes through which pours all-essential water for irrigation. The sun, with sultry authority, commands the stalks to stretch high.

The season progresses. The sky's indigo blue changes to hazy gray. My field's green begins to turn yellow brown, and on the tops of the straight stalks sit proud heads of grain. They ripen, pledging a rich harvest of grain sorghum. The men come again, with more machines; the brown and red-gold field gives up its wealth and becomes an expanse of stubble.

All this I can see through the year, contemplating the seasons from our front door. The tranquility and serenity of nothingness . . . then the birth of new life, the growth, the harvest . . . and again the waiting quietness.

It's a changing panorama that calms me, stills my anxieties and renews my confidence in the Divine Plan. My help comes from the Lord, who made heaven and earth, the hills *and* the prairie fields.

VERA DEAN WOFFORD

Awareness . . . in the garden

AFTER PLANTING SEEDS THAT APPEARED TO BE LIFELESS, AND LATER WITNESSING GOD'S MIRACLE OF RESURRECTION, I CAN NEVER FEAR DEATH

IRENE V. PETERSON

Prairie Men

*Hope swells in the heart of a prairie man
In spring, like sap that always finds the arms
Of maple trees. Each night and morning, from
The farm to the house, his burned-out yesterdays
And year-old dreams are trampled in the mud
Beneath his feet. Once more he works his fields
For planting time. Like winter wheat that grows
From sun-warmed ground, fresh dreams and hopes sprout green
In prairie hearts. Now life is good to all
Who till the earth—who turn black furrows up
To meet the sun, and prop small, new-born calves
On wobbly legs. This is a time for trust—
A summer-promising hour when men who plod
The knee-deep mud see phantom rows of corn.*

HELEN VIRDEN

More than a garden

Since our children are all grown and have homes of their own, I am often asked if I think it is really worth my time and effort to have a garden just for my husband and me.

Yes, I do! It's true, I know, that neither of us can eat radishes or onions anymore except when they are at their sweetest, most tender stages; that the peas are a lot of work for such small returns and that the lettuce soon gets wormy.

It's true, also, that I could use the time I spend in my garden on other things. However I have all winter to do other things. In the spring my nature responds to the call of the out-of-doors, and I am once more out there in "my sanctuary," planting seeds and sweeping winter cobwebs out of my soul.

CLARA YEAGER

Late Perception

His gardens have consisted, heretofore,
Of vegetables that did his countless hours
Of work and green thumb proud, and he was more
Than glad to let the women plant the flowers.
For "Flowers are women's business," he would say,
And never notice when the blooms were borne,
Fragrant and large and vivid, in the way
He paid attention to his beans and corn.

And so how strange it is to have him groom
His bed of pinks and candytuft, and sniff
The perfume, cherishing each dainty bloom
With his old eyes and heart. It is as if
He knows, for one so practical, just how
Tardy he is to harvest beauty now.

ELAINE V. EMANS

My catalog of dreams

The wind is howling from the north, a mixture of snow and sleet is falling and so is the temperature. An hour ago I fought my way to the mailbox, wondering if the result would be worth the effort. It was; for there in the mailbox was a breath of spring, a seed catalog.

Were there ever more luscious peaches or watermelons, crisper greens, more tender corn-on-the cob anywhere to compare with those you raise in front of a roaring fireplace during a January blizzard's raging?

This kind of gardening doesn't result in sore backs, late meals or delayed ironings. Nor does it bring children's grumbles over weeding. Your dream garden doesn't require much effort; of course you produce only dream food!

By contrast, real gardening demands that you plant, transplant, cultivate, irrigate, spray, prune . . . and you are required to do something with what you've grown. Freeze it, can it, force-feed it to the family, and you still have a surplus. You can't give the stuff away unless you're willing to pick and deliver it. I know.

Dream gardening is blessedly free of such difficulties and frustrations. Peas and corn don't get too mature, greens never go to seed,

15

radishes don't get pithy, tomatoes don't have blossom-end rot.

As my husband said when he saw this new seed catalogue, "Hope springs eternal." Next warm day I'll rebuild my hotbed and start another year's gardening-for-real.

CHARLOTTE A. SMITH

Green thumbs in snow time

Grow a garden in winter—in Minnesota? It's wonderful fun!

Last fall we stocked up on vegetable and flower seeds—some from our summer garden, some store-bought. Before freezing weather, we dug pailfuls of our best soil and planted our seeds in small pots.

You should see our zinnias blooming now! And the Indian corn, planted by 10-year-old Chuck, is several inches tall. There is also a mystery container with shoots coming up green, double-leafed, sturdy ... must be the "grape" tomato plants; we'll transplant them outdoors in the spring.

A three-tiered stand and a wide sill hold our miniature garden; the dining room's big window gets sun all afternoon. Kathy, four, is our watering chief. Both children are fascinated by how quickly the seeds sprout—almost overnight, it seems.

Just one problem: what to do when the squash vines grow too leafy and rampant for our window?

LORRAINE M. HALLI

Three rows of pleasure

When we planned our garden, I wanted three rows instead of just one for flowers.

My husband thought this was too much, but I planted zinnias, dahlias and gladioli. I tended them with loving care; every weed and blade of grass fell before my hoe. Finally the flowers began to bloom.

Now, who do you see walking down the colorful rows of flowers? My husband. "We'll plant more next year," he says.

I wonder if everyone receives as much pleasure from a few seeds and bulbs as we do.

GLADYS STEPH

Mary in my garden

When my grandmother came to this country from Germany as a young girl, she brought her exquisite little statue of the Virgin—and the tradition of growing a garden around it. Now, many years later, the statue stands in a place of honor against an old brick wall in my garden, watching over the flowers that I plant in Grandmother's memory. These are flowers which religion, folklore, and tradition associate with the life of Our Lady.

The garden begins blooming about Easter with violets and lilies of the valley. Violets are supposed to have sprung up in Mary's footsteps as she spoke the words, "Behold, I am a handmaiden of the Lord." The tiny lilies are sometimes called Our Lady's Tears.

In the shade, to the left of the statue, foxgloves bloom—Our Lady's Thimbles, the older folks used to call them. And here is rosemary which, according to legend, changed its blossoms from white to blue when Mary dried her baby's small garments on a rosemary bush during the flight into Egypt.

I have many roses in my Mary garden, and Madonna lilies. And when I kneel to work in this corner, I feel especially close to God.

KAY HEISTAND

Man vs. Morning Glories

No morning glories? What a pity!
  It isn't that they aren't pretty—
It's not because you don't like blue.
  And shouldn't we try something new?

You say they're such a mess by fall,
  I counter, dear, but aren't they all?
The gladioli, cosmos, phlox,
  And most of all, my hollyhocks!
Or could it be, my dear, that very
  Possibly you're just contrary?

KATHERINE TAUBE

(Could be what this is all about—
  He's spent the morning plowing 'em out!)

EDITOR

Perseverance

Most of us gardeners have days when we're sure that the weeds will inherit the earth, but we never give up. Tomorrow we'll be out there again, fighting the same old garden battle and taking pride in each little victory.

BONNIE KOPPMAN

Double pleasure in the garden

In summer I get more pleasure out of my flowers and vegetables both, because I sow flower seeds right along with carrots, beets and lettuce. The flowers give me beauty to feast on while I weed vegetables. As I pull a beet, I enjoy the zinnias.

Flowers that bloom all summer help cover up bare spots when the vegetables they've shared space with are gone. For example, my cosmos

17

are in bud at the time I pick green peas. The pea vines die away, but the cosmos bloom on into fall.

VERA A. THOMPSON

LIVING AND WORKING ON OUR FARM IS ONE LONG, CONTINUOUS SENSORY ADVENTURE

ON a summer evening, if you are very still, you can hear the earth cool. You can watch the wheat chaff dance with the breeze; if you turn west, you will see clouds meld into the sun. Rays of heat rise magically from the fields; watching them, you can drowse into the dreamland of your choice.

Harvest time means trucking time. Should the mood move you, sit on the edge of the truck box, ooze your toes into the freshly harvested grain, then sink to your knees in it. Five tons—quite a load! Each kernel shifts for place as you withdraw your legs from the grain's pressure.

Back to the cab! I hear the winged approach of flying ants—a swarm of black dots against the pink evening sky.

FRANCES McKENZIE ELLIS

Moving Day

When we moved in this morning
The house seemed strange, withdrawn—
Touched with the alien presence
Of those who have moved on.
But I've hung up ruffled curtains,
Put my plants along the sill,
Wound the clock and set it ticking . . .
Now the house is not so still.

I've hung up my favorite picture,
Found a cushion for his chair,
Set the coffee pot to perking—
Lovely fragrance fills the air!
Quick—a clean and pretty apron,
Plus a session with the comb.
Husband's waving from the barn door—
Suddenly we're home!

LULA LAMME

Morning bonus

This morning I left the house ahead of my husband for early chores. Mist and fog filled the valley below our hilltop home, so that the tree-tops looked like islands floating in a sea.

Did I ask for a miracle? I saw one: the silver of new-mowed pasture, a dark line of marching maples, a graceful streak of gold as our collie cut green trails through white dew.

A cow spoke low to her dancing calf, teaching her patience and faith. I listened as the corn prayed and a quail called amen. Already I have had my blessing this day.

MARY L. SCHOONOVER

Beauty in the commonplace

Brown, crusty loaves of bread freshly baked, a planter of scarlet petunias, sparkling windows that frame our farm scene, four small heads bowed in prayer . . . .

Ping, clatter, whoosh

Collecting stamps, salt - and pepper-shakers or antiques has never gripped my imagination; but I do have a collecting hobby; I col-lect sounds.

My sister started it when we were canning last summer. Listening to the sporadic ping of the jar lids as they sealed, she remarked that this was on her list of good sounds, along with others such as her baby's laugh and rain on the roof.

Since then I have been collecting my own good sounds: thunder on a summer day, wind blowing through pine trees, my husband's pickup driving in at day's end, our baby's contented sigh as she snuggles down to sleep.

Everyone has certain sounds that are special. My two teen-age brothers vote for the "come and eat" call. The most unusual favorite-sound comes from a friend. She says she likes to go outside after a heavy snowfall and listen to the stillness.

JANELL WHEELER

A variety of senses

A farm appeals to my senses. I like the distinctive odors of animals; the pungent smell of fresh silage, dust in the barn and new-mown hay; perfume of dew-covered lilacs and the light spring rain that empha-sizes their essence.

I like my feeling of relief when the last load of hay is safe from the sudden downpour. Sitting on a wagon full of bumpy corn, I am a prin-cess on a golden throne.

In my yard kittens play ring-around-the-rosy with their tails; the dog

19

tries to bully a toad into playing with him. I like to watch cool, wet weeds dissolve the dried mud on my boots.

Sounds on the farm are as numerous as the sights. The contented hog munching corn; the lonesome sound of a bullfrog; the terrified squeals of a gilt having her nose ringed.

Every sense is exercised as I become aware of things around me, and I know that life is good.

JEANNE SCHWARTZ

Prairie Mirage

Drouth has swept the prairie;
The grass is parched and brown,
Yet lakes of "water" shimmer
On the dusty road to town.
MARY DEAN WATERS

Everyday art

My favorite last-minute centerpiece: A bowl of white eggs—with light and shadow to capture their symmetry.

POLLY HUTCHINSON

Fruit Cake Baking

Step softly here, respecting royalty—
The queen of cakes is baking now! Yet sniff
Her fragrance without fear that you may be
Rude or uncomplimentary; catch the whiff
Of citron, lemon peel, pineapple wedges,
Of juicy raisins, dusky-hued and white,
Of cherries, walnuts, and, around the edges
Of fruit-scent, pick out cinnamon with delight.
She takes her own sweet time in baking, then
The mellowing will require time and care,
But she will reign majestically when,
With sprigs of green angelica for crown,
And long-awaited Christmas in the air,
Her court, anticipating her, sits down.
ELAINE V. EMANS

Awareness at breakfast

Do farm people become, through over-exposure to country living, immune to its joys? I'm afraid I did, till some house guests from the city spurred me to use my imagination.

Rather than the usual outdoor supper, which is often cut short by mosquitoes and evening damp, we had outdoor breakfast. We missed the sunrise by several minutes, but it was early enough that I didn't mind the oven's heat for baking muffins; and carrying the dishes and food outside didn't seem as tiring as it does at day's end.

Now we spice up our summer schedule by breakfasting outdoors on weekends and holidays. What a luxury to savor fresh morning air and birdsong as we sip our coffee!

BARBARA DREHER

Twilight Task

The children must be called in from their play;
Twilight is here. I open wide the doors,
And then the breath-arresting summer day
Comes plunging in to show its golden stores.

The fireflies start their ancient, sprightly dance
The grasses are astir with creeping things;
Our cat stalks prey with untamed glance
And insects sing or try small, gleaming wings.

What shame that little children must be led
From dewy grass, night smells and first-star sky
To such prosaic things as bath and bed
And furniture that cannot sing or fly.

MARGARET CHAPLIN ANDERSON

Fresh look at the world

We have a six-month-old baby at our house, and we can't wait to show her the world. She coos and coos over the little calves.

As we rush down a hilly path, she giggles—breathing in the summer breeze as if it were just *too* delicious. But we seem even more excited than she over the calves, the path, the breeze; I think we're taking lessons from our curious little bundle. Lately we sing every song we ever knew and create new ones just for her. Our baby has made us aware—to see, feel, taste and hear. By turning us "inside out," she's showing the world to *us*.

ELEANOR BREWER

Ice cream clouds

One summer we had three small children from Minneapolis staying with us—children who hadn't had much chance to enjoy God's out-of-doors.

One lovely quiet evening as the sun was slipping behind the horizon,

4-year-old Scotty came running into the house with a "Come quick," his brown eyes telling of some joy.

When I went outside the sun was casting its rosy glow on large, fleecy clouds. He stood enrapt: "Look!"

I'll admit it was beautiful—the more beautiful because a little child had noticed. I explained how my children had called those clouds "ice cream clouds." After a bit he nodded slowly and said—half to himself and half to me—"Raspberry."

KATHERINE MENKEN

Farm Kitchen

I like my kitchen. The big shining stove
With its friendly wood fire; copper kettle singing
Its contralto song; plump black pot
With its bubbling, savory stew. The rich, golden smell
Of corn bread ready to take from the oven blending
With the piquant spiciness of hot gingerbread.
I like the wide painted floorboards and the
Red geraniums in the windows; the little brown pots
With trailing ivy; the view of the road
Where I can watch the R.F.D. man drive up
To the mail box. I like to see the table
Set for supper, the red cloth, blue napkins
And cream-colored dishes. The cat lies curled
On the rocking chair cushion. Shep lies beside
The stove watching every move. Soon I'll
Hear his footsteps coming through the woodshed and the
Soft clink of milk pails. Storms may
Lash outside. Here in my kitchen all is warm and safe.

BLANCHE ELLIOTT PEARSON

A letter to Cassandra

We invited a nine-year-old girl to visit in our farm home last summer—through the *New York Hearld-Tribune's* Fresh Air Fund. It was an unforgettable experience that I can best explain with the letter I wrote afterward to our visitor.

Dear Cassandra: We hoped that we might entertain you and reveal to you some of God's wonders in nature. We wondered how you would react to the rolling green landscape in contrast to the city's tall buildings and fire escapes.

The two weeks we shared with you, Cassandra, were a joy to us all. Your happiness was evident in the tears you could not hold back when you said good-bye. We are glad you will hold pleasant memories of your vacation with us, but it is our family who is truly indebted to you.

How had we become so nonchalant about the lovely natural setting of our farm pond? Your squeals of delight, when you and our daughter, Jeaneen, swam together, turned our nonchalance into gratefulness. Exploring the fields with you, we wondered how the graceful swaying of the wheat and the green color of the corn had become so commonplace in our busy lives. With you, we thrilled again to a rainbow, and other wonderments we'd been taking for granted.

You have returned to the hubbub of New York, and we miss you. For you have given us something precious: a new awakening to God's wonders and a new zest for living. For this, we say, "Thank you."

JUNE JOHNS

Farm fragrances

After I received a delightful perfume as a gift, I listed some of the perfumes we can't buy by the ounce: freshly cut grass, homemade bread, laundry dried in the sun; moist earth after a shower, alfalfa or clover; a Christmas tree, flowers in pots or in the garden, smoke from a wood fire, candles burning, a tot in your lap after his bath.

GLADYCE SCHOTT

Monday—color it happy

This has been a blue Monday—and a wonderful one. My wash is drying under the bluest sky. I had coffee with a neighbor, out of a thin blue cup. I've filled my cobalt blue bottle with ivy—it looks lovely. And I'm just before putting the scissors into the beautiful blue stuff I got for kitchen curtains.

MILDRED BROWN DUNCAN

Awareness ... memories

TREAD SOFTLY ... THE YEARS ROLL OUT A CARPET OF MEMORIES FOR OUR HEARTS TO WALK ON

A professor once said to me, "As you live your life pick a bouquet of memories. When you are old, your bouquet will be your treasure. Pick a flower—a memory—and enjoy it. Think back on wonderful times. Some memories are not so fragrant, but they can be exchanged for others."

Based on his words, my philosophy has formed: Seek out the world's beauties; treasure worthwhile experiences as endless nourishment for the mind and spirit. This philosophy has helped me pick my life-time bouquet.

ALICE BURCYK

Water girl

The milk bottle filled with water and ice cubes was cold in my hand as I trudged up the hill. As I stepped across the prickly rows of cut hay, the water sloshed on my fingers. At the top of the hill I saw our orange tractor, followed by the red hay baler, followed by the wagon. Phil Anderson, our neighbor, drove the tractor, and my father stood at the top of the teetering load of hay, plunging hay hooks into the hard, rectangular bales as they emerged from the baler.

The two men stopped the caravan when they saw me coming, and climbed from their perches. My father took off the baseball cap he wore and wiped the ring of perspiration and hay chaff from his forehead. I handed him the bottle. "Um—good," he said.

I said, "Daddy, did you find any mice nests in the hay?" I was eight years old, and I was a farm woman.

MARYLOU WEBSTER THOMAS

Sign from heaven

Recently we moved into the house of my dreams, built on a high knoll. As we moved our final load, I held a large mirror and it reflected the night sky. That's how it happened that I approached our new home with a happy omen—a lapful of stars.

DAISY PAT STOCKWELL

I remember

Today I found one of my mother's old aprons. I took it from folds of blue tissue and tied it around my waist. The fine homespun material from Sweden fell almost to the floor—snowy white, bordered with crocheted lace. This was Mother's Sunday apron.

I remember her everyday aprons, too—generous lengths of calico or gingham. I can see her carry kindling, vegetables or eggs in her apron. The apron she always wore on baking days was a never-get-lost pot holder for taking bread from the oven.

With a vigorous flick of that apron Mother shooed chickens or animals from the garden. When unexpected guests came, Mother snatched off the solied apron, wiped my dirty face or did some quick dusting before she put on a clean apron and opened the door. Her apron was also a hiding place from which a shy child could peek.

And on cool summer evenings Mother would wrap her apron around me for warmth and protection from mosquitoes. Together we'd stand

and listen to the evening sounds.

What happy memories of childhood were brought by one priceless heirloom—my mother's apron.

ANNA KERTSCHER

Today I heard the corn grow

I laughed when my farmer husband told me, his city-reared bride, that corn makes a noise while it grows. But today I put on my sun hat, went to the field and listened.

Sure enough, the corn was making a crackling sound, for all the world like the purr of a happy kitten. When my husband comes in to dinner, I must tell him that I've heard our corn growing. It was a delightful experience, and a reminder of the presence of God in every living thing.

BESS DARNELL McKAIN

Four ages of sound

When I was 10 years old, my favorite sound was the call of the meadowlark as I walked across the fields to school.

At 16, it was the sound of cow bells jingling around the necks of my two prize heifers. At 20, I was quite sure I would never hear anything more thrilling than the foxtrot "Dardanella" played by the local Grange orchestra.

How was I to know, in those years of my immaturity, that the best sound of all my life would be three special "beeps" which my husband gives on the tractor horn each evening when he comes up the lane after a long day's work?

VIOLET PAULSON

To preserve the past

Recently we began tearing down the old red barn which has graced our farm more than 60 years.

As it came down, piece by piece, we shared the memories we associate with that weathered barn: the smell of animals and alfalfa in winter; sounds of calves slurping the last drop of milk; the exhilaration of sneaking up to the haymow to swing on the hay-rope trapeze (forbidden but fun!).

Now I'm making plans to keep these memories in tangible form. I have scrubbed and sun-dried pieces of board that are knotted, nail-holed, grooved and etched by years of exposure to the elements. I'll select pairs, trim them to 6" ·or 12" lengths (leaving the marks). Then I'll paint on them: field daisies, grapevines, horses with sleigh. My "old-barn primitives" will hang on the walls of our family room, linking past to present.

ELEANOR VOGNSEN

What price efficiency?

I promised myself that I would straighten up my recipe file today. I'd sort and discard, then type and file those to be saved. I'd even add an index.

But first I would bake cookies. It took some time to find the recipe— I knew it was written on pale green note paper. . . .

My thoughts went back to a rainy afternoon spent with Mary in her snug trailer house. Then I came across a recipe from Dot, one in Margaret's lovely handwriting and several others.

I couldn't destroy any of these! I folded them carefully, and put the box back in its place on the shelf. My memories were more important than efficiency.

ARDIS JOHNSON

Mending and remembering

Today, alone in the house, I've caught up with my long-neglected mending. Even repaired my husband's old work coat—it's been on vacation since summer arrived.

Where was I to find a piece of material to match the coat's grease-stained, faded green? It took quite a search, but at last I found something.

That torn pocket . . . I remembered the half-frozen, newborn calf that had caught its hoof in the pocket while being carried in Husband's arms to be thawed out in our kitchen. The gaping sleeve, snagged on a nail when Husband and I were building fence. Buttons missing—what farmer ever has time to wait for one to be sewed on?

Corn picking filled the coat with dust, and added more torn places. When Husband was too warm, he'd throw the coat on the ground; hence it's faded by the sun. Today, as I mended and cleaned this old garment for another season's work, I recalled how many purposes it has served: a "blanket" for a child napping in the field (our dog has even napped on it!); a cover to protect precious seed from rain; a shield for me when I'd forget my own coat.

I guess I am overly fond of old clothes because they call up happy memories. I did enjoy mending this ancient coat.

LUCILLE WYMAN

Weather or not

Our state is noted for its sunsets, but in the Sandhills of Nebraska we are more interested in clouds. I doubt if one in 10 of us can tell a cumulus from a cirrus or a nimbus. All we wonder is, do those clouds have rain in them?

BETTY CHRISTIANSEN

Awareness . . . philosophy

IT IS MUCH EASIER TO SEE GOD IN A
LOVELY LEAF OR A GROWING CROP
THAN IT IS TO SEE HIM IN THE RUNNY-
NOSED CHILD OF A NEIGHBOR WHOM
WE DISLIKE. YET, HOW MUCH MORE
IMPORTANT IT IS TO LOVE THE CHILD
AND TO LIVE IN HARMONY WITH HIS
PARENTS. FOR THE LEAF AND THE CROP
WITHER IN A SEASON, BUT WE SHALL
LIVE FOREVER

JOAN HAGEDORN

A S I stood in line at the grocery checkout counter, a little girl of
two kept pushing against me. She had her head down and I
thought she was just being playful while waiting for her mother.
When she hit her head against a rail, she whirled around and I saw she
was blind. I touched her to protect her from another bump.

Suddenly she grabbed my skirt and cried, "Mommy! Mommy!"

I bent down and put my arms around her. "I'm not your Mommy.
I'm her new friend." Her mother watched with grateful eyes.

As I watched them leave the store, I felt ashamed for having been
half-sorry for myself that day. God works in strange ways. I don't
know why He should deny a child her sight. I don't know why He
should deny me a child. I don't know why I should be called
"Mommy" for the first time in my life by a stranger's sightless child;
but I will never forget that it happened.

LAWANDA GUTHRIE

At the auction

I was at our farm sale today, and I overheard one woman's remark:
"It's a wonder they'd put that junk up for sale."

One by one the auctioneer held up my treasures. I had always liked
that dust mop; it was the only one that would go under Gramp's chair.

"Quarter! Let's hear 25¢!" the auctioneer shouted. "I'll throw in
the bedspread—now let's hear a bid."

While the bidding went on, I thought about the special "company
best" bedspread. I'd bought it before our daughter's home wedding,
had it on our bed when folks came to celebrate our 25th Anniversary,
and when they came to console because our son died.

Now, piece by piece, with laughter, people carried away our possessions. As I turned to my husband, he smiled at me and my heart filled
with quiet peace. Because my real, stored-up treasure folks can't see.

27

Exile

He was a country boy, and when he took
His leave, he stopped to give a last, long look
At the big red barn and silo, gray rail fences.
Now, overseas, he recalls with all five senses
The country things that he is fighting for—
A neighbor's friendly wave from a barnyard door;
The smell of hay in summer, and the sound
Of his pet colt's hoofs on the frosty ground
In winter; the taste of fresh, warm bread; the touch
Of wheat against his fingers.Oh, so much
He recalls! He aches to return, and will, some day,
When the reasons, the prickling conscience that took him away
Have been grappled with—and there's no more threat of harm;
Then he'll return—this exile—to the farm.

PAULINE HAVARD

Lesson from the birds

For two years a pair of cardinals have nested in a grapevine near our kitchen window. Watching them has given our family an insight into the love and consideration birds can show one another. I think the experience has made *us* more understanding and considerate.

IOLA EVENSON

Discovery

When I was a child, I thought that joy
Was a holiday or a bright new toy,
But when I was grown I found, instead,
That joy was the vow my true love said.
Yet oh, I was neither right nor wrong—
For joy may be a bobolink's song,
Or a kitten's unrehearsed ballet,
Or a glow in hearts at the end of day,
Or break with the morning, pure, starlit.
Joy wears the garb we make for it.

ELAINE V. EMANS

What's your treasure?

Just thinking about our quiet, peaceful creek, beautiful in its solitude, makes me feel good. When there are just the fish and I and silence, I can be myself, benign or ornery. For a short while I am nobody's mother and nobody's wife, nobody's 4-H leader, nobody's secretary, reporter or committee chairman. I am just I, with a couple of lovely hours to spend.

No wonder—when our speaker at club meeting asked us women what one precious possession we'd take if we moved to a country like Brazil—I answered instantly: "My fishing rod!"

FRANCES ANN JONES

Genesis

I often feel when God made pink
He must have also formed the rose—
Tinting with this tender ink
Cool flesh of petals; added scent
As delicate as heaven knows;
And blood-red thorns for covenant.
While in the bud, with Infinite art,
Was hid a golden crown for heart.

JANE CARTER

Tranquility by the river

As I walk past my windows and gaze at the river—calm and quiet, reflecting the trees and the sky—I feel tranquilized.

The whirlpool flow of the river inspires me to rush with my chores so that I can walk along the stream bank and renew my spirit.

My husband and I are thinking of trading farm locations to expand our operations. The idea brings sadness; "my river" may not be worth much to the busy world of finance, but to me it's beyond price.

MARCELLA MARTIN

My new, audible world

Those of us who are hard of hearing have a terrific problem. You don't enjoy other people when you can't hear. It's a strain to figure out what they are talking about. You get ill-tempered, and your friends get annoyed by having to repeat.

So what to do? Crawl in a shell and let the world pass you by, or buy a hearing aid and get in the swim? I bought the hearing aid.

That didn't completely and immediately solve the problem. After being fitted you can't just sit back and suddenly begin hearing perfectly. Hearing is one thing; understanding is another.

Some sounds you haven't heard for so long, you have to learn from scratch, as a baby does. I went for a walk and discovered that birds were singing; they hadn't sung for me for years! I listened to crickets chirp, the wind rustle in trees, the brook chatter. It all sounded lovely, once I learned to sort out one sound from another.

Voices—especially when several people are in conversation—can be confusing to one accustomed to relative silence. (One thing about a hearing aid—if voices blast the eardrums, you can turn them off!) But I didn't let myself get discouraged; I wore my aid everywhere I went. And although it has never become second nature, the inconvenience of it is petty when compared with my joy in rediscovering the sounds life offers all around us.

HELEN B. ZIERER

Of Things That Are Lovely and Fleeting

The dust on the piano keeps better than the flashing
Of loveliness, keeps better than the clean slant of wings
Across the cool garden, where the honeysuckle berries
Call the brown song sparrow that balances and sings.

The undone ironing keeps better than the beauty
Of the star-hung plum tree in the drying yard,
And the undarned socks will outlast the radiance
Of a sunset's glory to its last bright shard.

The tarnish on the spoons keeps better than the mischief
In a wee girl's eyes or the sunlight on her hair,
And the stacked supper dishes will long outlast the clinging
Of a small boy's arms and his little whispered prayer.

Ah, life is so short and earth is so beautiful,
And boys and girls are children for such a little while—
So we run in the orchard and look for four-leafed clovers,
And we know a spotless house isn't worth a baby's smile.

LEONA AMES HILL

A short visit to another world

Yesterday I walked into a winter-white world—and returned transformed. I had only to cross the road to our farm's South Forty. The day was calm; gray haze was silvered with sunshine.

As I followed the logging trail into the woods, I felt the snow compact beneath my boots. A solitary curled oak leaf, clinging to its mother tree, rustled overhead from the stirrings of some winged creature.

Moved by a passing gust, wild blackberry canes rattled against each other above the snow. The wind shook ebony elderberries like tiny castanets, then sighed away. Sheets of birch bark crackled softly, curling like paper in a fire.

Etchings made by little feet crossed the trail, and I knew that other creatures besides myself were here. White-bellied pack mice had been very busy; rabbit tracks cut deeply and a mink or weasel had left paw prints.

I sat in filtered sunshine on a stump to the leeward side of a small knoll. I listened, I looked up. Miles above, it seemed, the wind swelled to a low, dull roar like the bass tone of an organ. Yet near where I sat, not a crumpled fern frond moved. It was as if the wind was trying to tell me, here in this sheltered spot, about the greatness of the universe.

I held my breath to catch each fragment of sound; for winter woodland sounds can be quiet—everything is wrapped in waiting hibernation.

But unseen, unheard things are happening. Sap is rising, buds are swelling, inquisitive eyes are peering. Soon, with melting snows, winter must give way to spring.

Then I will return to this place of communion. Things will look different; but high above, if I listen, I will hear God's wind.

ELVERA OLSON

Why, it's beautiful!

"What's the most beautiful thing you can think of?" Dad asked us at the breakfast table. Mary said a rose; Bill said his new horse. Someone asked Dad what he thought.

"Young corn pushing up through red sandy soil . . ." Dad paused and looked down at his cantaloupe with its delicate shading of salmon becoming pale green near the rind. "Mighty pretty, isn't it? Sliced tomatoes are just as beautiful."

The younger children could hardly wait for lunch really to "see" sliced tomatoes. Soon they noticed their centerpiece—spikes of carrots, red cabbage leaves, sprigs of Queen Anne's lace.

Now at nearly every meal someone calls attention to everyday beauty we hadn't noticed before. We enjoy our food more—and each other.

LUCILE HUNT

Inheritance

We never grudged the endless time devoted
to rubbing highboys, keeping pewter coated
with frosty radiance, the paisley shawl
aired against threat of moth or mildew. All
were treasures of the household, legacies
from stout old generations. Tending these
was somehow keeping faith with men who poured
into this land their power's mighty hoard,
then at last their bodies.
Now we find

the other precious things they left behind,
hewn out of courage, moral fear and danger,
a valiant dream which welded foe and stranger
into one strength. These too are not bequests
to stow away in cupboards, attic chests:
The Bill of Rights, whose weathered doctrines age
the Mayflower pact, a single lucid page;
as sturdily as oak; that Declaration
handloomed upon heartstrings of a nation,
dyed from its veins—this heritage no less
needs the long patient care, the watchfulness.

F. B. JACOBS

Lucky girl

Somewhere tonight a millionaire sits smiling as he studies the stock exchange which has made money for him today.

I am rich tonight, too. I've just been sitting on our saggy sofa, thinking about my wealth.

The sun came out late this afternoon and the clothes got dry after all! The baby is fed and bedded down for the night. The older girls look like cherubs in their clean pajamas. They're eating now so they can see Disneyland on television. Ann's cough is much better today.

My husband is on his way home, bringing the sitter. We are going out, decked in our best (the cleaners did a beautiful job on the black dress I made over).

We are celebrating our 10th anniversary tonight!

MILDRED B. DUNCAN

Idea in a cloud

One long-ago day my toddler brother watched a dark, wind-propelled cloud momentarily sweep sunlight from the meadow. As he looked, he asked, "How can such a little cloud shut out a big, bright sun?"

To remember his wondering question restores my perspective at times. When confronted with trivial troubles and everyday "vexasperations," I remind myself: It's just a temporary cloud—too little to make a big or long-lasting shadow.

DORINE R. TUPPER

Family

We're an average family: We dislike war
between countries, strife between brothers
and weeds between vegetable rows. We like
a crackling fire on a blizzardy night, a
comfortable bed after a hard day's work,
and everyone sitting down to the table at
once when mealtime arrives.

Family

Family . . . traditions

TRADITION HAS IT IN THIS FAMILY THAT
EVERY GROUNDHOG DAY WE TURN THE
LIVING-ROOM RUG END ABOUT. WHY?
BECAUSE WE STARTED THAT PRACTICE
WHEN THE RUG WAS NEW. TURNING IT
MAKES LITTLE DIFFERENCE NOW; BUT TO
OUR KIDS, WHO LEND A HAND WITH
THIS SORT OF THING, TRADITIONS ARE
NOT CASUALLY PUT ASIDE

MARCELENE BELL

W E have family customs which we enjoy as a farm family because they are rooted in the soil.

The first day of spring, we go into the woods and pick wildflowers
to make bouquets for shut-ins. We also spring-decorate the church
with dogwood boughs.

In summer we work our experimental garden. Each member of the
family has a row where he can grow anything from mint to the latest
hybrid corn. We have a watermelon cutting on the Fourth of July,
and in the sweltering months we rent a cottage on the beach for one
weekend of deep-sea fishing.

In the fall we go possum hunting and for long walks in the woods
to gather pine cones and other offerings of the season. When we grind
our cane, we label one can of syrup Gingerbread Project. That's for
Christmas; during the holidays we make gingerbread boys and girls
for the children in a hospital.

Other customs which we enjoy are not exclusively the birthright of
farm families. Our two favorites are holding hands for grace at meals,
and setting the table with our best china on birthday mornings, for a
festive breakfast.

JO McGLAMERY

Antique swimming pool

When my husband's grandfather built a cement tank for garden irrigation on his homestead, little did he realize that he was providing a neighborhood swimming pool for generations to come. Our children are the third generation to enjoy his handiwork.

The pool is approximately 3' deep and 17' across. Each year with the help of the older children I patch-cement the tank and fill it for Memorial Day. That's when the clan arrives for our annual family reunion.

Our pool has been a nerve and time-saver to neighborhood mothers. The nearest town pools are miles away. And with the shortage of hired help, licensed drivers have been drafted for tractor duty.

The teen-agers enjoy the pool after work and on Sundays. When it is time to change pool water, they leap from their tractors at quitting time and jump into the pool, fully clothed, with shrieks of delight.

SARAH K. CARLSON

Camping in the barn

Hay is for horses and hay is for sleeping! "May Tim and I sleep in the hay tonight?" asked 12-year-old Bob. "Sorry," I replied, "the girls have reserved the hayloft. Tomorrow is boys' night."

And sometimes it's family night. Then, only two turtles, five guppies and a parakeet sleep in our lovely modern six-bedroom house. Mom, Dad and children, from the teen-agers to toddler, are in the barn.

We all have sleeping bags and enjoy camping, but the inconvenience of a time-consuming trip is eliminated when the family makes an exodus to the barn. Sounds of Little Paint and Rocket munching hay make a nice background for Daddy's story about "when I was a boy," and Dad's ears are first to sort out from other noises the hooting of an owl. Susan takes a bag of popcorn for a snack; we do some star-gazing through the loft door. Then comes sleep, only to be ended by Bubblegum, the banty rooster routinely saluting the dawn.

Togetherness? We've got it when our coal-black kitten Arthur Asphalt, and Shep the dog, join us to sleep in the sweet-smelling hay.

DOROTHY JOHNSTON

Reunion highlight

Although my 80 kinsmen are scattered over the U.S., most of us gather for the Labor Day weekend reunion we hold every five years.

In 1925, Uncle John, a lawyer and historian, organized a committee to preserve our fast-diminishing family ties. This committee arranged the first reunion, and over the years the members have helped to keep ours a lively organization. Each branch of the German Hauberg family is represented.

Because we meet only every five years, everyone makes a big effort to attend. The Committee takes care of details in advance, even hiring a cook and lifeguard. And my, what fun we have! We always choose a campsite near a river or lake to be sure of swimming, boat trips, nature hikes, campfire suppers and songfests. We've given plays and one year Aunt Katie demonstrated her skill on the spinning wheel.

On Sunday we attend church and if possible plan a tour of ancestral homes and burial sites.

The closing event is always a business meeting to arrange finances and make tentative plans for the next get-together. We also take time to collect pictures and family history, and to read aloud letters from the folks who couldn't come. Then we write up a journal of events to mail later to each family.

We go home with warm memories. It's wonderful to belong to a big merry family, and I think Uncle John started a tradition our people will want to keep for years to come.

HELEN SIMPSON

Fun at the dam

Fishing is a summer habit for our family—a nearby dam provides us with a pool. Our crew will settle for anything that bites. Or for no catch at all! Youngsters' cheerful jabber may scare away bass, but it's music to my ears . . . worth letting home chores wait.

NORMA BUSH

Family . . . happenings

A FAMILY HAPPENING CAN BE A ONCE-IN-A-LIFETIME SPECTACULAR OR IT CAN EXPAND INTO A CUSTOM

L AST summer we got extravagant and invested in a big, old-fashioned ice-cream freezer. It has paid wonderful dividends in inexpensive, friendly entertainment. It is equally popular with young, middle-aged and old. No one has yet refused an invitation to one of our freezer parties!

Our neighbors join forces with us, bringing their own freezers, ice or ingredients. Our city friends, too, love an invite to enjoy oldtime ice cream. In fact, one town couple says often: "Come see us—and bring your freezer!"

MRS. D. J.CARSON

Our camp has wheels

After haying was done and other chores attended to, we started our vacation, leaving the farm in our relatives' care.

With our five children in the back of our station wagon and a well-packed 15′ camper, we headed west to New York State via the Mohawk Trail, then on to the Great Lakes region, and finally on to Canada.

We climbed mountains, saw glaciers and lots of animals. I thought we would head home then, but my husband was closer to Alaska than ever before and couldn't resist an opportunity to make his dream to go there a reality. It was an adventurous trip up the Alaska highway: beautiful scenery, good facilities, meetings with other campers—even an old gold prospector. And we got in some fishing.

We arrived home after Labor Day, exhausted from seven weeks of travel. The children were marvelous travelers and campers; keeping them entertained was never a problem. The trip meant much more because the children shared the experience with us. So guess what? Now we're planning our next trip.

BARBARA BARTLETT

Snowbound interlude

In the winter my farmer husband works away from home, our two boys go to school and I attend to the house and chores. We seldom find time to sit down and just talk.

Well, as a result of a big snowstorm, we had four days of the closest companionship. It was my first experience of being snowbound. My husband, who has lived in this state all of his life, warns me every winter to "stock up, just in case." The storm caught me unprepared, though; we had to get along on limited provisions.

But what compensations! We got to know each other all over again. We played games the boys had received for gifts—games we grown-ups had never before shared. Between corn-popping and cookie-baking, we found that our 10-year-old is interested in how seeds germinate and grow; and that his younger brother is a whiz at drawing "treasure maps." We discussed big, improbable projects like turning our place into a fabulous, wealth-attracting dude ranch.

Now I'm trying to recapture "snowbound" closeness for my family at least one evening a week the year round. We can't rely on the weather to rescue us from separateness.

CLARA TELARICO

Back to taffy

Although I fondly recall impromptu taffy pulls our family used to enjoy on blizzardy nights in Montana, I never suspected that my youngsters' teen-age friends would go for such old-fashioned fun.

But last winter our son and daughter returned from a meeting of their church youth group with the news that they had to supply candy for a sale.

What could we make? I asked, what about my mother's favorite, taffy? So after supper we lit in. As word got around, teen-age friends dropped by, curious about the taffy. While we waited for the stuff to cook, we told stories and riddles.

When the bubbling mixture spun a thread from the spoon, we divided it on buttered saucers. Gingerly, five pairs of buttered hands started fingering the cooling taffy. Buttered or not, beginning pullers invariably got stuck—with lots of excitement over getting unstuck.

After the candy was pulled and shaped, we all agreed that for a spur-of-the-moment party for the high school crowd, you couldn't beat a taffy pull! Here's the candy recipe we used:

Combine 2 cups molasses with 1 tablespoon vinegar in a 6-quart kettle. Add 2 tablespoons butter; cook over low heat, stirring constantly, until the taffy threads from the spoon or becomes brittle when dropped into cold water. Remove from heat; stir in ½ teaspoon baking powder and 1 teaspoon vanilla; pour onto a buttered plate. When cool, pull until glossy. Makes 1 pound.

VERA LUND PRAAST

The day we won't forget

Thunder rolled in the distance on that warm day in June, as our teen-age daughter and her friend returned from a horseback ride. While they got ready for the high school's senior concert, rain began to fall, then hail.

Suddenly the warning came: Tornado! We huddled together prayerfully in the ominous quiet of our basement while destruction hovered and descended. Later, when we went up to ground level, we saw sunshine, and we saw something else: a white foamy tunnel rolled away across our fields, having wrought havoc on our home, yard, buildings, and crops. The cattle were wild, machinery twisted, our horses were dead.

We were lucky to be alive. And how thankful we were, not only for each other but also for the catastrophe's effect on our children.

Immediately they shared the heartbreak and work which are the inevitable aftermath of such a storm. When parents' patience wore thin, the 12-year-old would observe understandingly: "This summer was a hard one for you."

Yes, children can mature in a few weeks—sometimes faster and more drastically than they should. Yet, to become mature is to gain insight, and the empathy that will make them better human beings.

LOIS ROBINSON

A touch of graciousness

Meals are pretty informal at our house. With three children and little time, the easiest and most spillproof table setting seems best.

Then it was Easter morning, and I kept thinking of the family dinner we used to have in my parents' home. Best china, flower centerpieces, place-cards and the small frills that make a dinner complete. With a feeling of nostalgia, I went to work on my own family table.

Out went the plastic cloth, on went a good linen one. Our everyday dishes were replaced by the best china. Individual salad plates took the place of one serving bowl.

When we were ready to eat, the children acted accordingly. Barbara was so thrilled that she sat speechless. Gordon went back to recomb his hair before sitting down. Janice's manners became careful. My husband's "Sure looks nice" and quick hug made it complete.

All I could think of was, "Why haven't I done this before?" It didn't take 10 minutes extra time, the food was just what it would have been anyway (we always eat well) but was served more attractively. And we all received pleasure from our holiday dinner. Something tells me this will develop into one of our nicest traditions.

DOROTHY BROWNFIELD

Family . . . Dad

MY DAD'S A FARMER, A COMPLETELY LOVABLE GUY WHO IS REALLY ATTACHED TO THE SOIL. HE'S NEVER FOUND A PATCH OF WEEDS HE CAN'T CONQUER, OR A PIECE OF GROUND HE CAN'T BABY INTO GROWING SOMETHING

M Y dad works hard, and I love him—especially when he comes in from the field plumb tired, his balding flattop sticking straight up, and says "Let's all go out for a root beer."

When a crop is ready to harvest, Dad goes out to the field, grins all over his face and says, "Lookit all that money out there!"

Dad's proud of his work, and I am proud of him.

JOYCE CRANSTON

What keeps Dad young

Every girl believes that her father is invincible, yet a boy at heart. I'm no exception, though for a long time I worried about my dad because *he* worried so—over crops and money.

I often remember one dark, freezing night when Dad, with discouragement in his eyes, was hurrying to light smudge-pots in our fruit grove. Our whole family was running! The orchard looked eerie in the dark, as if warding off evil hexes and spirits.

My memory of Dad is variable, though. One dusk the next summer the farm was lighted up differently—with a huge, radiant sunset. There had been an electrical storm and the big thunderheads were just moving away. They seemed like great piles of raspberry and peach ice cream in pearl gray dishes. Daddy was outside, just standing as I was, staring at the magnificent spectacle. Then I saw that my father, so strong and serious, was a sensitive man—especially sensitive to nature's beauty. I'd never realized this quality in him before. I think this is what keeps him young, for he has never given up his dreams or the sensitiveness of youth.

HELENA FRACCHIA

Later than I thought

How many times I have wished that I had managed to be with my father more in his last years; that I had really settled down and listened to the stories he delighted to tell about his younger days.

I am the poorer for having failed to give my best attention as he unfolded tales of his rich, busy life; and he would so have enjoyed my being an appreciative audience.

I'd keep telling myself that some day, when things slacked up a bit, I'd get Dad to recount these stories in detail. I even planned to write them down for his grandchildren to enjoy. But it was always a thought for the future; the present was full.

He loved to talk of life in the Old Country; of his attack of "America fever," that intense desire to come to this land of plenty. Of his long, hazardous trip across the ocean; his trials as a Scandinavian in a new land. Of early logging days in Minnesota, settling a homestead, beginning a little country store, serving as postmaster, giving land for a church and helping build it . . . and, along with other things, raising a family of 10.

I only hope that those who still have their parents will spend more time really listening to their experiences. I wish I had.

MRS. F. W. ROSEBERG

Letter to my dad

Dear Dad: Do you realize that you help me—your teacher-daughter—pass along the values I learned on our South Dakota farm?

For instance, I can cope with tragedy and help my students face disappointments. How come? Remember the time our June's blue-ribbon calf ate too much ground grain, so that it bloated and died the very day before it was to compete in the Western Calf Show? You helped us learn from experience and look forward to another chance.

I've seen you walk through wheat fields that were ruined with rust, saying, "Next year we'll have a better break." (Most farmers live in next-year country.)

I encourage my pupils to develop your brand of courage and honesty. You gave me my first real lesson in truthfulness. . . . We were on a long trip. At a filling station June and I bought bottles of pop. A sign said: "2¢ deposit on each bottle," but we were sneaky! Well, 20

41

miles down the road, you noticed the bottles and asked, "Did you pay the deposit?"

We didn't dare lie. You turned the truck around and back-tracked so that two sheepish little girls could make amends.

Because you cared, Dad, I am now a teacher. You cared enough to drive me—50 miles round trip—to and from school. I have my degree because you and Mom so much wanted me to have a good education that you didn't own an overcoat and Mom wore the same green coat for nine years—to save money for my college expenses.

I believe passionately in America because you taught me to. You took a day off from planting wheat and took us kids to see the Freedom Train. You wanted us to see the documents of our nation's birth: the Declaration of Independence, the Constitution.

Dad, you are also special to me because you are a symbol of hundreds of farmers—men who believe in independence, who are responsible citizens and taxpayers, who have faith in the future. I'm trying to share your kind of faith with the Now Generation.

JOANE McKAY

Every year in springtime

The living room sofa has been converted into a comfortable sickbed. Teen-age daughter is fixing hot lemonade. Five-year-old Sonny is refilling the hot-water bottle. Mom rubs the patient's back and soothes him with loving hands.

Has there been an accident? No—"worst darn cold ever had . . . ache all over . . . feel awful . . . can't go through another day like this."

But family adoration is the best of medicines, and Papa quickly becomes his jolly, healthy self again.

NORENE RANNELLS

Priceless gifts

As a teen-ager during the depression years I longed for things which our family's flattened purse could not buy. Now I am aware of the many wonderful advantages our impoverished parents did provide for us children.

Many college graduates would give a lot for the training in English which we received from our parents, whose own use of the language was excellent. Now it is natural for us to use the effective word, the correct construction.

When we begged Dad and Mother for a radio back in the Thirties, our father bought instead a used phonograph with a supply of records. Listening to the recordings of John McCormack, Schumann-Heink, Fritz Kreisler, we grew to love and appreciate good music.

And our parents taught us to work. Although we disliked Dad's checking up on us, now we know why he insisted that the job at hand be done thoroughly.

Now that all of us children have ourselves become parents, we are deeply grateful to Mother and Dad for their unique gifts to us, for these gifts add up to a legacy that money couldn't buy.

HELEN CUBIT

Family . . . Mother

OUR MOTHER WAS BAFFLING, UNPRE-DICTABLE, INCONSISTENT—AND WON-DERFUL. HER ADMIRABLE QUALITIES INCREASED AS WE GREW OLDER!

I remember a dismal, blizzardy Saturday morning when a bitter wind invaded all corners of our old house. Dressed in sweaters, we children—all seven—gathered in the kitchen.

Through the frosted window we could see swirls of snow beating across the frozen garden, piling into gigantic drifts. We weren't happy to be shut in like that! "I want to make a snowman," Sharron whined. Nine-year-old Dick added forlornly, "I want to go outside and play." And younger brother Dave said, "We planned to dig a cave in a drift."

Mother stepped into the icy pantry and brought out a black iron griddle. "You'll have all winter to play in the snow. Put some wood in the stove, Bob, I'm going to make pancakes."

Seated around the table, we watched her beat eggs in the big yellow bowl, add the remaining ingredients and then start a saucepan of brown sugar, water and maple flavoring for syrup. The blessing was short and we attacked the pancakes with gusto. Mother, still at the stove, said, "I'll make you a pancake snowman, Sharron, since you can't go out and make a real one."

She dropped three globs of batter from the spoon, added two smaller drops for arms. A snowman began to form, bubbling merrily; Sharron was delighted when he was placed on her plate.

"Make me one!" Penny begged.

Mother spooned out more batter. "I'll make you an elephant." We watched, fascinated, while Penny's elephant took shape.

Our oldest brother Bob wanted to make one himself, so Mother handed him the bowl and spoon. While she ate her breakfast, we took turns at dipping batter and forming strange, lumpy creatures on the griddle.

By now the floor was sticky, the griddle caked with batter. Who cared? We had laughed and shared one of those "remember when" experiences and, unreprimanded, made a glorious mess. Not until years later did we begin really to appreciate our mother, who thought more of pleasing us children than of keeping a tidy kitchen.

BETH APPLEGATE

Mom's rule for child rearing

My first-born, Stuart, was five months old when I first went back to the farm to show him off to his grandmother. I had read Dr. Spock and was confident that I could rear my son with common sense and with a minimum of grandmotherly counsel. But my mother gave me a handy piece of advice that has become a family proverb.

Stuart was on her living-room rug making brave but not-so-effective attempts at crawling, talking to himself and to the rug pattern. My mother and I started to the kitchen to attend to woman work and woman talk. "Maybe I'd better bring the baby. He'll probably miss us," I babbled.

"Leave contentment be," Mother answered and put me to work.

Stuart is three now and Alison is six months, and I have learned to value those moments when a child has lost himself completely in a fascinating something. The most time- and energy-saving rule of child rearing that I know is "Leave contentment be."

SABRA MILLER

Mother-in-law's role

When my husband and I began housekeeping, I considered advice from his parents as interference. It wasn't until 20 years later when our own son married, that I realized our parents had tried to advise us only because they loved and wanted to help us. They wanted to keep us from making mistakes. But we young people wanted to try out our own ideas.

I'm sure our son and his wife feel the same way. So, if she wants to tint his hair green, I won't say a word!

ALBERTA VAN GILDER

"Ideal mother"—a teen opinion

We all admire a mother who isn't afraid to call the shots, one who doesn't fear that her discipline will lessen love.

When we're told to be home by midnight or forbidden to see a current movie, we realize your concern for us. We may fuss, "You don't love me," but we admire you because you're concerned. Once you've said no, don't back down—we have little respect for someone who doesn't stick to decisions.

Please don't try to buy our affection. Don't equate love with gift-giving—an outing with you or a special dinner will win over cologne every time. Your time and interest mean much more to us.

Most of all, we want a mother we can confide in—to share hopes and dreams; someone who listens and speaks out, too, so we'll learn more about each other.

You may wonder why we ramble on about the new boy in our class; but if we can't talk about our heart-throb, how will we be able to discuss the qualities of the man we might one day marry?

We can't always be mother's little girl—but sometimes we wish we could. At times we'll want your guidance (growing up is hard on us!). When it comes time for us to leave home, try not to worry. With your upbringing and encouragement, we'll become worthy of your love and confidence.

How could she do that to me!

It was a little thing that brought on this outburst. As little as a baby tooth hanging from the middle of a black thread and displayed for the umptieth time by my husband's mother, at my expense.

We were having company—people John and I hadn't seen for years. Inevitably Mother, who lives with us, must show her souvenirs. Our Ray, nearly 15, squirmed with embarrassment as she held up the two clothespins with which she "hung up his first little didy." But it was *I* who squirmed when she dangled that tooth!

"Lillian (that's me) always put up such a fight to keep everything about her children sterile," Mother jibed, "and then didn't she pull Ray's first tooth with a black thread!"

Everyone laughed, including me. But for a long time my laughter has had a hollow ring when my children's grandmother brings up something to belittle me.

She—my mother-in-law—is a fine person. She would have to be, to bring up as wonderful a man as my husband. I love her dearly—but I wish she'd stop making me out to be a simpleton.

Family ... grandparents

SOME LUCKY KIDS HAVE DISCOVERED THAT GRANDPARENTS ARE EXTRA PARENTS—WITH TIME ON THEIR HANDS AND UNDERSTANDING IN THEIR HEARTS

HOW do some families get along without a grandmother in the home? When our children were small, their grandma was their ally. She could always spare time—to build with blocks, hold the baby, read a story out loud, play dominoes, or tell true stories of her younger years.

As the kids went through adolescence, she was never shocked by their confidences, although they *tried* to shake her up. Let one of them win an honor at school . . . Grandmother produced a batch of herfavor-ite-doughnuts and held a celebration.

Grandmother's presence has taught our children, first hand, some important lessons in love, respect and tolerance. She has given us all the experience of three generations living together happily, each learning from the other.

Of course she is sometimes cross and bossy, and so are we all!

Turnabout

In Grandma's kitchen, after Sunday church,
The huge old oven warmly browned its pies,
As reverently Grandma'd pat the dough and perch
Her light bread on a window sill to rise.
Translucent glasses spoke of hilltop berries;
The milk would cool, the chicken pop and sing,
And eagerly I'd climb the dictionaries
To slip the napkin from its silver ring.
Now Grandma's first to notice and applaud
My paper napkins or new mats of plastic,
While heaps of golden drumsticks lately thawed
Find her, each Sunday, more enthusiastic.
And twinkling eyes acclaim a bright granddaughter
Whose angel food springs magically from water.

ALICE BOYD STOCKDALE

All in the point of view

At 44, I am about to become a grandmother. How thrilling it will be to be young enough to enjoy my grandchild, to be his friend and be able to enjoy the things he enjoys.

I feel sure that grandmothers in general aren't as old as they used to be. I remember my own gray-haired grandma—she'd have abhorred a dye job. We children loved her enormously, but we didn't think of her as fun. Then there was my own mother—grandma in her turn. She spoiled our youngsters, rocked and sang to them and humored their every notion. How patiently I taught them to respect her age and save her strength by running errands for her.

Being an elderly grandparent must be a rewarding experience that helps fill the long, inactive years. But I'm glad my grandchildren will have a young grandmother to remember.

Excuse me a minute—here comes my seven-year-old son with question marks in his eyes. What did you say, dear? Will I still be alive when you get married?

Well, goodbye, folks. This is where I came in.

MARY RUTH DULING

46

Unsung grandheroine

Where the stork goes, there goes Grandma. That's especially true of today's globe-trotting grandmas.

Baby books instruct young mothers-to-be to pack their overnight bags several days in advance of B Day; Grandmother usually packs hers at the same time. If the expectant family already has children, she goes sooner, to wipe noses, pack school lunches and keep everybody fed while Mama is in the hospital.

Grandmother never feels more welcome than when she is met at the station—or airport—by a nervous new father who drives her home, where a wan, uncertain young mother (with infant in arms) awaits her arrival.

If Grandpa goes with Grandma, he has an heir-raising good time. He polishes up his baby-burping skill and warms bottles like crazy. He doesn't mind; he'd rather bottle and burp Baby than feed himself from the freezer while Grandma attends the new monarch.

No doubt Grandpa—influenced by Grandma—has spent lavishly on the layette. But there's one compensation: Grandma always finds some feature about the beautiful baby that causes it to resemble him!

JANE BAUMAN

December romance

Grandfather had been alone for several years when he announced to the family that there was going to be a wedding—his.

The very idea! Why couldn't an old man act his age?

After the wedding, our family relations limped along until one day our six-year-old said (oh, the simple wisdom of youth!): "Aren't you glad Grandpa got married? He's so happy now!"

Ashamed? Yes, I was, and after that Grandpa's new wife became truly part of the family.

First grandchild

When our Erin Eileen was born, a first grandchild, she got a letter from her grandfather, an Iowa farmer. Here's the gist:

Dear Erin Eileen: My, what a pretty name—ethereal, poetic, musical—and so are you! I am your grandfather, dedicated by tradition and intent to pampering and spoiling you. I bid you welcome to the Funny World of People.

But it's about your dad, Erin Eileen, that I am writing this letter. Dads are grossly underrated by their womenfolk. The pangs of fatherhood linger to the end of time, and Dad's throat is due for many lumps along the way.

At your baptism, for instance, he will dedicate himself, rather than you, and with a big lump of pride and humility. In a few years your

47

front teeth will drop out, costing your dad 10¢ each! All too soon you'll spend hours primping in the bathroom, more hours on the phone.

You'll make remodeling dad a major project, sometimes giving up in despair. You'll master the Withering Look which has wilted dads since dawn of parenthood.

Daughters seldom know of the sleepless nights when Dad wrestles with mortgage payments, bills for dental braces and music lessons, formals, and, finally, for that silly old tribal custom, a wedding. Somehow Dad always manages to come through with flying greenbacks.

His biggest lump will come when he answers the question "Who giveth this woman?" Forcing a smile that fools nobody, he goofs a bit and mumbles, "Her ma and me." All of these years he has been prouder of you than you can ever know. Suddenly you have become to him a reprint of your mother.

So you will grow up and acquire children and wisdom and stature and favor with God and with Dad, and his pride will overflow for he will know that all his lumps have been tremendously worthwhile. Typical of him, he will give the major credit to your mother.

Perhaps when his lumping days are over and the good green grass has healed over the scar made by his take-off for the Long Journey, his little girl will say: "Happy landing, Dad, and many thanks for everything."

Love and kisses from Grandpa,   CLARENCE S. HILL

You can see why the letter is one of our prized possessions.

SUE HILL

Grandpop was a forecaster

I have strong childhood memories of Grandpop Cummings' knees. Partly because I used to be forceably bent over those knees whenever I misbehaved; but mostly because they made a comfortable place to sit while Grandpop smoked his pipe and forecast the weather.

His 87 years of living, deep in the heart of Hoosier woods, gave him seniority in the matter of reading weather signs. I was on the job with him, sitting on his knees or hiking with him through the woods. Either way held adventure, for Grandpop was an easy talker and an observant walker.

In the summer he would sally forth, my starched pinafore crackling with the bobbing of my short legs, as I skipped along trying to keep up with Grandpop's big strides. Smoke would come out of his pipe in furious little snorts.

Maybe we'd come suddenly upon a flock of field larks. If they flew away in a covey instead of scattering, Grandpop would pronounce: "Rain before night." If he could find a maple tree with its leaves turned upside down, that cinched the matter.

In the fall, "Find me a nice fat caterpillar," he'd tell me. He would examine the fuzzy creature thoroughly. If the brown bands on its body were narrow, we were in for a long, hard winter. He would confirm this opinion by noting that the squirrels had unusually bushy tails or that the molehills were extra deep this fall.

Grandpop could tell almost to the hour when to get in extra firewood. "See the animals," he'd say. I'd look at my kitten and at Sam, the hound, sitting with their backs as close to the fire as they could without getting singed. If Sam happened to be licking his chops— "Tasting snow," Grandpop would say.

A pain in the stub of that finger (bitten off by an ax years before) would bring forecast of an early thaw, especially if water in the teakettle boiled away in record time or if the cat licked its face before breakfast. Rain on Easter Sunday? Then rain on seven more Sundays in a row!

But Grandpop pooh-poohed the idea of a groundhog forecasting by its shadow. How could a common old groundhog tell anything about the weather?

JUANITA STOKES

Child size

"I like to walk with Grandma, she takes little steps like me," our preschooler said. Perhaps we should remember more often that a "grandma walk" with time to listen and communicate can be a time of renewal for both child and grownup.

GLADYS MARZAHN

The spoiler

My mother spoils our son Robin. He is our only child, three years old. We live in the country and he has no regular playmates; but he isn't lonely, because he has Grandma.

When he first wakes up in the morning, he makes a mad dash for Grandmother's room, snuggles up and begs for a story. He gets it. If he wants a tiny piece of candy to go with the story, he gets that!

During the day I am often too busy to notice Robin; but Grandmother always has time. Her cake batter, sampled raw, is a treat! When she child-sits at night, so that my husband and I can go out, Robin never goes to bed on time; he and Grandmother are having too much fun.

You may think this kind of pampering is all wrong. But we believe it is good for both boy and grandmother—and for us parents. Grandmother can now do for our child all the funny, tender things she never had time to do for her own family of eight. She is reliving motherhood in a perfect way, and our son is storing up memories to strengthen his spirit for a lifetime.

PRISCILLA SMITH BOTTI

A FAMILY NEEDS, UNTO THE GENERATIONS, A TALENT FOR RELATIONS WITH RELATIONS

A recent magazine article blamed the high divorce rate in the U.S. mainly on the prevailing lack of communication.

How true this seems! Haven't you often said, "You just don't understand what I mean!"?

Why can't we learn to express ourselves so that we can be understood by those closest to us? Perhaps we were not taught to communicate as children . . . only to talk.

Do you find time to listen, with heart and mind as well as ears, when your children tell you what is going on in their world, and how they feel about it? Before you know it, those children will be men and women. How ready will they be to communicate—with mates, children and the people of this wide, wide world?

RUTH LEE

Shower for Mom

Once upon a time I kept some useful articles in my kitchen: a small meat saw, a set of screwdrivers which fit perfectly into one large one, and a quart cup.

Over and over I made it clear to the family that these were not to be taken outside. Yet one by one they vanished.

I found a long-missing ice pick on a piece of farm machinery. The quart cup was just the thing for measuring oil. I've bought dozens of pie tins; yet I have only two left. They're fine for warming the kittens' milk. Where do you suppose my lost darning needles are—and for what are they being used?

I'm making a list of lost articles; it will be a long one. And when the family asks what I want for my birthday I'll present my list. I should have quite a shower.

NETTIE H. REISTE

The very nearly unkissed

As I watch TV dramas and ads, I observe that wives and mothers are constantly getting kissed by their families.

Is it because I am not a glamor girl in maxi skirt, but a chore girl in jeans and sweatshirt that I'm neglected?

The typical departures at our house go something like this: My moonlighting farmer—"If the lime comes, have it spread on the lower 10." Our son, taking off for college and dormitory living: "Mom, tell me again how to bake potatoes." Our high school senior daughter:

"Remember I'm bringing some girls home for dinner tonight."

The next son is juggling books, lunch pail, glove, ball, bat; no chance for a kiss from him. Next-in-line is looking for a strayed shoe, while precariously balancing a dozen fresh eggs packaged for her favorite teacher.

Finally, though, here comes my kindergartner with a moist, warm kiss that leaves me in a glow. Guess I'm not neglected after all!

MARCY MARTIN

By their gifts . . .

Our son's new bride was very shy, and we had no relatives around to help her feel at home. I hit on an idea: I'd have an apron shower for Cecelia and invite our relatives to contribute by mail.

When all the packages had arrived, I had Cecelia over for a little tea party. Just she and I were present. What fun she had unwrapping her gifts. Over the red wrap-around apron I told her about Aunt Inez, who'd sent it; about Aunt Annie (organdy party apron); Aunt Mabel (likes to be different, so she sent dish towels).

And I told her about Grandma, who—dreaming of great-grandchildren to come—sent a huge terry cloth bath apron.

My new daughter-in-law ended up with more than gifts, for now she really feels a part of the family.

MELVINA HATCHER

Mysterious partner

My biggest problem as a farm business partner is that I'm married to James Bond—or a reasonable facsimile. He's handsome, exciting and very secretive. While I'm aware of the financial and long-range aspects of the business, I know nothing of the day to day work.

The barn and fields are off-limits to me. Everything is mechanized and can be run by one man—the secret agent man, that is. The details of his feeding and milking routine can be found only in his head. The field work is top secret, too. In 15 years I've been unable to find out how to start a tractor.

I am frightened at the thought of my husband ever being unable to work. In sheer desperation, I have organized our children as a ring of counter-agents. While sweeping the barn, they keep their eyes on "Mr. Big" to see which button makes the silo unload, which cows are fed more grain. They are instructed to tag along in the fields and report what they learn: "We ran over a woodchuck today." . . . "Daddy said a bad word when the baler got stuck." . . . "A lady with red hair stopped her convertible and talked to Daddy."

Very enlightening! Someday, though, we'll crack this operation wide open. In the meantime I hope our secret agent stays as indestructible as his fictional counterpart.

MARY JEAN PARSONS

51

Rapport in the shade

We have two Jeffs at our house, and they are the best of friends. Recently I heard one say, "Let's move our chairs to the shade where we can talk."

They, like the walrus in "Alice in Wonderland," talked of many things: the first day at school, what to name the puppies, why there's snow on Pike's Peak in the summer.

Their ages? Six and 76.

LYDA A. PERRY

Generation gap

Today is our 25th wedding anniversary and we've invited my husband's old-fashioned parents to a party. They won't like our having spent for refreshments (too extravagant). They will complain about the children staying up late and their own loss of sleep. But the main thing is, they will come and they'll enjoy themselves.

They cannot break a lifetime of habits any more than we could live their lives. They struggled hard for many years but forgot to enjoy what they achieved. We younger people try to make the most of our todays. We have enough money to get by and savings are put away regularly, so we aren't the spendthrifts they may sometimes think we are.

We humor them and let them have their say, because we know we won't satisfy *our* children 15 years from now. Already our teen-agers think we're old-fashioned!

Five on the honeymoon

To celebrate our Twenty-fifth Anniversary, my husband Irwin and I had made a romantic plan—for a second honeymoon that would retrace our wedding trip. But we hadn't reckoned on the children! Phyllis, our registered nurse, and Nancy, away at business school, eagerly planned vacations to coincide with ours; said they'd love to come along and bring their young brother, our still-at-home Wilmer. They'd pay their own expenses, of course.

Take a honeymoon trip with a family? But then Irwin and I laughed together and agreed, why not? We visited Niagara Falls, crossed by boat to Detroit, toured the Ford plant and nearby Greenfield Village, a place out of the past.

My husband has been gone 15 years now. But still, at a family get-together, one of our children will say, "Could you ever forget our honeymoon trip? My first train ride." Or, "Remember that night we crossed Lake Erie? Stars bouncing on the waves, Dad and Mom trying to be alone on deck, romantic music by the orchestra . . . ."

We two would have missed a lot if we'd gone "honeymooning" alone. And how much it means now to have some who shared the trip —to relive it with me in memory.

ANNA WENGER

Atten . . . hut!

When we were first married, I told my husband that I hoped I'd never become a nagging, bossy wife and mother. My ex-G.I.-husband suggested a way of preventing that. Whenever I *order* instead of *ask* a family member to do something, he snaps to attention, salutes smartly and with a twinkle in his eye, bellows, "Yes ma'am!"

MILDRED KAIN

On a Son's Marriage

She's such an unversed child—so very young
How can she understand him, read his face?
How learn to know his thoughts, his flash-fire tongue
When angered? Keep abreast of his swift pace?
Oh, he was such a very special lad!
He could be led, but balked if pushed or urged—
And when he fell, too proud to cry. I'm glad
Of course, to see he keeps his man-fears scourged.
Without his knowing, will she learn to lead
Or how to follow when he makes the plan?
Oh, I would show her, gladly intercede,
And teach her that he is half boy, half man.
But no. . . For lack of years, love will atone;
Oh lonely, meddling heart, leave them alone!

MAUDE RUBIN

Please let me know!

After our children were old enough to go places alone, I had trouble getting them to call home if they were going to be much later than expected. I'm not particularly nervous, but I do feel better knowing they're all right.

They always had such good excuses (they thought), such as "We were in such a rush," or "There wasn't any phone handy." Even their father was guilty occasionally of failing to inform me that he'd be delayed.

One afternoon I got everything ready for supper so a few minutes would finish it, and went into town. I shopped, then went to the movie. Nearly an hour after mealtime I showed up.

You should have heard them! "Where have you been? We've been so worried!" Also, "We didn't know what might have happened—you should have phoned!" I just stood there and looked at them, and finally they got it. They didn't care for my method, but now they usually call if they're going to be late.

KATE HENNING

Neat retreat

When we moved on our present farm, my husband and I mistook a small room at the far end of the house for a spare bedroom. But bedroom furniture was never at home in it; so we've converted it to a "recovery room," a tiny haven where any one of the family can recuperate in private from the trials of daily living.

Part of the room's magic lies in its "escape" equipment—a rocking chair, bookcase, magazine rack, sewing machine, typewriter, blackboard and desk.

Every wife and mother needs such a place to have a secret laugh or to cry unseen; to catch up with her sewing, write a letter or read. Dad, also, needs a quiet spot where he can retreat to cloudland or do down-to-earth bookkeeping without interruption. The children find refuge in this retreat of ours when they grow weary of a rough-and-tumble world. Denied radio, record player and TV, our recovery room is a perfect corner for dream-spinning—a place where we can listen to ourselves think. Come to think of it, I've used up my turn here. Who's next?

MARY ANN GOURLEY

Argument for losing

Hail to the art of losing, especially of losing a family argument.

Our whole society is geared to winning. Win that game! Hurrah for the Yankees! Bring more A's on your report card! Our children grow up with win. But how often are they instructed in the joys and benefits of losing?

Recently I began an experiment in losing arguments. I had grown to adulthood feeling well satisfied with my store of accurate information. The only trouble, the man I married had just as much confidence in *his* facts. Each of us considered it a matter of personal honor to convince the other. It even got so our children added their versions.

I realized, finally, that I became exhausted trying to stay on top. There was no reason why I had to be the winner. The topics were seldom that vital.

In losing an argument, I have developed a whole new vocabulary: "Yes, dear, how nice! You're so right. . . ."

And the whole family has become concerned about my welfare when I lose. They go out of their way to make it up to me. Actually, I've never had it so good!

BERTA S. BEHREND

Woman's World

A woman's day is filled
With little things,
Or so it sometimes seems
When tasks are small:
Cleaning the kitchen,
Making rumpled beds,
Sewing a button,
Dusting in the hall.
Yet when these little things
Are added up,
The sum is order
And a home that brings
A welcome to a husband,
Meets a child
With love that quite transcends
These little things.

LOUISE DARCY

Woman's World

A FARMER'S WIFE, DEFINED

A farmer's wife is a woman who . . .
Always has time to—
    Search the countryside for a repair part,
    Hold a "frozen" bolt with a wrench while Dad removes the nut,
    Admire a stand of corn.
Finds beauty in—
    A new litter of pigs,
    A bushel basket of freshly-picked green beans,
    The graceful contours of a just-plowed field.
Usually knows—
    How much fertilizer was used on the east eighty,
    The amount still due on the farm mortgage
    Where the latest farm magazine is hiding.
Doesn't mind—
    Waiting until "next year" for that new living room chair,
    Sheltering a new-born calf on the back porch on a zero day,
    Listening to complaints against the agriculture department, state
        or federal.
A true-blue farmer's wife knows that the farm is where her heart is,
    and she's glad!

DORTHA SCHAEFER

Handiest farm gadget

Modern science has come up with many labor- and time-saving devices. But the most useful on our farm is a gadget my husband acquired some 25 years ago.

He has programmed it much as a scientist does a robot. It is trained to operate a car, a truck and the farm machinery. It can deliver vise grips, tin snips or the needle-nose pliers on command.

The gadget is helpful when repairing fences, sorting hogs, loading planter boxes with grain, ripping open fertilizer sacks, hauling grain to the elevator, keeping books and picking up junk around the farm.

The gadget can talk, and occasionally gripes that it is not fully appreciated.

But my husband is smart. When he sees signs of trouble, he oils up the gadget with dinner-out or some spending money. He knows that if he gives it kind treatment and loving care, the gadget will serve him for many more years.

I hope I can, for I enjoy being the handiest gadget my husband has on the farm.

ZELDA JENKINS

Coverall catchall

The back door opens and my husband pops his head in. "Honey, I forgot to tell you—there's a check in the pocket of that coverall I wore yesterday."

A rhythmic swish-swish from the utility room proclaims that the washing is underway. It also pushes the panic button for me, this farm's bookkeeper and Girl Friday.

My farmer's coverall—whichever one he is wearing—is a filing cabinet, tool chest, glove compartment, pencil holder, lunch box and knickknack holder. In addition, its pockets store an assortment of corn, beans and pelleted feed.

Innumerable business cards are thrust in coverall pockets. Sometimes I remember to rescue them, against the day when I'll hear the man call: "Say, honey, phone that disk-sharpening service, will you? There's a card in my coverall . . ."

ANNE CORRIGAN

Pigs are like people

Since I've been helping with the care of our Yorkshire brood sows, I've learned that hogs are more like humans than I'd ever dreamed. One unpredictable young matron won't spend her confinement in our modern "maternity" quarters; she prefers a nest under the lilac bush.

Sows make faithful and protective mothers. If separated from their youngsters, they fret piteously until they are reunited; then their expressions of relief sound almost human.

At feeding time, the frantic females remind me of a department store on bargain day. They crowd from one bin to another, rooting to outdo each other for the best buys in rolled barley. And they do get peeved at each other—like their human counterparts.

Also like humans, pigs are perverse. Driving piglets is like trying to marshal a cloud of leaves in a fall wind. But they'll follow me if I carry a pail of fragrant buttermilk. I kind of relate to perversity; I'm not easily driven, either.

IRIS BUAKEN

Roses to share

The June sun shone brightly on the just-plowed furrows of young corn. My red roses were in their glory. With a light heart I cleaned in preparation for our women's club.

But June is also a time for picking peas and strawberries. I was also involved part time for my farmer, running errands. So as my day fled, I found myself with much still to be done.

When my guests' arrival drew near, I had a bucket of blossoms but not a single bouquet. So on each milk-glass plate I placed a rosebud as an eye-appetizer. My guests' gracious response made me feel that I'd been right creative in a crisis!

SHIRLEY WENZEL

Plaint of a hired man's wife

My husband has been a hired hand most of his life. But clever, modern farming made his day not shorter, not easier, just busier (more and larger Holsteins giving much more milk), faster (four milking machines going at once). And, oh, the cruel hours—11½ a day, at top speed.

With other folks making bigger pay from less work and having so much time off, our treadmill finally seemed ridiculous. He quit. Now he has gained weight, and we can relax together like other people.

But how he misses watching moist, dark furrows fold over neatly behind the tractor or sea gulls from the beach circling his tractor as he drives it in the welcome sunlight. And our young daughters no longer have personal acquaintance with little calves and with other natural miracles in season.

Somehow we've lost something.

Will there ever be an eight-hour day for farm workers so they may see home and family each evening—without being too weary to enjoy them? If this could come to be, you'd find my husband back in the tractor seat!

EVELYN W. KENYON

Scrub pail—plus

In this age of nuclear power, jets, computers, push-button feed mixing and instant foods, what is the most important helper you own? Mine is a lowly, plastic scrub pail.

I can't list all its uses, but here are a few: It holds tomatoes from the garden, gives a drink to a mother pig and her babies, waters a new tree out of reach of the hose, cleans the small stock tank and fills our car radiator.

When the pail was missing last Saturday, I was sure my son had taken it to the University for car washing. But, no, I found the pail in a field holding soil samples.

Sometimes I think my pail travels more than I do—and that's my problem. I can never find that pail when I need it for its most important job—scrubbing.

HAZEL KRUMWIEDE

Hands I love

How many different kinds of hands a farmer possesses! Mine has gentle hands that help the heifer at calving time, firm hands that put a ring in the sow's nose, tough hands that tighten the barbed wire fence after the colt jumped it, and calloused hands that swing an axe.

He has quiet hands that calm the calf whose head is caught in the feed bucket, skilled hands that operate equipment for sowing and reaping, strong hands that set the post and straighten the sagging roof, and tender hands that pick the first bloom from our prize iris.

He has comradely hands that throw a ball to our 10-year-old son, and confident hands to hold a bat or bait a hook. He has praying hands that count blessings and give thanks, and loving hands that set my world right with a touch that leaves no need for words.

DORIS KEARNS

Woman's World ... feminine point of view

MY FRIEND'S HUSBAND SPENT $1,500 ON A MINK COAT FOR HER BIRTHDAY. NEVER THOUGHT I'D BE IN THAT BRACKET. BUT I SHOULDN'T HAVE BEEN SO PESSIMISTIC; MY HUSBAND JUST BOUGHT ME AN $1,800 HAY BALER FOR MY BIRTHDAY

CHARLOTTE McGOOCH

SO long as it matches my lipstick! Seriously, would, you believe I drive a pink tractor? Having driven tractors for 20 years you'd have thought I'd learn to get along with them as they are. But one thing bugged me—their colors, mostly garish green, red or orange.

So now I have my own tractor. The dealer thought I was crazy, but pink it is. It is my very own—I'm paying for it myself. My husband uses it too, of course, and he brags it's "far out."

ELIZABETH P. LAMPKIN

Unused treasures

When my husband's parents retired from the farm and moved to town, I helped my mother-in-law sort the things she had stored over the years. The upstairs of her home was nearly filled with new—or, rather unused—possessions.

She had beautiful dishes carefully tucked away; the ones in use were cracked and darkened with age. Cooking utensils lay shiny and bright; those in her cupboard were bent and worn. Drawers and boxes contained bedding and towels; her linen closet was full of ragged, mended ones.

When she proudly related how carefully she had always kept everything, I could have wept at the waste. All the beauty others had selected for her had been hidden away, never brightening her life. The givers had never known the joy of having their gifts used and appreciated.

Someday, someone else will enjoy these treasures. How I wish it could have been my dear parents-in-law.

Farm consultant

When my husband has a problem with farm machinery, he calls me into "conference." We hold our consultation under the tractor, over the hay conveyor or half inside a baler. The atmosphere is perfect: No hard chairs to sit on or cigar smoke to get in the eyes!

After I dig out the operator's manual and offer a few solutions (none of which will be correct), he hits on the trouble himself and goes about correcting it. I go back to the kitchen, refreshed.

I wouldn't miss these barnyard conferences for the world!
BARBARA BAKER

Clubs aren't for me

Our Extension home economist wants me to join a club. She is wonderful—hearty, bubbling over with ideas for getting people together. But I am not a joiner.

Nor am I shy! I like the human race, but prefer its members one or two at a time.

When I need help, for instance in making slipcovers, I'll most likely learn from a magazine. I am not limited to magazines, of course, but it does seem that an alert editor is as likely to have good suggestions as a teacher with a government pamphlet. Magazines have color illustrations, too, and explain in simple language.

Within 50 miles (easy cruising radius) there is a DAR chapter to which I am eligible, an Extension club, a PTA, a chapter of Grange, a soil conservation group and a cattle breeders' organization. All going strong with no help from me. (That "with no help from me" does twinge my conscience; but unfortunately we faulty humans seem divided into two extreme categories—over-participators and non-participators.)

Maybe you predict that I'll have a lonely old age. I bet I won't! Besides a desire to appreciate people in singles or in pairs instead of in herds, I have a library card, a perennial border, a collection of antiques, a huge dog and a devoted husband who enjoys not having to get his own meals every second Wednesday.

JEAN K. BOONE

No green thumb!

Since I am a farmer's daughter, the instinct for growing things should have been bred into my bones. I'm sure there should be a grand feeling of thriftiness in seeing those jars of relishes lined up on the pantry shelf. But now it's time to confess. Tending all the little vegetable plants and later bottling up the vitamins are projects that bore me stiff: There, I've said it! This distaste for gardening has been heavy on my conscience for years.

Since I've always admired beautiful gardens and watched my mother plant hers tenderly, nostalgia used to prod me to sow my seeds each spring. I would tell myself, "This is the year! Come July, I'll be deluged with luscious green peas and corn-on-the-cob, and there will be a green and yellow vegetable (fresh, frozen or canned) for every day of the year." But my inspiration was always short-lived as the garden rows began to wither and wilt. Then my lethargy would come like a blight, and the villain ragweed always took over.

I've given up hoping for a green thumb, but now I have an alibi. Teaching at the school my children attend leaves no time to garden. Who'd ever plant vegetables in late June when school is out? So I am off to my books with a free heart and the knowledge that my particular "plants" seem to thrive in the classroom.

FRANCES BEESLEY

Acute timing

After the birth of our fourth child, my husband came to my hospital bedside and said, "You are the best farmer's wife in the world. You not only picked the right hours for the baby to arrive, so it wouldn't interfere with chores, but you also picked a rainy day!"

FERNE TIFFANY

Serendipity

My sister-in-law gave me a set of oil paints for my birthday. "This will be a good way for a busy farm woman like you to relax."

For my first painting I began a still life using a vase of brown-eyed Susans on the kitchen table. No sooner had I applied the main colors to canvas, than I had to chase the cows out of the corn. I returned to the painting—oh, what a state it was in!

The wind had blown it down from the window ledge, and my 4-year-old was smearing the oils with his fingers. The yellow was streaked through the blue in the vase and all this was blended into my red background. On sudden whim I framed the painting as an abstract and called it "My Day."

PATRICIA SCHULTZ

The woman's touch

At our place things mechanical lie in wait until the men are at work on the South 40. Then the gadgets act up. Our centrifugal pump is temperamental. If a bit of flotsam the size of a gnat's brow gets under the foot valve, the pump loses priming. So I've added a crochet hook to my tool kit, to remove such particles.

And the lawn mower—that brazen hussy purrs like a kitten for men, as the salesman blithely demonstrated. But I can pull the cord till it's threadbare and nothing happens. Or else the motor starts with a jolt of fiendish delight, hurling rocks at the bewildered dog and cat, and exploding my eardrums.

I can take a hint. Power mowers are for men only!

HAZEL DAVIS

Woman's World . . . farm life

WE CALL OUR FARM NEVER NEVER LAND, BECAUSE WE'D NEVER NEVER WANT TO LIVE ELSEWHERE, AND BECAUSE IT SEEMS WE'LL NEVER NEVER GET IT PAID FOR

BEVERLY CHRISTIANSEN

EACH year that we stay in farming, I appreciate more and more one asset—the solitude offered by our countryside. Relative isolation is relative relief from tensions. My solitude is companionable, though, shared by my family and animals—cows, calves, ducks, dog— and my special friend, a huge red-tailed hawk. He is so graceful and lovely as he soars over our hayland, I reflect how we humans dreamed through the ages of sailing aloft like that, and how man is incredibly freeing himself from his earthbound condition.

One day as I watched Mr. Hawk coast high over our yard, nobody was around to call me an idiot, so I called out to him. He ignored me at first, but finally he came circling down, down, down . . .

I had quite a "conversation" with my friend as he drifted over our flower border. But then he saw pooch Charlie coming, and beat a hasty departure. When he had gained altitude the hawk seemed to look down at me as though saying, "Thank you for the visit."

THELMA RODEKOHR

Sentiment wins

Some people, Lady Bird Johnson for instance, would definitely not approve our farm's contribution to the environment. The house by itself is a rather pleasant-looking ranch-style residence perched atop the highest hill along our roller-coaster road. The problem is that the house *isn't* by itself, and that all our farm machines stand out in stark relief against the horizon.

To give you an idea: one bulldozer, three tractors, one combine, several plows, a tank wagon, a manure spreader and other items too numerous to mention. We have considered moving these eyesores downhill and out of sight. This would be impractical, though, since "out of sight" would put them half a mile away and in the creek bed.

And that's not all. From the variety of old-model cars clustered around our house, you would think that we are having a perpetual reunion of impoverished relatives. Such isn't the case—it's just this thing my husband has about cars. He can't bear to part with one— from Little Red, our 1935 Ford pickup, whose rings and bearings gushed oil like ruptured ulcers, to Baby Doll, an inverted-bathtub which carried us for 200,000 miles before succumbing to total fatigue.

After all, Husband reasons, who knows what might happen to his cars, thrown to a cold, cruel world? You do understand now (or do you?) that we would like to help with junk removal, but we just don't see how our treasured necessities could possibly be considered junk.

LOIS FIRMIN

Our day in a free country

Yesterday my husband Ralph and I had an early breakfast while we picked up the world news. Then Ralph went out to feed the drylot steers while I got the older children off to school.

We like farming and we love our country. Ralph enjoys the freedom he has to hire men, repair machinery and decide which new crop varieties, herbicides and insecticides to try. We have the privilege of opposing government plans for us, and we do (we voted against the wheat referendum).

I plan meals (without worrying over ration cards) that call for pro- duce from all around the world: cocoa, tea, rice, pineapple, nuts, tapioca, spices . . . plus our good farm standbys meat, eggs, vegetables, fruit and so on.

It was a busy day, interrupted some because I take care of our two preschoolers instead of sending them to a communal nursery. I spoke my mind freely in two telephone conversations, wrote to our congressman and helped Maryanne and Paul hang the flag on the front porch.

All these things we do routinely.

After supper Ralph turned over the PTA books to the new president (he had freedom to call a meeting), I took the children to junior choir practice and Bible study. The church rang with hymns of praise; what a privilege in a world where half the people aren't permitted religious freedom.

When an unexpected frost warning came over the radio, no secret agents questioned our turning on lights, hooking up waterhoses and spraying the garden at 3 a.m.! We saved the plants and got a little more sleep before beginning another day of free enterprise in a free country.

DELIGHT B. WIER

First in his thoughts?

The temperature soared near the hundred mark today. Nonetheless I was in the hay barn preparing wool for market. Some mutterings from outdoors caused me to peek through the slats in the wall. My husband was urging a cow: "Come on in the barn now; the sun's too hot."

A few minutes later I heard a humming noise. Wiping the perspiration from my face, I investigated. In the heifer shed I discovered our huge oscillating fan, the cow lying contentedly in its cool breeze.

I just shook my head and returned to sorting wool. After all, the cow was expecting!

HELENA YOZWIAK

Lost in space

For adventure, I climbed into our empty 60-foot silo before we filled it again. Now I know how it feels to be the last olive in the jar.

SHIRLEY HOWE

Communication deluxe

We love our intercom. The whole house is wired and the barn, too. I use the speaker to wake the children every morning. Or I can talk to a youngster who is sick in bed without leaving my work. When I go outside, I turn up the volume so I can hear the baby if he cries.

JUANITA YARGER

Limited compromise

My dreams of a new farmhouse started out on a grand scale and they have shrunk. But I have firmly decided on three necessities: a large kitchen, a large utility-mudroom and 150 closets.

JUDI BURNETT

Second fiddle

Our farm demands 27 hours a day of my husband's time. His wife demands the rest.

GENIE DeCOU

Woman's World . . . safety

COULD BE TOO MANY OF US HAVE A BLIND EYE TOWARD HEALTH AND SAFETY ON THE FARM FRONT?

THE other day a ravel on my husband's overalls caught in the washer wringer and got wound up tight. How fortunate that the ravel hadn't caught in the belt when he ground corn.

These days with everything mechanized, think of all the machines that seem to reach out for torn overalls and fluttering apron strings. A neighbor got three fingers taken off in a cornpicker accident because of a torn glove.

A farm wife's job is to be extra sure her family's clothing isn't tattered and floppy. We must watch for rips and tears, and find time to mend them.

I've looked for dangers to avoid. Neighbors tease me because I refuse to let our 11-year-old boy drive the big tractor. Oh, he's learning the fundamentals, but no field work. Would you let an 11-year-old take the family car to town for repair parts? No—too dangerous. Well, I can't see much difference?

Please don't get me wrong. I am not the clucky-old-hen type of mother. But our four children, yes and their father, are my responsibility.

IRENE SMALL

My mind went thataway

Last week as I was frying chicken, my skilletful of grease suddenly caught on fire. In my panic I did the worst thing possible—threw water on it.

Fortunately I wasn't burned, but by the time I got the fire under control I had a new color in the kitchen—black!

Later when I confessed my stupidity to my neighbors one told me of a similar experience: "I had turned on the vent fan so that flames were sucked into the attic and set the roof on fire." Another yelled for her husband who started to the door with the pot, dropped it when the flames burned him, and spread fire all over the kitchen.

Our fire chief says the best thing to do in such circumstances is to smother the fire with a lid or throw salt or soda on the flames. Never use flour—it sometimes explodes.

RUTH BALL

No time to live

As a teacher-mother, I have become increasingly aware of a flaw in our American way of life. Our sons and daughters are working days of seemingly interminable lengths . . . six hours in school, followed by chores, home study, Scouts.

The good student often overworks. I notice nervous symptoms, frequent colds and fretfulness in my ninth grade classes.

What can we do about this? PTAs, church groups and teachers organizations must be made aware of the danger of "early burn-out" in the minds and bodies of our young people.

VERA EDWARDS

Overfed, undernourished

"Our teen-agers are starving in a land of plenty." This statement, coupled with a nutrition film I saw at a state school-lunch program, startled me, and concerned me deeply.

I learned that many of our children are building their fast-growing bodies with ice cream, candy, potato chips and soft drinks, rather than with well-balanced meals.

Malnutrition is often hidden, so that youngsters appear to be well-fed. However, lack of good diet often shows up in later life.

What can be done? We mothers can promote good food habits at home by serving well-balanced meals. We also can urge more emphasis on nutrition at school.

IONE MAXEY

Cancer with a happy ending

Recently I read where breast cancer still tops the list as number one killer in the cancer deaths of women in my state.

This seems odd to me, for breast cancer is among the most easily detected forms, and is usually quite evident before it reaches the fatal stages. Why then, do so many women not heed those warnings until it is too late?

I believe it is because most people hear far more about the tragic side of cancer and fatal cases than they do of the cured cases. Is it any wonder that most people become panic-stricken and frightened if confronted with the possibility of cancer? To combat this, I believe that people who have been cured should talk openly about their illness.

I speak from experience, for this year I became a "cured" cancer patient. This means that five years have elapsed with no further complications.

Five years ago I knew very little about cancer, and my imagination greatly exaggerated the danger. I also had a horror of breast cancer surgery, not understanding that a woman's life can still be satisfying and rewarding after such an operation. If I had only known some of these things, I would have been saved many hours of useless worry and fear.

BERNEITA GOODLOVE

Girl on highway

The other night after 11 o'clock I saw a girl walking slowly along the highway. The dance was over and the lights in the school were out. My sons had walked to their grandparents' where I had waited for them, and we were on our way home.

I passed the girl before I realized that she lived out our way, and as I turned around I saw another car pick her up. They were probably neighbors and she may have been waiting for them. Nevertheless, I think the highway is hardly a place for a girl to wait late at night. Some terrible things happen as the result of trusting the wrong driver.

Last year we took a ninth grade girl home when her father didn't come for her. The next day, her father laughed at my husband for his trouble, instead of thanking him for seeing that the girl got home safely. Is this the general attitude of parents of girls today?

Woman's World . . . homemaker

FOUR-LETTER-WORD DAY: WASH, IRON, SHOP AND BAKE; LOVE, LIKE, GIVE, AND TAKE; GOOD, TRUE, DEAR AND CARE, WITH NO-NO SPRINKLED HERE AND THERE

LOLITA B. HIRSH

WHEN you have six children (and I do), you are neck-deep in two dozen careers!

I am a nurse. But rather than gliding along hospital corridors, I ponder whether the flush on Joannie's face means over-exertion or measles—meanwhile reviewing the complications of notifying 22 children to call off tomorrow's birthday party.

I am an artist, music master, dancer, singer: I draw dogs and paper dolls on demand, encourage young Anthony at the piano, practice dance steps with teen-age Cordelia, sing Brahms' *Lullaby* to the baby.

I am a religious leader, trying to give my family spiritual guidance. Although the antics of our youngest at evening devotions may cause the recording angel to smother a smile, let it be written that we did kneel down to pray.

I am bookkeeper and banker for a busy husband; nutritionist and cook, seamstress and photographer. I am maker of dolls, repairer of toys, counselor for broken hearts. I am a teacher, baseball umpire in season, vegetable gardener and grower of roses. I am hairdresser, chicken and rabbit raiser, sometime athletic coach. I am a story-teller and reader of poems. (My college course in speech pays off in a way I hadn't anticipated.)

I am often tired, sometimes discouraged, seldom free for contemplation, often distracted, never up-to-date with the reading I want to do.

What's my pay? A home crowded with affection. A man under whose gentle guidance our family blossoms as obviously as the fields respond to his touch. And moments like this—when my husband saves up and buys me a nice maternity dress, because "if you're going to be the most pregnant woman in the community, I want you to be the prettiest."

JUANITA YATES

Bride's box

One of the gifts I received as a bride several years ago was a large box filled with small household items; some new, some used and some that never could be purchased in a store. My friend had collected these useful household items for me from her own home.

Included, among many other things, were soft cleaning cloths, a mending basket fully equipped, a box of assorted buttons, ash trays, matches, a soap dish, clothespins, jars of strawberry jam and a mouse trap.

I have used every single item in that box (even the mouse trap) and some of the things are still used every day. If I were a bride again, I would wish for just such a box, although it probably cost my friend very little in actual dollars and cents.

LAURA PALMATIER

Junk or gem?

Collecting old, blue canning jars is a fad now; I have always loved them; they remind me of stout, pioneer ladies. My mother had some and every time she sent me to the cellar for jars, I'd get several of the blue ones. She would always make me take them back because they were old and impractical and, besides that, they were for canning pickles. I couldn't argue about the practicality of them but I decided if I ever canned, I'd use the blue jars for everything.

Years later I realized my mother had chosen their use properly. The blue glass made peaches look green and pears moldy, but pickles are enhanced by the color.

BARBARA MALLOW

Inherited philosophy

As a girl, I sometimes heard women ask my hard-working mother: "Do you *like* to wash dishes?" "Do you really *enjoy* housecleaning?"

Her reply was in this vein, "Not especially, but I like the result."

Now, as a mature homemaker and mother, I am convinced that much of the worthwhile work in this world is done by people who are not ecstatically happy while accomplishing their tasks, but who do enjoy the result of having accomplished.

NANCY C. VIAL

Timeless task

For my grandmother, baking bread in a big wood stove was a routine but pleasurable job. My mother, who worked outdoors a great deal, managed to bake homemade bread.

I have a modern kitchen, visit the hairdresser regularly, drive a car, truck and tractor and I still make homemade bread. My daughter may have a pilot's license as well as a driver's license and use solar heat in her kitchen—but I hope she'll still find pleasure in the aroma of freshly baked bread.

JANET CHESTER

Reorganization ahead

I'm making some changes in my household routine, and I'm going to be in charge. Here's my list of decisions:

Out goes everything that can conceivably be used as a water gun —home permanent neutralizer containers, shampoo squeeze bottles and plastic doll bottles included. A household of six children and an arsenal of water guns in wintertime is a bad combination.

I will never wash and store another coffee can, jelly glass, or peanut butter jar as long as I live. I don't need them, I don't want them cluttering shelves.

I will never eat another thing rather than see it go to waste. It's my waist it goes to!

JEAN CARTER

Playing it by ear

Since we started a new baby, our doctor has ordered bed rest for me until 10 o'clock each morning. Our busiest hours! Steve, Suzy and

LuAnn are on different shifts at school; they and their dad all leave at separate times; hence, separate breakfasts.

So—I get up early and wake Steve, our junior highschooler; cook up a big pot of cereal in the double boiler; set out juice and some bread for toast; make four lunches and go back to bed.

I've developed acute hearing! I control everything from my bed— sometimes in shrill tones, I confess. I can hear Steve let the dog out, and if the door doesn't slam just right I know it will blow open. I can hear him get the milk out, pop the toaster, slurp his cereal, and I can tell if he forgets to put his dishes in the sink or to put the milk back in the refrigerator. I know whether he brushes his teeth good or just hits 'em quick.

If I hear him sniffling and sniffling, I holler "Blow your nose!" I can hear him pick up his books and lunch sack and make sure the door is closed good.

Suzy is at a satisfactory do-it-herself stage, and self-reliant. After she leaves, I wake LuAnn and the whole thing starts over, plus I have to button and comb her.

The only thing I can't quite hear is if someone forgets to screw the toothpaste cap back on.

JEANNE LOHBECK

Keep it or toss it

Each spring I move to another house—just in my mind, of course. I start with the drawers and proceed to the closets, cabinets, basement and attic. When I find worn or unused items, I think: "If I were moving, would I keep this?"

By answering my own question I decide what to keep, throw away or sell to the second-hand store. As a result, my housekeeping is much simpler and my house looks better, too.

CATHERINE JENSEN

Help wanted—female

Oh, that housekeeping had the same appeal as an office job, so it would be possible to hire household help occasionally. Maybe a short course in homemaking, with a diploma, would dignify the position of hired girl.

DORIS KNORR

Filing purse for homemakers

My hope for 1966 is that a real business-type purse will come on the market. Then men can't laugh at us women for emptying the entire load to find one article!

My pocketbook right now contains 41 items (count 'em) ranging from a pair of gloves to indigestion pills. And there's not one thing that I don't direly need at times.

What I want is a capacious purse with many accordion compartments labeled for the articles I carry. Money is the least of these, but a hidden compartment for that might be okay, too.

VERA LUND PRAAST

I recommend dabbling

As a writer I am a fizzle; as a seamstress I'm mediocre; as a maker of ceramics I'm less than good. I hold no cooking records. But at just plain dabbling I am tops!

I've dabbled in all the arts mentioned with little success. At times I'm as deflated as a punctured balloon.

My latest effort was in creative writing. This was a thrilling challenge. Hadn't I always received excellent grades in English composition, and hadn't I always had the desire to write? Alas, it was the same old story; even to me my writing sounded immature.

But don't feel sorry for me, please! Each dabble has been rewarding, and after all, it is we also-rans who most keenly appreciate the great—or anyway competent—authors and artists.

I hope that some day our true worth will be recognized and merit ribbons handed out for dabbling. I'm sure mine will be blue.

LUCILLE HULL

Valentines I'll Never Get

Roses are red
Violets are blue
Your son got five A's
Hats off to you
Principal, Fairview High School

Roses are red
Violets are blue
This mink coat
Belongs to you
Your loving husband

Roses are red
Violets are blue
We can use your verse
Here's a check for you.
The Editors
JANE K. SHOEMAKER

Loaves of love

Not long after our marriage, I discovered my husband dearly loves homemade bread. I never expected my bread to be as good as "Mother used to make," but I tried.

I discovered that bread-making is not nearly as complicated and time-consuming as many women seem to think, and never has such a small thing reaped such big rewards. A loaf of my homemade bread has brought an it-was-so-nice-of-you-to-remember smile from an elderly friend, shown concern for the sorrow of wonderful neighbors and prompted my small son to boast, "My mom makes all our bread!"

Most important, however, a row of freshly baked loaves tells my husband he is loved and appreciated.

MARILYN BITTLER

A job for daughter

Today some friends discussed what they wanted most to teach their daughters about housework. Some said sewing, gardening, cooking and how to be a good mother. Because my daughter is only four months old I hadn't thought much about it.

This evening, while I did the supper dishes, I decided the most important thing I can teach my daughter about housework is *to enjoy it.*

First, I want her to learn to take pride in her home; even if it's not the most modern house in the area, I hope she'll add little extra touches —a bouquet of flowers in summer, bowls of fruit in winter.

Next I'll teach her to find something that interests her about housework—to save for those days when nothing goes right. I'll tell her how important it is to let everyday work go once in a while and do something she's been looking forward to.

Last, and probably most important, I'll tell her that nobody's house is always clean; everybody's children have dirty faces once in a while. So even if the work piles up, the baby is fussy, and her husband needs help all at the same time, I shall tell my daughter, "Count your blessings, have a cup of coffee, count to ten and then dig in. There will be a new day tomorrow."

KATHY HILE

Knotty, Nutty Problem

Cashews, peanuts invite, entice,
And appear entreatingly nice.
When you sit beside a dish full,
You are merely being wishful
If you think, when once begun,
You can stop with only one.
COLLEEN STANLEY BARE

HAPPINESS IS EVERYONE BEING ABLE TO FIND BOTH SHOES IN THE MORNING . . . SUNSHINE AFTER TWO DAYS OF DOWN-POUR AND ONLY TWO DRY DIAPERS LEFT . . . 15 OF THE 16 DUCK EGGS HATCH-ING . . . THE SOUND OF MY HUSBAND'S TRUCK COMING DOWN THE ROAD. AND NOT LEAST OF THE FASCINATIONS INHERENT IN MY JOB IS ITS LITTLE IRONIES

FOR example, it beats me . . .

How three teen-age boys can fill to bursting a room which holds three adults comfortably;

How our daughter, who has always been a bottomless pit, can suddenly go on a no-sweets, no-fats, no-soft-drinks diet when she reads that it will help her complexion.

Who leaves the basement light on;

Why unexpected company never drops in when we have fried chicken and angel food cake for supper;

Why twin babies aren't twice the work of one, but are twice the joy.

FRANCES WOLD

As I thrash it out with the lawn mower, I may sometimes reflect . . . Why is it that a child who can't remember that three times six equals 18 can tell me the name, time and channel number of 35 TV programs?

Since I spend a good part of every day cleaning house, how come I can do it in 20 minutes if I hear the magic words "Company's coming!"?

How can a teen-ager who has nothing to wear have it all over her room?

What do I do about a man who promised me Arpege and ended up giving me Airwick?

SARALEE LUCHANSKY

Open to Discussion

All cartons, containers, boxes
And such I'm grimly opposed to:
That tell you plainly "open here"
But tear where they're not supposed to.

BETTY ISLER

That's gratitude?

I coddled and fed the birds all winter, served them trays spread with suet, crumbs, seeds. Come springtime, the little stinkers feed on my planted garden—uproot my inch-high corn, pull out the squash plants and deal havoc in general.

VIOLET FELDMAN

Marriage Statistics

In nine short years of wedded bliss,
I think there is some truth in this:
That if I'd stacked the dishes up,
Plate on plate and cup on cup,
Pot on top of pan and then,
Laid the diapers end to end,
I'd have made sufficient track
To take me to the moon and back.

GLENNA HOUKOM HENDERSON

If we were seven

In this age, husbands are prone to tell their wives, "If you'd only put your work on an *efficiency* basis!"

When I attempt to draw up an efficiency schedule, I realize that the average country home needs a staff of seven wives (what am I saying!), the duties of each to be nicely balanced between executive type and underling.

Wife one would have charge of the food department and kitchen. She would market, cook, bake, plan the meals, serve the meals, pack lunches, wash dishes, do canning and jelly-making . . . and so on.

Wife Two (clothing custodian) would do the washing, ironing, sewing, mending, garment-purchasing, cleaning and pressing, airing, putting away . . . and so on.

Wife Three (interior specialist) would sweep, scrub, dust, wax floors and polish furniture. She'd shine windows; clean the closets, cupboards and dresser drawers; make the beds . . . and so on.

Wife Four (nurse) would take care of the children: their formulas, feeding, baths, naps, training, discipline, recreation . . . and so on.

Wife Five (outdoor specialist) would look after the garden and yard; raise the chickens; gather, clean, candle and market the eggs; take care of the milk house and equipment. She'd harvest the fruits and vegetables, care for the domestic animals . . . and so on.

Wife Six (public servant) would work in P.T.A., Mothers Club, Red Cross, local politics. She would teach a Sunday School class, serve on committees . . . and so on.

Wife Seven (sweetheart, pal, partner) would assist her husband in the business, entertain their friends, attend social events with him, listen to his problems, love and cherish her mate.

Each of these wives would have a full-time job, with little overlapping of duties.

So who'd give birth to the babies?

It's doubtful that the efficiency system would allow any of the seven wives times for that. Bearing young can be a full-time job in itself—a job which the average inefficient homemaker manages to squeeze into her many-sided program, for all her lack of system.

MRS. J. J. MORTIMER

Exceptional Child

How is it that when mothers look
For guidance in a child-care book
They find advice for every case
Except the one that's taking place?
CORINNA MARSH

Boob-tube frustration

There's a four-legged monster in our living room, whose square TV face is always telling me what I am missing. For no handsome gentleman plays Chopsticks while I dust the piano; I have no look-alike daughter with whom to compare non-dishpan hands or Size 12 figures; the plumber does not come to scour my sink . . .

There isn't even a friendly giant in my washer!

Worse yet, the box has my husband believing a lot of unlikely things: that I can scrub floors mirror-bright with no effort, clean the oven while wearing white gloves, eat a meal that fills me up, not out . . . and that I can wash a curl right into my hair.

Who believes that fairy-tale commercials chase away gloom?

MARY ANN GOURLEY

Washday Nightmare

(Or, Why I Need a Dryer!)
The wind was brisk, the sun shone bright.
I hung my clothes with great delight.
But as I finished with a sigh,
Some big dark clouds came drifting by.
The sun was gone—I felt a drop,
I picked the clothes, took down the prop.
I limply sagged into a chair,
And then I saw the day was fair!
ANGIE MURPHY

The Lighter Side

I caught a glimpse of myself
in a mirror one day and suddenly I realized
that I'd been walking through my
days with a face of gloom.
Since then, I've resolved to
focus on the humor that abounds
in my life; I don't have
to look far to find it. . .

The Lighter Side

The lighter side . . . Mom's chuckle file

THE OTHER DAY I HEARD ONE OF MY
BOYS SAY TO THE OTHER, "ONE GOOD
THING ABOUT MOM IS, IT DOESN'T TAKE
MUCH TO MAKE HER LAUGH."

ARDES DIUR

W HEN the service man arrived to repair our garbage disposer,
our five-year-old daughter explained the problem: "It chews
up the food, but it doesn't swallow it."

ANNE DIRKMAN

Animal welfare

I was reading from a book: Some wealthy Hindus endow places to
take care of old cows. "Well, what do you know," said my son,
"Medicow!"

PATRICIA PEAK

It's in the air

I'm 13 years old. Just lately I discovered that there are two things you
can't hide—smoke and love.

CINDY KILL

Early exhaustion

Slow to waken one rainy morning, our first-grader murmured, "I've
got tired left over from yesterday."

SYLVIA VAN DYKE

No choice

One little tyke came to my door on Halloween and said, "Twicks or tweats." I asked, "What will you do if I tell you to trick me?" He said, "Soap your windows, if you have any soap I can use." He got his treat.

EDNA GEORGE

Creative stitchery

Our daughter, five, had been sewing scraps of material together all forenoon. She followed me all over the house with requests for help: "Thread my needle, tie a knot." Out of patience, I asked her to quit sewing and play with something else. "I can't stop now," she said. "I have to find out what it's going to be."

VALANE GEIER

Unique breed

At the local 4-H Fair I explained to my five-year-old son that the black and white cows are called Holsteins. As we moved on to another exhibit, my son suddenly exclaimed, "Look, Mom, there's a genuine Holstein rabbit!"

BERTHA DREW

Color it snow

When it began to snow, my three-year-old wanted to know, "Mommy, why is it raining *that* color?"

HELEN PRESCOTT

Sleuth in my kitchen

While baking cookies one day, I took some out of the oven and placed them on my kitchen table to cool. After they were cool, I stored them in the cookie jar. Before I had a chance to clean the table, my four-year-old son came over and asked "Mommy, what are those marks on the table, cookie tracks?"

DIANNE EVANS

Masked youth

My Patsy, age four, listened in on grandma's sewing bee to hear "we girls" this and "we girls" that. Later, when I told Patsy I was going shopping with the girls, she asked, "Are you going with the girls that have grandma faces?"

FLORENCE CLIFFORD

Mini-sympathy

Our son, when about 3½, rushed to his grandmother after she twisted her ankle. She was sitting on the floor; tears were streaming down her cheeks. He put his hand on her shoulder and said, "It's okay, Grandma, we just laugh at little things like that"—the very words we use when he takes a tumble.

ELIZABETII KYLLO

Hybrid variety

Several years ago when we asked our three-year-old how she liked her new sister, she replied, "Oh, she's okay. I'm special though—I'm adopted and she's just homegrown."

MARGE RANDALL

Mileage magnified

We were driving our two grandchildren to their new home quite a distance away. Finally, after traveling for several hours, the six-year-old heaved a sigh and asked, "Are we still in America?"

MABEL MAAG

Home improvement?

A vent over the range seemed like a good idea in our country kitchen, but our small daughter slowed down the project with her woeful lament: "But then our mouths won't water from the good smells, Mommy!"

OLIVE FISCHBACHER

Wrong way

The Sunday-school teacher talked about Lot's wife who looked back and turned into a pillar of salt, when my neighbor's child interrupted, "My mother looked back while she was driving and turned into a telephone pole!"

LILLIAN CONRAD

Taken aback

Thinking that my "baby" would be frightened on his first day of school, I suggested that I go with him. "An old woman like you?" he said. Well, it's like I've always said, it takes a family of growing children to keep you in your place.

NELLE GILG

81

I GET UP AN HOUR EARLIER THAN EVERY-BODY ELSE AT MY HOUSE, BECAUSE IT'S SO NICE TO HAVE ALL THAT TIME TO LOAF

DORIS W. DURST

LAST night my Mom went to one of those parties where the hostess gathers her friends together in order to sell them something. Mom came home with a special brush to reach behind the bathtub without stretching, a brush to clean walls without reaching, a mop to mop floors without stooping and some wax to shine with without rubbing. She was very pleased with all the work she was saving herself.

Today, using Mom's new gadgets, we wiped the walls without reaching, cleaned the bathroom without stretching, and mopped without stooping. But before she started to wax the floor without polishing, Mom tuned in on a reducing exercise program. For 15 minutes she reached, stretched, stooped, bumped . . . .

Doing her exercises, you know. Only Mom says she *likes* to exercise to music; stretching to clean the bathtub just doesn't feel the same.

ELIZABETH WEIMER

PracticeWhat I Preach

I tell him little soldiers aren't afraid
Of thunder, bull dogs, barber shops and jeers
Of bigger boys—the endless ambuscade
That keeps a guy forever fighting tears!
I must not let the little sergeant see
What bandaging his finger does to me!

PHILENE HAMMER

Hen with house privileges

My parents pampered their pet banty hen to the point of allowing her in the house at times. Our pastor, who grew up on a chicken farm, also took a fancy to her, but she'd never let him pick her up.

One day the pastor came when Father was out. While he waited, to his great delight he induced the banty to perch on his knee.

Mother still enjoys telling of Father's scandalized expression when the pastor greeted him with the world, "Well, I held the little lady on my lap for a few minutes."

NELLIE COX

Better than rose-colored glasses

This morning as I looked in the mirror, I couldn't believe my eyes. Overnight I had become a beauty! The chin was curved and soft, the eyes enchanted and tender, the cheeks without blemish or freckles.

What brought about such a magical change? The new hormone cream? The boiled-egg and carrot diet? The poem I had learned while doing dishes?

None of those, I discovered; I'd forgotten to put on my bifocals!

MURIEL MENZEL

All Sales Final

I love sales. They are fun,
Except that when I go to one
I always manage to succeed
In buying things I never need.
Perhaps someday I will learn,
A sale is a place of no return.

COLLEEN STANLEY BARE

Call it superior

Have you ever noticed that phrases like "Farm-Fresh" and "Country-Style" are used to advertise something special? What a nice compliment to us farm people.

VIVIAN DANZ

Through the kitchen window

A duck is a bird that walks as if it had been riding a horse all day.

MARY LENTZ

Book end

This book has an ending that cannot be beat;
It set me to laughing and grinning;
Arousing my interest to such a degree
I think I will read the beginning!

CAROL GELBER

Exchange

When I surprise my daughter with freshly baked cookies, she gratefully presents me with a mud pie.

RUDY BLAIR

Fresh furrow

I think that when God created sound, he did so with little boys in mind. My 10-year-old son can imitate a tractor so well that I am certain my dining room floor is being plowed up.

DORIS KEARNS

Mother-in-law

According to warnings I have read,
"Mother-in-law" is a name to dread.
But I, for one, never felt that way—
Without his Mom I'd be single today!

WILMA MARSHALL

Who, me?

Some of us never have time to get old, then, all of a sudden. . . . Well, recently I was caught in a mob of youth that belched forth from a bus. A young voice rang out: "Stand back and let the old lady get on!" Bracing myself, I looked to see what old lady—and to my chagrin, discovered it was I!

EUNA CHARNOCK

Gift Hint

With thanks I will take it,
As I've been taught,
But do try to make it
The gift—not the thought!

MAY RICHSTONE

In Dad's footsteps

If my husband's not in the field he's sure to be at a meeting. Perhaps that's why our little girls, when they dress up in play clothes, pretend they're "going to a meeting." They don't know there's any other place to go!

MARLYS WICKSTROM

Day After Christmas

Here stands a woman all forlorn,
Tallying up, while the little ones play,
The toys dismantled, dismembered, torn.
Is this what they mean by "the break of day"?

ANITA RASKIN

Time passes . . .

It seems like only yesterday that I was sewing capes for Superman and Zorro. My Superman and Zorro are now 18 and 16.

This morning, my four-year-old Batman waited anxiously by my side while I repaired his well-worn Batman cape.

MARGARET PETRICK

The lighter side . . . teens

WHY CAN'T ALL THE PROBLEMS OF LIFE HIT US WHEN WE'RE 17 AND KNOW EVERYTHING?

LOUISE DOOLEY

Problem's Child

She worries a lot about the world,
She worries about it all.
For her no issue looms too large,
No topic lurks too small . . .
Air pollution, Unemployment,
Whether the bomb will fall,
Common Market, Classroom Crowding,
Khrushchev and DeGaulle,
And whether the simply darling boy
She met last night will call.

ANITA RASKIN

Menu conflict

It is difficult for my family to agree on a diet plan. My husband wants steak and potatoes. My son would like to live on ice cream and bananas, and my 16-year-old daughter won't eat anything that doesn't resemble a hamburger!

JEAN DAVIS

Mentor

At discipline, I'm a dismal flop.
It's time I taught my son to stop
Behaving like a boor, I know—
His older sister tells me so!

MAY RICHSTONE

85

Sign of age

My daughter is growing up. This morning she hadn't time to lick the frosting bowl—she wanted to hear the latest Beatle record instead.

MARIE EVANS

Teen in between

Growing pains: Young enough to want mother to kiss you good-by and too old to have your friends see her doing it.

VELMA JOHNSON

The lighter side ... Merry Christmas

A FUNNY THING HAPPENED ON THE WAY TO CHRISTMAS

TWO days after Christmas I came home from an errand to find our tree retrimmed. The 18- and 19-year-olds had removed all the decorations and started over. Result: a group of teardrop-shaped ornaments at upper right and an enormous concentration of icicles at lower left. Not a thing else!

Their teen-age companions thought the pop-art effect was "real cool" and I—well, I was impressed!

HELEN GOODHUE

Deep secret

What a situation! Our six-year-old Amy won't tell us what she wants for Christmas. She says she'll tell Santa at the department store, and we'll find out Christmas morning.

JEAN BISHOP

Peripatetic chair

Our daughter has a well-traveled red chair. My parents gave it to her at our Christmas family gathering in a relative's home.

We left the party, but forgot the chair. My parents took it back home with them. Later, they carried it to church and asked another couple to pass the chair along to us. (We were to attend a gift-exchange at this home.) Again, we forgot the chair and it traveled back to my parents, who then sent it to my grandparents. We missed it at that stop, so back it went to my parents. A month later we arrived for dinner and put the red chair in our car trunk *before* we sat down to eat. The chair still travels. Daughter carries it all over the house.

MRS. HALL H. MOXLEY

Exit—face first

After hours of baking, I packed a dress-box full of fancy Christmas cookies for my daughter to take to school. I felt so good when she went out the door. Then I saw her run for the bus, trip and fall down —right on top of the box.

MRS. RICHARD GEISLER

Help-yourself trick

Our daughter and son-in-law were describing tricks their dog could do, so we let Shep inside to perform for us. I had just baked a layer cake which was cooling on a kitchen counter. Shep walked on his hind legs, begging for a treat, then waltzed right over to the counter and took a bite of cake.

MRS. BROOKS H. BAKER

Business as usual

On our December trip to see Santa, my young grandson usually asks for a new piece of farm machinery "like Daddy's." This year as he climbed onto Santa's lap in the crowded department store, he said, loud and clear: "Please bring me a manure spreader."

NORA ANN KUEHN

Well cast

On our church's Christmas program I was in charge of the "shepherds." These lively nine-year-olds filled their time in the wings by using their crooks to trip each other and catch any unsuspecting actor by the neck.

The shepherds' cue to walk onstage was: *Rugged men they were . . .* To which I added a spontaneous and fervent Amen.

RUTH POTTER

Poster protest

A couple we know decided that their children had outgrown Christmas stockings. Their eighth grader did not agree. He waged a campaign with posters in unexpected places. When you opened a closet door, for instance, you might see a sign: SAVE OUR STOCKINGS. He won his campaign. Stockings still hang on that family's mantel, sure as Christmas.

MARY CANTWELL

ALL OF US HAVE DAYS WHEN WE FEEL LIKE A COFFEE BEAN—IN A REGULAR GRIND

MARVEL PAGELER

Gay Day

Did I have a pleasant day?
Yes, dear, it was very gay.
(Up at seven, burned the toast,
Put two chickens on to roast,
Combed the baby's golden locks,
Picked up 97 blocks.
Washed the dishes, scrubbed the sink,
Gave the baby another drink.

(Found the bread box filled with ants;
Changed the baby's soggy pants;
Swept and dusted, mopped the floor,
Shooed a salesman from the door.
Thought I would catch forty winks,
But Baby wanted forty drinks.
Hurriedly I changed my clothes,
Dusted powder on my nose). . .
Dear, I'm sorry I'm a mess—
Baby spit up on my dress!

JANE K. SHOEMAKER

Worth of a farm wife

I can't place a value on jobs I perform for my husband, but he can.

Last month, Rob said he'd give $100 for a good, soaking rain. I washed the car, it rained, and Rob said, "Thank God!"

He told me he'd give a pretty to find his old work pants, so I bought them back from the rummage sale. He gave me a pretty smile.

Rob mentioned that he'd give a week's pay for some young turnips, cornbread, green onions and cold buttermilk. I fixed some for him, but I didn't gain a week's pay—I gained two pounds.

My husband puts a high value on me. I know, because I heard him say that he wouldn't take a farm in Texas for me. But come to think of it, no one has offered him a farm in Texas. . . !

MARGARET MONTGOMERY

Paradox

Isn't it strange that a man who thinks nothing of working around—and often in—manure, refuses to change his baby's dirty diapers?

BETTY COMBS

CedarChest Soliloquy

The first child's clothes
Are stored away,
Their future uses reckoned;
But all unnoticed
Goes the day
They were due to fit the second!

ANITA RASKIN

Cheers from the gallery

During summer vacation, I Tom Sawyered the girls into helping me paint the house. The biggest help my busy husband gave was encouragement—to finish the house so we could paint the barn.

BARBARA WOOD

Just a BigHam

We have a big old watchdog
Whose growl is low and mean,
Whose teeth appear quite able
To take a leg off clean.

And when we're home, no peddler
Comes near this vicious beast.
He'd scare most robbers out of
A full year's growth, at least!

But people who come calling
When we have left the house
Report he's gentle as a lamb
And quiet as a mouse!

HAL CHADWICK

Wrong reading

Yesterday, as usual when a new magazine arrives, I dropped everything to read "just one article." The one I picked told how I should make my husband happy at homecoming: I should greet him in a clean house and pretty dress, with children quieted and smells of delicious food wafting from the range.

My rancher husband's homecomings are unpredictable timewise, so he may be greeted by screaming tots, stew boiling over and me in the midst of some messy job. But John had said he'd be home for supper about six o'clock last night, so I decided to make him happy like the magazine said.

I showered, and changed from jeans to an orange dress with zing. As I brushed my hair and put on lipstick, the three-year-old wailed, "Why do you have to go somewhere?" I cleaned up the children and the house, and the kids wouldn't stop asking who was coming for supper.

In the kitchen I laid out ingredients for a chiffon pie, a very fancy omelet, and a French soup I couldn't pronounce. This supper was going to be something!

In exactly an hour the pie was done—a masterpiece—and I started the soup. I was timing everything, because the article said husband's despise to wait for meals.

At 5:20, a dirty, slimy creature whom I could barely recognize as my husband stuck his head in the door. "Sweet thing," he said, "I'm digging out old Charley's septic tank again, so you'd better feed the cows and have supper ready after I milk."

You may have noticed that The Man *didn't* notice anything different about this temporary homecoming. "But I'm fixing a party supper!" I wailed. He didn't hear, and anyway neither his attire nor his aroma was party indicative.

Oh, well. I got into my jeans again and headed for my barn assignment. Later I shook the hay from my hair, opened a can of corned beef hash and set the table. When John came in from milking, we ate supper.

After he returned to chores, I discovered that the pie was still on top of the refrigerator and I was still in jeans. The odor of septic tank lingered faintly.

That article, I decided, was definitely written for a different element of our female population. Give me a magazine that faces up to life as we live it here on the ranch!

PHOEBE CRANOR

Filched warmth

At Christmas I received a beautiful electric blanket, pink and satin-bound. I cherished that gift, because winter nights are cold in our part of the country and we don't have central heating.

Shortly afterward I was called to a neighbor's house to look after her small children while the mother was in the hospital with pneumonia. When I returned home, our own young daughter announced: "Mommy, guess what: Miranda had babies while you were away." Miranda is one of our sows, and her piglets numbered 10. "They were cold and shivery, so Daddy brought them in the kitchen."

That wasn't quite all of the story. "Daddy plugged in your electric blanket and put it over them, Mom, and they snuggled down and went to sleep."

Aren't men the most?

MARGARET CAREY

90

No hogs in my heaven!

Any woman who thinks she's smart enough to chase hogs is either a bride or plain dumb. A woman just isn't built for hog chasing—yet, in a pinch, I have to do it!

Years of being a farmer's wife have taught me some signs that precede moving hogs, sure as tadpoles come before frogs. If hubby makes grim efforts to appear cheerful at breakfast, I know there are hogs to be moved. A peck on the cheek and a comradely spank mean they *all* have to be moved.

Sure enough—"Got some time?" he asks. Rolling a wary eye, I mention yeast rolls to be mixed, milkers to be washed. "This'll take only a few minutes," he says.

I know I'm hooked. Soon, in jeans and flapping overshoes, I trudge Indian-fashion, 10 steps behind him, toward the hog pens. I'm trying with scant success to look only half as ornery as I feel.

He clambers over the plank fence ahead of me and says, "We'll put that bunch in that door"—nodding toward three pens and four hog house doors. "You let 'em out."

Not wanting to appear stupid, I start toward the gate of the pen he's looking at. "Not those!" he yells. "I want the batch that farrowed the last of March!"

Walking slowly, I scrutinize the row of too-human eyes peering at me from between the planks. I try to divine the hogs farrowed the last of March from those farrowed March first. After two false starts, I open the only pen left.

Now the fun begins.

The hogs in front of the gate won't budge; then, as if at a signal, they pour through the gate, all 35 at once, heading in all directions. "Head 'em off!" Husband shouts over his shoulder, tearing after one bunch at a fast sprint.

I throw my head back, clench my fists and, knees high, give chase. I'm still in pretty blamed good condition for a 47-year-old, I tell myself. I get my pigs turned and, trying not to wheeze, trot back to the man. Do I rate a pat on the head? Not so. "You chased the only ones headed in the right direction," he says glumlike.

Instant blindness sets in among the hogs. They can't see the right door, or even the hog house. Suddenly one starts at a determined run toward the gate she just left. "Stop 'er!" Husband yells. "If she goes back, they all will!"

A hundred and fifty pounds of pork and I clash at the gate. We are about pound for pound; but except for an irritated grunt, the sow doesn't know she's hit anything. I'm sitting in a mire of hog manure—with a tromped-on foot and blood trickling down one arm.

Eyeing my adversary from her own level, I holler: "To heck with these stinkers!" Husband hollers back. "It was stinkin' hogs like these that paid for the water system and your walk-in linen closet! Now you grab a board and whack 'er a good one!"

The sow, who has backed into a corner, glares at me balefully, head down. I grab a board (with, oh, joy, a nail in it) and I sock it to her. "Not there," husband wails, "you'll damage the pork!" (I'd like to embroider her ham with a rivet gun, think I.)

The sow decides I need more exercise, so she shoots past me out the gate as if jet-propelled. Husband, with the aid of snow fencing, has corralled the other 34 hogs at the right door, and obviously he can't leave them. So, giving full throttle, I chase after the runaway. She stops, turns, walks sedately to the hoghouse and into the right door. . . .

Smelling more like those hogs than their own mothers do, I limp toward the house, the Medi-quik and a change of clothes. "Thanks, Ma—that wasn't bad, was it?" Husband calls after me. Feebly I wave back. It could have been worse; I could have broken a leg.

I am aware that, for our earthly consumption and profit, hogs are a necessary evil. However, when ultimately I cross the Great Divide, there hadn't better be a pig in sight. There will be no hogs in my little patch of heaven!

ETHELYN PEARSON

Rueful Re-decorator

I always am intrigued by "before" and "after" scenes
Appearing in the ads in the household magazines.
I re-do and re-decorate, with muscles tired and sore,
And end up with a room just like the picture called "before."

CECILIA STANLEY DERRY

Cheaper at the store?

Faced one morning with a large quantity of rapidly ripening tomatoes, I focused my attention on a recipe which would use up the greatest number of tomatoes—one called Deluxe Ketchup.

I searched out all available canning jars—mostly quarts—and in a few minutes had them sterilizing happily on the back of the range. Out came the five-gallon canning pot, strainers, colanders, pots of scalding water and other equipment.

I scalded, peeled, dipped; boiled, stirred—and stirred. I strained and pulped; mixed herbs and spices, savory vinegars and sugars. I was spent. The kitchen was spattered red from wall to wall.

Five or six hours later, I peered into the large pot. Somewhere way down in the bottom of that great container lay a residue smelling wonderfully like ketchup!

After the mess was cleaned up and I had put away a number of empty jars, I looked with pride on my product. It was like vintage wine—not to be opened casually but saved for a special occasion when I could serve it triumphantly.

In re-reading the recipe, I discovered a small note I had overlooked —printed at the end: "Yield, two pints."

ANN ROSE

Favorite quick supper

Measure 3 c. flour into large bowl; answer telephone; take large bowl off small son's head; sweep up flour.

Measure 3 c. flour into large bowl. Measure ¼ c. shortening; answer door bell; wash shortening from son's hands and face.

Add ¼ c. shortening to flour. Mix well, rock crying baby for 10 minutes.

Answer telephone. Put son in tub and scrub well. Scrape flour and shortening mixture from floor, adding enough tears to relieve tension.

Open 1 can of beans and serve with remaining strength.

LEE WALLACE

The lighter side . . . children, faintly saintly

SO FOOLISH THOSE FATHERS AND MOTHERS / WHO THINK THAT THEIR CHILDREN ARE SAINTLY. / NOW, OURS SHOW THE SAME FAULTS AS OTHERS / (ALTHOUGH, TO BE HONEST, MORE FAINTLY)

ANITA RASKIN

AS a measure of self-preservation, I wrote Bulletin No. 26385 and tacked it up in our kitchen. I am not willing to vouch for its effectiveness, but here it is:

ATTENTION, COWBOYS, INDIANS, RUSTLERS!
1. Speed limit through the kitchen has been reduced to three (3) miles an hour.
2. Roller derbies and basketball practice will no longer be conducted in the dining room.
3. No cowboy will wear guns to bed.
4. There will be no shooting of cap pistols at the Chief Marshal while she is washing dishes.

> Your loving (sometimes)
> Mother

P.S.: Don't use my earrings for checkers anymore, either.

SARALEE J. LUCHANSKY

Persistence

Little boy's motto (who won't take NO for an answer): If at first you don't succeed WHY, WHY again!

EMELINE ENNIS KOTULA

Silence can shout

There is a certain stillness in our house that always causes me to stop what I'm doing and listen. This silence, with small children in a house, is like the ringing of a warning bell. Have you ever noticed how "noisy" some quiet pastime can be? For instance:

A red crayon writing on a living room wall (you're in the kitchen);
A small finger etching the frosting on a freshly baked cake;
The unwinding of a roll of toilet paper;
Pouring of sand down a heat register;
Smearing of lipstick on a round little face.

KAREN ANDERSON

New School

Yesterday I visited school
And saw, to my surprise,
Green blackboards and some yellow chalk,
Desks that adjust to size.
Coral wallboard, soft tiled floor,
Windows wall-length wide
Conspire with all of nature
To let outdoors inside!
But pupils do not change, I find
As I reflect again—
That soundproof ceiling overhead
Blots out the classroom din.

DOROTHY ROEDER

A case for four-handed people

While fixing one of those stir-constantly-while-heating dishes, I thought, "Lucky I have two hands!" Then: "Three would be better, though, or why not four?"

Having two hands is not man's adaptation to a world of two-handed jobs. Vice versa! We have tried to break down the world's work into two-handed bits, *because* we have two hands. There are still operations that cry out for a third and fourth hand. Package tying is one. Answering the phone when both hands are messy with dough is another.

I do wish the biologists would work on how to get four hands for a man—and especially for a woman.

Excuse me now. I have five two-handed jobs screaming for attention. No, I don't want 10 hands for everyone. Think of the increased resistance of small boys sent to wash all of them.

RUTH CAMP

December

While children eagerly await
The Twenty-Fifth's arrival,
Parents eye the twenty-sixth
And hope for their survival.

HELEN LEMMON

Bright side up

When our little son Timmy knocked my sister's picture off the desk and broke the glass, I scolded.

Timmy watched solemnly as I brushed away the small pieces of glass, then he looked carefully at the picture. "Don't worry, Mommy," he said. "She's still smiling."

ROSELLA HOUCK

See It His Way?

He wouldn't be so rebellious a lad,
So quick with sudden rage,
If our young son had a mother and dad
Exactly his own age!

THOMAS USK

Distress au naturel

I thought that if I didn't worry about the Joneses, sooner or later they would catch up with me. Now they've done it.

In a mail order catalog I came across this: "Apply antique finish in a day with a new 'distressed' look."

Got that? All you need is some ambition and this kit which includes a distressing liquid and crayon to use for the look of "worn elegance."

Our furniture has always had the look of worn elegance, and with no effort on my part. To start with we had Early Attic; and by the time we could afford new furniture, we had our own distressing kit— two boys and a girl.

BETTY COMBS

Advice to a Dinner Guest

Choose wisely every word, my friend,
Take care what jokes you tell,
Since you were here last year,
Junior's learned to S-P-E-L-L.

ELIZABETH-ELLEN LONG

Letter to the teacher

Many a school morning I want to send a note like this with my 12-year-old Robert:

Dear Miss Smith: I want you to know that the way my child is dressed does not necessarily have the approval of his mother. (signed) HORRIFIED MOTHER ROBERT LEFT AT HOME.

P.S. He's the boy with the new wool shirt no matter how hot it is the first day of school; the boy who's minus a raincoat in the rain, without a jacket during a cold spell, capless during the big freeze. But his hair isn't shoulder length yet.

ROBBIE PRUITT

Early birds

My husband and I told our two boys we'd all wait and open gifts on Christmas morning instead of on the Eve as was customary. So the fellows set the alarm clock for "morning"—exactly one minute after midnight!

LURA COX BRAND

The lighter side . . . for better or for worse

MY HUSBAND IS SO TOLERANT OF ME. ONLY RECENTLY HE SHOWED ME THAT I'D HOOKED HIS SUSPENDERS THE WRONG WAY 676 TIMES SINCE WE WERE MARRIED JUNE 14, 1941 TO THE PRESENT WASHDAY

JEANNETTE THORMAN

DO our husbands see us as we are today, or as we used to be? Recently, I noticed a new acquaintance looking at my hair. Curious, I asked, "What is it?" She laughed. "Oh, nothing. Only your husband said you had coal black hair." Touching my hand to my graying locks, I laughed too. It's been years since my hair was black.

LETA FULMER

Consolation

I'm another farm wife co-ed who does it the hard way. When I seem discouraged, my husband says, "Smile, honey, when you have to help milk. Remember, you're working your way through college!"

SOPHIE ZIFCO

Catch-up vacation

My husband usually gives me a special birthday gift—a day's work to accomplish some of the odd jobs I've been wanting done around the house.

HELEN PARKS

A new religion

My neighbor and I had been assigned to canvass a small town in a countywide church census. We were courteously received in most cases, but one woman was reluctant to give her husband's religious affiliation.

Her husband, who had been reading a newspaper within our view, called without looking up, "Tell them I'm a hypocrite." My partner duly filled in "Hypocrite" then dryly inquired. "Is that liberal or orthodox?"

BERNZIE BEVAN

To the Mother of the Bride

Today I gave the bride away,
Now you and I are left alone,
But we have gained a son-in-law,
A bathroom and a telephone.

ANNA M. GASSER

Risky raiment

Not long ago my husband asked: "Why don't you ever wear a dress around the place?"

I'll admit I'm partial to my old jeans because they're warm, practical and comfortable. But I try to please, so the next morning I put on a dress.

All was fine until I was in the midst of breakfast preparations. I turned from the range to see our two-year-old David reaching for the butcher knife. A chair was between us, but I leaped to the rescue. Dresses were not made for high jumping. My thud on the floor diverted David from the knife.

The next dress incident occurred when I was gathering eggs. I had the egg pail in one hand, and lifted my dress with the other so I could step over a feeder. But I concentrated more on my skirt than on my footwork, stepped on a chicken and fell in the watering pan.

I should have called it quits then, but didn't. When I went out to feed the pigs, an old sow caught at my hemline and up-ended me.

So, Husband dear, that's why I never wear dresses except for church or when you and I go out in the evening. For a working day on the farm, my old jeans seem safer.

PAT HUGHES

Handwork versus footwork

My husband came in from chores the other day and saw me embroidering. (I enjoyed this hobby before marriage, but three small children have occupied my "spare" time until recently.)

When he asked how I happened to be doing stitchery, I told him I had decided to grow old gracefully. . . . He took me bowling the very next day!

CAROLE TOPP

I Need a Book to Cook

A dash of this
A pinch of that
A scoop of flour
A dab of fat . . .

I tried it once
And what I got
Practically broke
Our marriage knot.

CAROLYN BECKNER

No competition

There's another "woman" in my husband's life. Sometimes his tender loving care toward her makes me a little jealous, yet I don't really mind. I can cook—"Alice" Chalmers can't.

KATHLEEN PALMER

He's thinking ahead

My husband Bob and I were expecting another member in the family. I wanted to plant my garden as usual that year, but Bob vetoed my wish. "No garden for you. The weeds are due at the same time you are, and I'm the one who would be tending both!"

NANCY NORMAN

Farm-style flattery

One day I arrived from the beauty shop with a complete hairdo instead of my usual haircut-only. I was clipped, curled and sprayed to the teeth. As I stepped from the car, my husband whistled then winked at our two boys. "Say, your mother's really combed and curried! She looks like a club calf ready for the fair."

Everyone laughed—but I know a compliment when it comes my way from the man I love.

FAYE COOL

Brighter each year

My husband's hair used to be very curly and dark brown, but right now one of his most polished points is on top. His pate used to shine through thick, but now shines through thin.

IRENE VICK

The lighter side . . . big little thoughts

I KEEP PAD AND PENCIL HANDY FOR JOTTING DOWN THE THOUGHTS THAT FLASH INTO MY MIND. MY BRAINSTORMS WON'T REVOLUTIONIZE WORLD OPINION, BUT THEY MAY ADD TO SOMEONE ELSE'S STOREHOUSE OF INSPIRATION.

WHY is it that when we are *against* something we are always willing to fight? When we are *for* something, we aren't so eager to stand up and be counted.

GEORGIA LAARMAN

Coffee-cup diplomacy

I have the feeling that if only I could get Mrs. Khrushchev in my kitchen over a cup of hot coffee and a plate of sugared raised doughnuts, all warm and cinnamony, and could get her to talk about how she makes borsch or some other Russian specialty, and if that meeting could be multiplied by thousands, we might get somewhere with negotiations. Something about a kitchen makes the human race kin.

ETHLYN GORSLINE

What's behind the blue?

The white trail left by a jet plane looks like a gigantic zipper across the curtain of sky.

EDNA FLEMING

Blacktop rule

Wish people would be more considerate of others on the highway. If they would only try thinking, "I'm in the car in front of me," maybe they'd take fewer chances with their lives!

GERALDINE CLARK

Awakening

My father took me by the hand when I was six and led me into our public library. Thus began my lifelong love affair with books. They've helped me widen my horizons, deepen my understanding and learn how little I really know.

JUANITA YATES

Conditional existence

As a farm mother of seven, I have known this fact for years, but recently noticed that, literally, *life has a big "if" in the middle of it.*

BETTY STEARNS

Other pasture

My husband Jim has a theory he calls "the greener grass." To be satisfied and successful on a farm, you need a taste of doing something else.

DIANE MAXWELL

What price progress

Why do farmers have so many back ailments nowadays? I believe it's because they work too long hours—today's tractors are *always* "energetic" for work. In early days, a farmer quit working when the horses got tired.

BEATRICE MARSHALL

Vanished comfort

When we relegated the rocker to the attic, one sure way to relax walked out of the American home.

NINA W. OGILVIE

Earmarked for youth

It's impossible to guess what this year's fads will be with our teens—the twist with a new twist, multi-colored fingernails, fringe on blouses and socks, everybody wearing the same color—who can say? But I'm glad teens have their fabulous fads—it sets them apart from the adult world.

BETTY McJUNKIN

The
Four Seasons

Spring's air is clover honey,
   Soft as silk;
Summer air is rich and sunny,
   Jersey milk;
Ginger ale is air of fall,
   Sparkling spice;
Winter has no taste at all—
   Flavored with ice!

ALTHEA WAGG HALLOCK

The Four Seasons

The Four Seasons ... rhythms

IN THE COUNTRY, EACH OF THE FOUR SEASONS HAS ITS PARTICULAR RHYTHMS

TO the exile in the city, spring is for remembering how March, with its handspring winds, can giddily confuse a young crop. Every transplanted farm boy or girl must feel the pull of some crop's seasons. (Does one from Iowa yearn to "hear the corn grow" again?)

KAY DAVIS

A Farmer's Notebook

SPRING: half-cold, half-warm, the April wind
tugs at the chestnut's mane; he sets his hooves
deep in the earth and furrows are left behind.
Swallows call wildly to their wheeling loves.

SUMMER: the tall corn talks in the amber day;
the tiger-lilies bloom in the river-marsh.
The hay is in, the timothy meadows sway
beneath the crows' black crying, slow and harsh.

AUTUMN: the heifers come down from the golden hill;
the dooryard rose-hips have the hardness of coral;
supper-smoke rises straight and the nights are chill;
beneath red maple leaves the ground lies sorrel.

WINTER: before green dawn the lantern light
in the breathing barn casts a circle the color of honey;
hills climb through stars, my acres are drifted white;
and my heart knows the taste of a good year strong and sunny

FRANCES FROST

Back-porch calendar

Some new farm houses I've seen have only one small back step. What do people do without back porches?

Mine is like a calendar. In the fall, when school starts, I see baseballs, bats and mitts. In October I stumble over hunting boots and coats, boxes of shells and yellow hats.

At Christmastime the back porch is a haven for tree decorations and unused trimmings. The day after Christmas I can hardly walk through the wrappings and ribbons. Then there's a lull until I give baby chicks the "sun lamp" treatment.

My favorite time is when we get out the gardening equipment and flats for starting seeds. Then come the fishing poles, bait and fish baskets. This we move in time to haul out the portable barbecue, the ice chest and hamper for picnics.

Yes, you can tell the season of the year by what's on our back porch. I couldn't do without it.

AMY BAKER

Seasons

The weather, that great friend of man,
Follows a check and balance plan.

The winter frosts me all about,
Then summer comes and thaws me out.

When summer's warmth begins to strain
The winter cools me off again.

A splendid plan. All honor to it.
The trouble is, both overdo it.

CLARENCE E. FLYNN

You can go home again

Today I visited the old farmstead where I grew up, and found it under the spell of new-fallen snow.

There were no shoveled paths across the circle formed by barn, shed, pump, chicken house and farmhouse. Not one human footprint—the expanse of white was broken only by trails that had criss-crossed as busy rabbits hurried to their committee meetings, or wherever it is that rabbits go.

How quiet it was! The only sounds were subdued chirpings of birds and the rhythmic crunching of snow under my stride.

Crossing the farmyard, I looked up and saw pure artistry—winter pine branches etched across the sky's deep blue. I walked alone—yet not alone, for this was a familiar part of God's creation and I was companioned by memories.

AUDREY WINSLOW

I KNOW THAT SPRING IS HERE WHEN THE NEW GRASS IS PINNED TO THE HILLSIDE WITH YELLOW PEGS OF DANDELIONS

ARLEY CLARK

Dandelion

I think that Dandelion's
just what his name implies:
the summer's first gate-crasher
with gold dust in his eyes.
He springs up here,
he springs up there,
formality despising,
rubs elbows with
the nobler flowers
by brash self-lionizing.
He lingers late,
a puffed-up ghost,
to tell the season's done,
to blow about his gilded past
and seed five hundred sons.

JANE CARTER

Rebirth of a season

On an early morning walk I witnessed the mystic yet unmistakable return of spring.

As I climbed a steep hill near home, my breath sent puffs of vapor into the clear, nippy air, and my boots crunched on the heavily frosted ground. Despite the calendar, spring seemed very far away.

Pausing at the hill's crest, I gazed down at the valley, still and colorless in the pale morning light—a black and white etching on nature's huge canvas. A delicate pink glow on the horizon hinted at the sun's arrival, and suddenly in awesome silence—the crimson sphere slipped into view and struck the world with brilliant fire.

Instantly—like millions of tiny mirrors—all frost-tipped twigs, and spears of grass sparkled with brilliance and I felt as if I, too, radiated their light.

As the sun rose higher, gaining in intensity, I became aware of a faint, almost imperceptible hissing all around me—as if the earth were breathing. Puzzled, I leaned close to the ground, looking and listening, and then I understood what caused this strange sound.

Until dawn, each particle of soil had been encased in a capsule of frost, but with the touch of the first warm rays the ice released its grip and melted with a gentle sigh. It was this sigh that insistently proclaimed winter's end.

Beneath the thawing crust of earth I sensed a stirring force: fragile tips of grass probing towards the sunlight, seeds straining to split their husks, grubs uncurling to begin their tedious journey to the surface and another life cycle—all bringing a new beginning to a waiting world.

JILL TAYLOR

Company

Our spring visitors: Three starlings (they got in the house); two baby woodchucks (they got away); a rabbit (also got away); a lost and confused coot; 11 unbelievably tiny mice (they died); a snapping turtle (we let him go).

MADELINE M. DODD

It's Spring!

It's spring—let's roam the woods a while,
There'll be beauty there to see,
A bed of purple violets,
Or an anemone.
And such enchanting sounds to hear—
Out there where it's so still,
A solo by a hermit thrush,
The brook beneath the hill.
The velvet moss is emerald green,
There's charm in everything.
The dogwood tree is budding white,
Let's roam the woods—it's spring!

LUCY HOUGHTON JEWETT

Farmer's sixth sense

I cling to winter like a barnacle hugs an old hull. But my husband is different.

Paul is like a dormant plant coming to life with spring. Without my being aware that he's even thinking about farm work, I find him out acting on some idea that smoldered all winter. This inner stirring that moves my farmer never ceases to surprise me.

He gives himself completely to winter—loves his teaching job, the lying in late, the relaxing days. But he never loses that primal instinct that says, "Get off dead center; spring is in the air!"

PATRICIA P. LEIMBACH

Great expectations

April on the farm is full of promise. Corn now is a lot of yellow kernels three-eighths of an inch across and one-eighth inch thick— not yet a crop to worry over or maybe replant. I hope that in heaven it is always spring.

PAULINE DOANE

Good-bye to Winter

My spring came this year as I stood
in the falling snow and listened to the
wild geese proclaim the approaching season.

SABRA ISHAM

I'll take the dirt

I almost envy my sister and her city apartment every spring when it rains and six kids and hubby too, track up my newly waxed floors.

Then I start thinking: Can her husband delight his kids by bringing home a new hatch of pheasants from the field? Does she hear "Hey, Mom!" from young son 50 feet up in a tree? Does her teen-age son frighten her by dropping a tiny rabbit in her lap? Or does her teen-age daughter ever come in from pinch-hitting on the branding crew—jeans smeared with dirt and blood—only to emerge an hour later in party frock ready for a date?

From my point of view I'll take the country, the mud, and the unexpected pleasures that spice my life.

LETTIE ROBBINS

Spring's wonder

A heart would be dead indeed that didn't beat faster at the thought of spring. Today I heard a crow, or thought I did. I shouted to the man who was making me cupboards, "There's a crow." And he said, "You're crazy." Then he yelled, "No, you're right; there it is . . . there are two of them. What do you know?" His voice held wonder and joy. His face lifted and his eyes traced their flight over the frozen lake.

There it is again, spring's wonder.

This fellow has been seeing crows every spring of his life. He doesn't even *like* crows, but here he is, this raw spring day, lifted with joy at the sight of two black crows sailing over the fields.

EDNA JAQUES

Spring happening

On the morning her husband says, "Today we sow oats!" every farm wife knows spring has arrived.

The spring field-call is like the migration of birds; it cannot be denied, changed or ignored. One day the world is frozen; next day the frost mysteriously comes out of the ground. Everything is "go."

We part-time "field fillies" get called into service because of the farm labor shortage. So my husband patiently explains again this year that (1) this button is the horn, not the starter and (2) there is not enough space to drive the tractor between fuel pump and corn crib.

Would I like to drive the tractor or would I rather shovel oats into the seeder? Driving sounds easier until I remember how difficult it is to keep the engine operating at the right speed, count the corn rows correctly, and turn the tractor at the end of the row at a safe distance from the fence.

So I shovel and sing. Drowned out by the protecting blast of the tractor engine, I'm equally great at blues, rock 'n' roll and gospel.

By the end of the day, oats are in and I'm all in. But a wonderful feeling of accomplishment envelops my farmer and me as we share our spring happening.

MARYON ANDERSON

Because of Spring

Because of daffodils upon the hill;
Because grape hyacinths are breaking through
The snow; because of wings that fill
The vast sky's infinite extent of blue
With eager onward joy—because once more
Earth grows more beautiful than I had dreamed
It could become again, my praises soar
To God, and I am stronger than I seemed.
I could not find a lovelier way
Through life's bewildering sorrows, than with the sight
Of blossoms gold and blue I see this day,
And April birds' exhilarating flight.
I find fresh courage for my journeying
Through every troubled year, because of spring.

JANE MERCHANT

Hurry the season

A good way to bring on spring is to buy a cord of wood. After this purchase, cold days seem to vanish. A second way to hurry spring is to put off doing your income tax. Relax, do nothing and the deadline arrives in nothing flat.

HENRIETTE B. SCHULZ

THE BUSIER MY SUMMER, THE MORE FIRMLY I AM CONVINCED THAT I AM MISCAST AS A HURRYING, TENSION-HARASSED FARM WIFE. MY NATURAL JUNE ROLE IS THAT OF A CHILD

Likeness of a Boy

Stretched full-length upon his side,
Deep in the summer grass,
For a golden century he watched
An ant procession pass.

Then he followed with his eyes
A lizard's winding way,
And spent bright aeons pondering
What crickets have to say.

A bullfrog called him to the pond,
And squatting down, he sat
For a cool green generation there,
Observant as a cat.

And so he spent the sun that day,
As one might spend a dime;
Indifferent to the ticking hours,
A plutocrat of time.

JENNIE D. WOOD

Inspiration from the stars

Some summer nights, tired as I am, I find a dark spot on the lawn to stare into the star-filled sky.

I may start with the North Star, Polaris. This fascinating pinpoint of light is eight times larger than our own sun, which is 300,000 times larger than our earth. Not only is our sun immense, it has periods of swelling and receding. Why does it pulsate? Scientists have never figured out.

Next I may seek Orion to locate Betelgeuse, one of the largest stars in our visible universe. I tell myself it's 300 light years away. Knowing something about a particular point of light in the heavens gives meaning to the vast panorama; and trying to grasp the immensity of our creation is good for the soul.

Studying the stars (I recommend a book like Fred Hoyle's *The Nature of the Universe*) makes me feel humble. If you want to put your petty problems in perspective, step out into the dark and glance up into the lovely and infinite sky.

OLIVE SMITH

Appropriate apparel

Now is the time when mothers put away the long pants and little boys wear shorts and Band-aids.

MARGARET HUNHOFF

Summer Shower

The rain began staccato
With sharp, bright dots of sound;
Continued in legato,
Until it soaked the ground.

The sun came out crescendo
Forming colors, till we found
The shower diminuendo,
With a rainbow tied around.

ISABELLE HOOPER HAIGHT

Stored beauty

Summer's harvest of flowers, grasses, and fruits enriches the farmhouse with winter beauty.

At the beginning of summer, I start collecting for winter bouquets. Some of my wildflower favorites are tansey (both the yellow flower and the brown fruit), goldenrod, yarrow, pearly everlasting and joe-pye weed. Later on, at end of the summer, I collect pods. Glorious crimson sumac, milkweed pods, poppy heads and Siberian iris pods make interesting additions, along with honesty's silver fruits and bright orange Chinese lanterns.

I cut many varieties of grass growing along the roadside. By now my collection needs only beech leaves, cut in early fall and kept for a few weeks in glycerine and water to make them stay supple and bright all winter.

To preserve flowering plants, I pick them when they first come into bloom, bring them in, and immediately strip off their leaves. I tie the flowers in bunches of a dozen, and hang them upside down in a dark warm attic to dry. Grasses must be dried upright, loosely arranged in a basket or vase.

The arrangements I make from these treasures give us enjoyment from Thanksgiving until spring's first blooming.

CONSTANCE M. NIX

Child in Summer

Out of the golden heart of summer came
The child, and what his age was, or his name
I did not know. Juice of wild blackberry
Stained his fingers, and his eyes were merry.
On his bare, brown arm a pail was slung.
August was sweet and rich upon his tongue;
A honeycomb of hours that he had spent
Among the fragrant grass and wild-rose scent.
I see him plainly still, his blue eyes bright
And ignorant of time's momentous flight,
As in a green and secret world he stands
With childhood's magic touchstone in his hands.

PAULINE HAVARD

Bird-bitten

Once I was bitten by a bird's song, and I have never lost the fever. Treatment: Instead of coffee breaks I take bird breaks.

I'll be pondering world problems over my kitchen sink, when through the window I catch the flash of a blue wing or the metallic glint of a golden breast. I hear a few silvery notes, an unfamiliar warble or a new arrangement of an old, old song.

Was it a bunting, a bluebird, a tanager? Or was it a bird such as I've never seen before? It's very important to me to know whether that snatch of song was sung by a bird father-to-be to his mate in the lilac bush or maybe a mocking bird's mischief.

I cast a guilty look at my taskmaster, the kitchen clock; then Audubon (pioneer historian of American birds) never sped more fleetly in his moccasins than I in my sandals. His paint pot and note sheaf were never more carefully clutched than my basket loaded with binoculars, reference books and note pad. Work, war and other worries get along without me while I stalk a song and a flit of feathers.

In an hour or so I'm back at work—disheveled and dusty; but happy, because now I know which bird sang that song! As I finish the dishes I whistle a few bars of my newly learned bird ditty, the world's woes forgotten.

RUTH M. JACKSON

Dry Summer

Day follows day in parched monotony,
Its sights and sounds etched subtly on the brain.
The dying fields lie gasping in the sun.
Above them floats, as if to ease their pain,
Suspended there in haunting harmony,
The robin's poignant, plaintive prayer for rain.

MARIE OLSON

111

TO BE IN THE WOODS, TO HEAR NUTS DROP FROM TREES AND SEE LEAVES FLUTTERING TO THE GROUND, IS TO KNOW WHY WE CALL THIS SEASON FALL

To All Who Cherished Summer

November's fallen leaves and widened skies
That shine through branches' candid filigrees
Are seldom deprecated by the wise
Who love essential inwardness of trees
And never have enough of heavenly space,
Whether it be festival of blue
Where celebrating clouds perform with grace,
Or chastened gray with silver shimmering through.
What though the jubilee of leaves is past
And only muted grays and browns remain?
To all who cherished summer it will last
As long as they; and they accept the plain
Bestowals of November with thanksgiving,
Habitually enjoying all of living.

JANE MERCHANT

Autumn . . . a beginning?

Did you ever notice that the new year begins in September instead of January? It really does, you know.

What's newer than new school clothes in September? New lunch-boxes, new faces . . . books, teachers, pencils, erasers, sunburnt faces and unscuffed shoes?

After the hard spring work, long hot dusty days of haying and field work, 4-H and county-fair, what's newer than the beginning of a new school year?

MRS. GEORGE OLTION

Harvest

To look upon these fields of ripened grain,
Stirs eyes to tears—somehow we sense again
The need of earth's poor hungry to be fed,
Who cannot pray with hope for daily bread.

ELSIE BERG

112

Breath of fresh air

It was a lovely fall day with the leaves turning tawny and crimson and gold. I had promised my small granddaughter, who was visiting me, that I would take her for a walk down by the creek. But I kept busy with my cooking and other duties.

She waited patiently for me for quite a while. Finally she took hold of my hand and pulled me along. "Come on, Grandma. Stop working. Let's go outdoors and get some use out of the world."

MRS. GRACE McKEE

Cricket

His is the voice of summer at its end,
After the bird songs drift on southward wing,
And over deserted nests stripped branches bend,
While to the bough the hardiest leaves still cling.
His is the summer's requiem—on a note
Defying frost he strums his valiant song,
Tuned to the voice he heard in a thrush's throat;
At the edge of doom, he cries it will not be long
Until the transient will again return.
His jacket shines and he is not afraid;
Though autumn's russet tinges leaf and fern,
And flowers are vanquished by the rain's chill blade.
This is the bravest fiddler of the season,
Crying on winter in the name of treason.

ELEANOR ALLETTA CHAFFEE

Worthwhile work

The yearly job of preserving food for the winter is upon us. Some farm women revel in the art of preserving; others wish summer would never come, or better yet, wish for an eternal summer, so there would be no need for canning food. I'm in between—neither relish the chore, nor do I despise it.

When I'm elbow deep in green beans, I'm so thankful that I have a freezer to put them in. (I remember my mother spending hours over a hot wood stove and steaming kettles.)

Some city cousins may ask, why go to all that trouble when you can buy food in cans with no work? Ah, but they don't know how comforting it is to work along with Mother Nature.

Canning and freezing seem worthwhile to me when the snow and cold wind are here, and we sit down to a meal prepared almost entirely the summer before. I nearly burst at the seams, when someone says, "Those beans taste like they were freshly picked." Or, "Those are the best pickles I ever ate."

FRANCES BURKHARDT

113

Hiatus

Nature rests in the beautiful days of September and October. Growth slows and harvests are over; winter is coming. But today the haze hangs blue and dreamy over the hills and the golden leaves are idle on the resting trees.

MAE URBANEK

Seasonal Surrender

*In our backyard stands
a young apricot tree
quivering and naked in a
small pool of golden leaves.*

JUNE KNIGHT

Fourth season ... winter

I LOVE WINTER

WHEN the temperature drops, the wind rises and snow splats against the window panes, I settle down to enjoy the contentment season.

We have popcorn and stories by the fire, games on table or floor. Winter is a time for cooking special things and serving them with tempting dash. It is a time to let the children help with kneading and cutting, and to set the table early so that we can have supper and get to our games.

It is a time for creating things with the children; for pasting and cutting, for talking things over without hurry. It is a time to pet the kittens and toss a ball for the dog; a time to look at slides in a darkened room, with the radio supplying appropriate music. Of course this is the time to romp in the snow, and to visit with the animals in the quiet barn.

All these enjoyments repay me for winter's inconveniences. Winter brings blessings of relaxation, togetherness and meditation that no other seasons provides.

MILDRED REINHART

February in Minnesota

I don't know about April in Paris but February in Minnesota is my brand of enchantment.

If the snow tosses into drifts that look like breaking ocean waves outside my window, it makes me all the more content to stretch out in the big chair with a book. Or I get out the scrapbooks and paste away, sit down at the sewing machine to whip up some doll clothes or finish other odds and ends—all the things that I have tucked away during the busier parts of the year. For February is truly my catching-up month. I consider it a "vacation at home."

MARY JO BOOTS

Winter Whimsey

Our garden lay, a page of white,
Without a mark upon it,
Until two playful rabbits wrote
Some hieroglyphics on it!

WANDA E. SWIFT

Repose

The orchard in winter is a quiet, sleeping place. Trees stand like soldiers, row on row; no colorful income to harvest now, just a somber gray. Rough, horny branches twist and thrust against the sky. No birdcalls here, but if you listen carefully you can hear squeaks of mice scampering through the burrows beneath the mat of snow.

KAY SEXTON

January moments

January has bleakness; naked trees with cold rain dripping from them. It has drabness; violence; sharp, bitter winds; and the colored magnificence of ice, too. But sometimes it has moments of tenderness that are not surpassed by the compassion of any month.

One of these is that moment when night has just barely come but day has not altogether departed from snow-whitened hills and fields. When lights come on in the farmhouse then, one looks from a warm, lighted room into an outside world turned suddenly bright blue.

Against the glasslike clarity of that blue sky, bare trees loom up in blackness. A line of fence posts rises up blackly from fluffy cascades of black weed and brush. The last, late birds, hurrying from feed pans to wherever they go to sleep for the night, are small black pebbles tossed against the bright blue air.

This moment forgives the day all its shortcomings.

This late, bright blue moment of early evening is reward for one's having ploughed laboriously through snow all day, to the barn, mailbox, henhouse, to neighbors' houses, to woodpile or cistern or wherever one went that day. The blue world lasts only about ten minutes, fifteen at most; even the busiest of farmers can spare the time to accept this tenderness from January's cold hand.

RACHEL PEDEN

January's for me

There is something about this month that guilelessly ushers in an untried year. Solitude, for one thing. Tons of drifty, blowy snow may accumulate on the road until the white stuff is knee-deep or deeper. We may be gifted with two or three days of isolation.

It pleasures me to enjoy January for its serene contrast to the rest of the year. Take summer:

June brings showers for the bride, parties for the graduate, schoolmates staying for one last pre-vacation overnight. July and August find me working twice as hard so I'll be ready to "do nothing"—picnic, fish, entertain city friends who come visiting often because *it's so relaxing in the country!*

In summer I'm picking and freezing vegetables; keeping weeds out of the garden and kids out of each other's hair. Ultra-busyness can cause me to overlook this season's special lovelinesses.

I'll pass over the proddings of other months, except November and December: football, cooking, overeating, entertaining friends and kin. . . . Yuletime can be too much a time of guessed-at-sizes and corrective exchanging. Festivities are laced with tensions.

But January—there's a month of blessed nothingness. If the school bus can't get up the road, The Man can't get down it. My family and I snuggle close in our white cocoon; we have time to relax, to discuss, to rediscover each other.

Happily do I put up with 11 months of hubbub, because I know that January, the calendar's delinquent child, waits in the wings.

MARY R. CONNELL

The Seasons in Haiku

Ever since I discovered haiku
I have been obsessed with composing
these word pictures. This is foul-
ing up my house cleaning, meal
schedules and other regular duties—
but I feel creatively fulfilled.
It amazes me that so much can be said
within the confines of 17 syllables!

CONSTANCE FRALEY

The Seasons in Haiku[*]

Spring

Last year's fallen nut
swelled with its own importance
sprouts and splits its shell.
          RUETTA McGRAW

Little yellow balls
on the lawn become quivers
of downy arrows.
          HELEN RUNYAN

Plum tree confetti,
flung in spring's carnival, strews
orchard ground with white.
          GAIL BROOK BURKET

*A short poetic form consisting of three unrhymed lines of five, seven and five syllables. Haiku comes from Japanese culture and refers in some way to one of the seasons of the year.

Silver-needled rain
stitches flowered tapestries
over earth in spring.
MAURENE McDONALD

Toadstools button up
the sweater of spring. Daisies
embroider the hem.
HELEN E. RILLING

A robin broadcasts
from a TV antenna—
spring is his sponsor.
LOU PHILLIPS

Summer

Traffic to and from
food supply to open doors—
the ant trail highways.
GENE M. EDWARDS

Garnet petals are
threatening to expose black
onyx poppy heart.
VERA A. SCOTT

Sighing at her work
the tidy sea scrubs a beach
tracked up by small boys.
LOU PHILLIPS

Racing raindrop beads
on a clothesline abacus
count my storm-spun dreams.
MIRIAM WILHELM

Sand- scented sun couch,
cadences strong and rhythmic . . .
sea psychiatry.
ELAINE BRADSHAW

Night came cool. I touched
a stone, still warm, that held the
summer sun long gone.

Rows of minarets
in my common garden. . . . Oh!
onions gone to seed.
SIBYL LEUTENEKER

Bright curse, lightning rips
the voile clouds. Thunder's needle
sews them up again.
MARJORIE ROONEY

Stilt-legged kildeer
quilting lightly the brown dust . . .
squatter in my field.
MARY ANN BRINKMANN

Autumn

Amber glass is sun
filtered through the sassafras
leaves first touched by frost.

MRS. L. M. ABBOTT, JR.

Gold, green, brown, it stretched—.
a carpet-covered farmland —
contour at its best.

DOROTHY LEIGHTEY

Dark milkweed pods burst—
feathery white darts scatter
on the autumn breeze.

HELEN RUNYAN

Dandelion seeds
bail out like parachutists
in a swirl of white.

LYDIA O. JACKSON

Thrifty patchwork quilts
loam-plump and tied with corn shoots
sun on the prairie.

MARION S. GEBHART

Splendid the autumn
storehouse warming our senses
for bleakness ahead.

EMMA RUTH MURRAY

Gaily galloping,
the stalwart stallion summer
nears the stable death.
JERRY WHITE

Field, yeast, flame, and I
have made one loaf to join all
women throughout time.
FLORAINE STARK

A mateless goose calls
black against the shadowed moon
remembering still.
ANNE SULLIVAN

Winter

Snow painted peach by
the sunrise, a golden path
to start the new day.
JEAN SACKRIDER

Scalloped tops of trees
lace in dark needlepoint the
camisole of night.
JERRY WHITE

Billowing snow drifts
designed in light and shade by
wind, the artist's brush.
EDNA G. SCHROEDER

123

Bare trees at sunset
make a black lace overskirt
for the sky's gold gown.
CELIA L. PUFFER

On winter's white spread
ice-bedazzled weeds become
crystal on damask.
ALMA SMOCK

Rows of snow-capped posts
go marching across the fields,
white helmets sparkling.
DALLAS JOHNSON

Lace drifting downward
perhaps tatted by angels.
embroiders tall pines.
ADDIE ABELE

Silver-veined rose leaves,
pearl and crystal mosaics,
inlaid by Jack Frost .
META PFEIFFER

Angels give us snow
from feathers that have fallen
from their pillow fights.
KATHY NELSON

Love
and Marriage

Will you love me in the morning when my
hair's a frizzy sight
Just the way you did last evening underneath
the pale moonlight?
Will your cheerful smile still linger when
the eggs are fried too brown,
Or the pocketbook's deflated after I have
been to town?
Will your clear blue eyes still sparkle,
will they dance in sheer delight,
When the baby wants his bottle in the
middle of the night?   EILEEN WIKEL

Love and Marriage

"HIS" AND "HERS" MAY BE ALL RIGHT AS TOWEL MONOGRAMS, BUT DECISIONS AND ADJUSTMENTS IN MARRIAGE SHOULD BE LABELED "OURS"

ALVIDA WILLIAMS

WILL someone please help me to understand my wife? Her approach toward getting things she wants always follows a pattern.

She will say, "Henry, that living room rug looks terrible." I will answer, "Oh, it'll do for another year."

"Well I'm simply ashamed to have our friends see it," she will say.

I can tell by the gleam in her eye that once more she's trying to inveigle me to spend some cash. She takes her time. I'll get my favorite dessert a few nights. I get high praise for anything I do around the house. I get a superplentitude of caresses. By this time my girl has already decided on the color of the rug.

Naturally, after a reasonable time I'm defeated. My wife is so pleased that she won the game, and in no time at all she's campaigning for something else she would like for the house.

I kind of thrive on all this. I'm conceited enough to believe she thinks the game is one-sided and that I don't know I'm being maneuvered. Then, again, perhaps she knows I'm wise to her tricks. It's hard to tell. Women are plumb hard to understand.

HENRY BRAND

Who should farm?

My husband and I both grew up on farms, and when we were married we supposed we would spend the rest of our lives on a fruit ranch in California.

Not my husband Bob's choice, though. He wanted to be an engineer, but lacked the education and training.

After we'd been married a year I began to understand how thor-

127

oughly miserable Bob was. He tried to compensate for his dislike of ranching by working (and worrying) extra-long hours. Making decisions about when to thin, spray, or harvest the fruit brought nightmares for both of us.

But at the ripe old age of 30, a man couldn't switch from the only occupation he had been trained for. Not when he had a family to support!

To get his mind off his troubles, I encouraged him to take some correspondence courses and night classes. He never finished the correspondence assignments, but those A's were worth every penny they cost as morale builders. Bob finally got around to writing to several companies about an engineering job. At last opportunity came: an offer of a good job plus a chance to finish college at night school.

This was what we had hoped and prayed for. It wasn't easy to leave family, friends and relative security, but we left!

Oh, how much easier it is to live with a man who is happy with his work! Bob goes to school four nights a week and studies prodigiously at home. I manage house and garden, and look after the children. That college degree is not far away; soon we'll have more time for life's enjoyments.

We both hope there are not many young couples who "fight farming"; but if there are some misfits like ourselves, we hope they'll find courage to take the bull by the horns and find a new way to make a living.

MILDRED R. BAKER

Emergency Rations

Today we're going to the lake,
My angler spouse and I.
He said: "Just take some coffee,
And a pan in which to fry
   The trout."
   But I,
   In doubt,
And having had experience
With camping trip cuisines,
Will add a slab of bacon
And a can of pork and beans.

RUTH KUNZMANN

Meet me at the barn

For the first two years of our marriage, it seemed I never got to see my dairy farmer husband. When I told him that he spent more time with his 33 cows than he did with me, he apologized but didn't know what to do about it.

Finally I decided that I would have to go where he was—to the barn.

At first I just stood around talking to him as he milked. But soon he employed me to grain the cows, change their belts and let them out when the milking was finished. Next thing I knew, I was feeding calves and washing milkers!

My husband praised me so often, saying I really helped speed up chores, that I began to feel almost indispensable. Now I even get up at 5 a.m. to help him with chores.

It's definitely worth the extra effort. Not only do I see my husband often but now I feel better qualified to help him make decisions.

CONNIE WRIGHT

Good Line

Lesser women undoubtedly do
Require fine fashions, costly and new,
But with your natural loveliness,
You, dear wife, need no new dress!

THOMAS USK

Second wife

When I married Bill, a widower past middle age who had a farm, many friends were sure our marriage wouldn't work. "You'll never be able to take his first wife's place," they warned me.

I had no intention of trying to "take her place"! To compete with her 20 years of devotion seemed absurd to me. And so I have followed a course in accord with my own nature and with my husband's happiness in mind.

Her photo remains on a dresser, as a matter of course. Would I expect Bill to forget his parents, or a child. . . . Then why expect him to "forget" a loved wife? If he reminisces about some trip they took, I listen with interest, for his former experiences are part of the man I love and have married.

My pride is that their son has come to accept me as his father's wife. And though he calls me by my first name, his children call me Grandma.

ALICE DARLENE MILLHAM

Financial plan III

When Grant and I were first married, I wanted many new things for the house. So my husband and I decided that I could have the proceeds from selling every bull calf we had that winter—buy what I could with it, and that would be that. He'd claim the heifers.

Well, one after another all 13 cows freshened. And one after another they produced a total of 13 bulls. Oh, boy! My husband accused me of pre-natal influence.

I bought steel cabinets for the kitchen, a double-bowled sink with a sliding drainboard, and I forget what all else. Oh, yes, I bought a lovely new coat. (Which I'm still wearing, because after the bull fiasco we dispensed with *that* system.)

Our next system was for me to sell young stock for him on a commission basis. But that didn't work out, either. Because my commission was seasonal, and meanwhile my husband had spent his share for a tractor.

Finally, we arrived at our present system, which, so far, is workable:

I get 10% of the income. That isn't too bad—with milk, eggs, vegetables, and meat free from the farm, 10% for groceries and do-dads.

Big undertakings take mutual planning and family-wide financing, as they should. The 10% for me suits my husband because, since 10% of a lot is more than 10% of a little, I make a real effort to promote the general welfare of the farm. If I manage to feed our family of five well, and still have enough left over for a leopard skirt (fake), my husband can't complain.

Now, I don't think that this is the last word on systems. The only conclusion I have about family financing is that, no matter how you do it, mutual honesty and integrity are absolutely necessary.

MARYANN SHORES

The Space Age

Outer space is a problem they're working on now,
With whom to divide it and also just how;
But an inner space problem that causes more strife
Is the closet a man must share with his wife.

SYLVIA PEZOLDT

We made our marriage work

My husband and I are of different religions and he is seven years my junior. I am Scotch-Irish, he is pure American Indian. When we married, he was a widower with two small children.

My friends warned that our marriage would not last six months. But I turned a deaf ear, because I believed that love could surmount any barrier.

For us the latter has proven true; after nine years, our love grows deeper. If an argument comes up, we never bring up race, religion or age. We mend our disagreements with compromise and then forget them.

The children are growing up to be lovelier and lovelier. My husband and I share with the youngsters as we share with each other. We find time to take them to band practice, to music and dancing lessons. The children and their father go to their church, I go to mine—a comfortable arrangement!

No marriage has a chance unless two people are working at it. The odds against us were 99 to one. But with love and common sense, we've evened those odds. Doesn't that prove that almost any marriage can be happy if both partners do their best?

ELEANOR CROSS

My Husband's Favorite

Its collar is worn, its sleeves are frayed,
Its brown is faded to purple jade.
But giving that coat to the rummage box
Would be putting my marriage on the rocks!

MAUDE RUBIN

Help for a non-rememberer

During the almost 20 years of our marriage, my husband has never failed to remember our anniversary. Why? Because I remind him—after all, am I not his true and loyal helpmate?

Sometime near the date I'll mention the approaching milestone and ask, "What shall we do to celebrate?" With five children, some sickness and financial problems, we haven't always been able to do spectacular honor to the day. We may have friends to dinner or go visiting. Once we took the children to a state park. One year we just celebrated with homemade ice cream sodas.

Whatever else, we always read together Ephesians 5:21–33, as we did on our wedding day: *For this cause shall a man leave his father and mother* . . .

So why make an issue of anniversaries? Better to give that nice, if forgetful, man a little help. It works for us, and I'll bet it would work for you.

ANN COULTER

A turn at glamor

John and I needed a vacation, but what with long working hours, three rambunctious children and the extra work of remodeling our old house, we couldn't take the time off. So we decided to have a fling near home.

We got a couple in for the weekend, to look after the children and stock, and we went to town for overnight. We registered at a good hotel, changed into our glad rags and were off, pleasure bound.

We had a leisurely dinner; we danced, held hands by candlelight and finally went back to our hotel for luxurious sleep. We awakened late and, for the first time since our latest child was born, I had breakfast in bed. It was wonderful not to have the children jumping all over us; we could really read the Sunday paper!

After going to church in town and doing some placid sightseeing, we went home, rested, and glad to be engulfed by three pairs of eager arms welcoming us back. The children seemed to benefit as much from our vacation as we had.

That was our first weekend vacation. Since then, similar weekends once or twice a year have become our custom. They help recapture the romance which can to easily slip away from a marriage.

MARY MAGNUSON

Vacation Shopping

I bought a cute pattern
Some silk and two suits—
My husband came home
With slick fishing-boots.
I found stylish slippers
With the dancingest heels—
While hubby was shopping
For spinners and reels.
Next winter I'll wear
My new duds at the Grange—
'Cause now we are heading
For the wide open range.

RUTH EVERDING LIBBEY

Mama's secret bank

We sell our cream and eggs for cash, and my wife picks up the check for them when she goes to town.

It used to amuse, and occasionally irk me, to realize that she was holding out money on me and hoarding it in a spot that I've never discovered. If I mentioned needing money for something she considered foolish, she'd keep a poker face. If I needed it for a wise investment, the money would appear.

Last month our son was run over by a tractor and severely injured. He had to be flown to a city hospital, to be operated on immediately by an important—and expensive—surgeon. I had less than $5 cash; but Mama's hoard paid for the operation that saved our son's life.

I'll never object when I miss a few dollars and know that my wife is holding out on me again. In fact, I slip her some extra money when I can. We never know when we'll need to dip into her secret place to tide us over a real emergency.

BURL CAMPBELL

Mother's helper

I'm the type of person who never seems to avoid that last-minute rush. But I am lucky enough to have a husband who never yells "hurry up" when I'm already near bursting with tension. Instead, he helps.

While I work off my head of steam on the muscle jobs—mopping and cleaning— Pop takes over the frills. You should see him decorate a Christmas tree, fasten buttons on a tiny dress, take the curlers out of a little girl's hair or arrange a plate of cookies.

He thinks these chores are a to-be-expected part of the husband-and-wife trip. I am so grateful that I'm married to a man who doesn't shy away from a chore because it's "woman's work."

BETTY HATCH

Love and marriage . . . the seamy side

MARRIAGE, LIKE LIFE, HAS ITS SEAMY SIDE. SOME WEAR IT RAW-EDGES-OUT, OTHERS WITH STYLE DEBONAIR

I cut my love from whole cloth,
The splendid, irridescent stuff of dreams.
Gayly, recklessly, I fashioned it,
Neglecting to use caution at the seams.

This insufficient thing, a little dull,
Is not the garment visioned in my heart;
Love must be wrought cannily, with skill,
If it lose not its sheen nor strain apart.

But I'll piece out my love with stitches fine,
Place some beguiling patchwork here and there
To cover flaws; perhaps none will suspect
The makeshift if I wear it with an air.

Mutual adjustment

We had a problem. My husband is a farmer through and through. I am not. To me, summer meant long hours of hard work and little more. I dreaded for that busy season to arrive.

Most farm women enjoy their gardens, but not me. I was an outcast and I knew it. Winters were fine; we had time to watch TV, to shop, to visit relatives and friends, to see a movie. But in summer it was rush, rush to get the crops in, keep them clean and then harvest.

Bless my husband! He didn't expect that I do all the adjusting. He adjusted his summer work enough so we could get away now and then. And to rest me from child-rearing tensions, he took (still takes) the children with him when he is doing safe work.

I discovered the fun a family can enjoy by having meals outside, so I keep a table in the back yard under the trees. And I took a course in journalism. Now I'm a writer!

On holidays my husband doesn't feel like driving a car on long trips—after all, he's been on a tractor all week, chances are. He also doesn't feel like pushing through crowds at the beach. The children and I love a day at the beach, so we go by ourselves—on a weekday.

Now I've begun to find extra satisfactions in farm life. We have privacy and a closeness with each other that are hard to come by in the city. Our adjustments took time, but we've made them, and I feel that we are now among the "happiest people."

NORMA SULLIVAN

In defense of "having it out"

I am not convinced that a marriage without any quarrels is necessarily a happy one. Just as a quick shower can clear the air, a brief go-round between husband and wife can often wash away angry or hurt feelings.

My reasoning is influenced, in reverse, by my Aunt Dora, who's fond of saying, "I lived with the same man for 30 years and we never had a cross word." Then she adds primly: "And that includes the day we got the divorce."

CHRISTINE WILSON

Is getting ahead worth it?

Two years ago, with our savings, a loan and some help from my husband's parents, we bought our farm. For those savings I have to thank my husband. During these first seven years of our marriage, Keith has worked day and night, in factory and field, to provide for our family and to get ahead in the world.

We drive an ancient-model car, have good food, good clothes, and we've acquired lots of machinery and equipment besides the farm.

That's the material side. But have we been living, or merely existing?

Mornings, when Keith comes in from the factory, he goes right to the barn or field. He works until suppertime, sleeps from supper until 11, and is off to the factory again. During planting and harvesting, especially, days go by when he doesn't have time to speak a word to me. Weeks pass and we've never gone out or enjoyed another's company at home.

There have been some good times; but I can't truthfully say we are getting what we should out of our marriage. I want more than money can buy: time with my husband, time to go bowling and square-dancing.

If we are granted many years together; I may feel that the effort of getting established was worth the effort. (Or will we have forgotten how to enjoy life?) But I can't forget how, instead of living, we've thrown away seven precious years of our youth.

LOIS EMENHISER

Husband heard from

Women are forever asking, cajoling, pleading and yelling for more storage. My wife is no exception.

If women would clean out the storage they've got, if they could ever bring themselves to *throw away something* (which no female seems to be able to do), they'd have storage.

The same goes for cleaning out chest-type freezers. The woman who hasn't seen the bottom of her freezer for three years is loudest in complaining that there's no place to put anything."

I figure nothing can change all this, but then I thought maybe a little diagnosis of the problem wouldn't hurt.

GEORGE Z. WHIPPLE

What price wife protection?

My husband and I have been married eight years and we have four children. We are buying our farm and barely making ends meet. Hanley has never had life insurance—until this month I finally talked him into getting a policy.

After he'd signed up, all he said was "Are you satisfied now?" He contends that he doesn't have to pay someone to save his money. But if anything happened to him, I'd be left with four children and debts as high as the silo.

My husband is resentful, so I am miserable. This breach between us seems a cruel price to pay for my "victory."

My almost-hero, but . . .

Good-grooming is hurled at TV and radio listeners and readers of magazines. Alas, my husband Frank pays little attention; usually he is working or dozing over his newspaper.

Most of my friends' husbands—white-collar workers and farmers alike—shower and shave daily; but my farmer resists even Saturday-night scrubbings. A thimbleful of nudging arouses his Irish, as when I

135

chide him for too-infrequent haircuts and black-bordered nails.

Greasy overalls and frayed work caps arouse *my* Irish! Also start me casting verbal barbs. Some attention to grooming niceties—for instance, using a deodorant—would rid him of my nagging, but he elects to endure it in stony silence.

And yet . . . otherwise my man rates high in marriage quizzes. I love the guy, and want to keep him. So please don't tell him that I've broadcast my complaints!

For brides and grooms

When Alan and I were married, 35 years ago, the husband of an old friend told us: "I only hope you two will be as happy as we thought we'd be!" Apparently he considered his marriage something less than a success.

His words discouraged and frightened me. And, remembering them, I was disillusioned when the inevitable misunderstandings came. Maybe our marriage, too, was a failure. For I, in common with many another newlywed, had expected 100% happiness.

A good many heartaches later, I read an article entitled "Eighty percent Happy," which helped me change my outlook on marriage and on life. As I remember, the article's gist was:

You don't expect 100% returns on other investments—why on marriage? As children we learn not to be disappointed if we get a *B* instead of an *A*. A baseball player who makes a hit a third of the times he comes to bat is rather well satisfied. It's unrealistic to expect total perfection in any walk of life.

Couples do themselves and their marriage an injustice if they regard their partnership a failure because it doesn't produce perfect bliss. *Life* doesn't produce total bliss!

So here's my advice to newlyweds: Be happy. But don't expect to be 100% happy; settle for 80%. If you can't hold that score, try for 70%. Just be sure you're playing with all you've got. And don't drop out!

MRS. I. A. DYKKESTEN

Eye-opener

Several years ago when my husband displeased me about some trifle, I decided to soothe my hurt feelings by writing down all his faults.

To be fair to my husband, I decided I would first list his good points. They seemed few at the moment, so that shouldn't take long.

I sat down and began writing; soon my list was so long that I was astonished. By now I was ready to catalog my husband's faults. But (more astonishment!) I sat and sat, thinking, and finally I gave up. I couldn't think of one fault worth putting down.

Often since then I've been glad that I listed those good points first.

Now when I'm tempted to be angry with my husband, I remember the day I counted his many good qualities and tried to list his bad ones. Then my anger is short-lived.

MAY PAUK

Who put the "t" in paint?

"Win four gallons of paint!" the ad cajoled. "Tell which of our colors you like best and why."

After living for five years with a color that could only be called Desperation Yellow, telling the manufacturers why I wanted another color—any color—would be easy.

"Won't do you any good," remarked my husband. "I'm not doing any painting, and that's final." Pooh! Who ever heard of a husbandly "that's final" being final?

"Tell us simply, in your own way!" Simple! That was me all over. How well they knew me!

Six weeks later, I got four gallons of paint. I won by confiding that "my favorite color is Spring Green because the most wonderful thing happened to me one Spring; he was tall, dark and handsome—and I married him."

The flattery got me nowhere at home, however. My years in art school weren't wasted after all. I'm a painter at long last.

LEOTA HESHMATI

Golden years—for whom?

Ever since I can remember, I've dreamed about the day when my farmer husband would retire and we could both take it easy—perhaps do a little traveling. Now at last, he has retired. But *I'm* just tired!

Since we are living on retirement income, I am expected to pinch pennies to keep us within our budget. I grow a large garden, can and bake (to save on our grocery bill); I'm the family barber and seamstress. I do the house painting inside and out since we can't afford to hire it done (Hubby says he dosen't know how to paint—besides, he's retired).

These "spare time" tasks keep me from getting bored when I'm not baby-sitting eight hours a day to supplement our finances. When exhausted, I comment, "Gee, I'd like to retire." Hubby replies, "What do you mean? You've been retired all your life." That's when he makes me understand what "women's liberation" is all about!

No time for life

My husband Bob can't be bothered with skating parties, birthday surprises or even an afternoon swim. He has a farm to support.

His corn yields are higher than our neighbors'. He fattens more hogs on less feed; his cows have a higher percentage calf crop.

Bob's work is never done and his long hours leave him so tired he dosen't seem to know his family exists. If the children will just be quiet and let him have his hour in front of the TV, he's satisfied.

Before marriage, Bob toured the West and vowed he would take me to see its wonders someday. Almost twenty years later, he has hardly been off our farm. The year we were chosen to represent the county at the State Fair, Bob sent the children and me alone—the only family minus a father.

Our five children are rapidly maturing. They respect their dad for his integrity and industriousness. He taught them to work; why can't he learn to play with them?

The Exception

When someone says to him, "Think big!"
  My husband will agree.
He loves high mountains, towering spires,
  Redwood immensity.

The wide horizons suit him well
  And wider yet, blue sea.
But his big thinking stops quite short
  At added width on me!
                    ELOISE WADE HACKETT

An ounce of honey . . .

In honor of June, marriage month, may I offer some workable marriage wisdom? Husbands are pretty well molded by the time we marry them. We aren't likely to change them much, but praise will carry more weight than criticism will.

Why nag the man about the warped top of your ironing board? Iron in the valley a few more months (or get a new board) while proclaiming your joy over the lake cabin he built. And don't act martyred when he goes hunting with the red-suspender set. He needs a man's world now and then!

Equal time for husbands: Don't mention to your wife that she washes dishes only once a day (she knows it), but brag that she has the best-looking yard in the neighborhood. Forget that the front room needs scrubbing, and praise her artistic centerpiece.

Here I am writing this when I should be mending my Other Half's shirts. Hope he won't bring up "nothing to put on" again. He might say, instead, that not *every* wife can get her marriage-wisdom letter published!

                    ANNE NORBY MILLER

What is it?

If it slumps in an easy chair and says, "Would you bring me a glass of cold water? I've had a tough day in the field" . . . *and*

If it demands a few hours' help around the machine shed the same day I'm getting ready to entertain my women's club . . . *and*

If it must have the family auto for an errand just when I'm about to drive in the opposite direction to attend the P.T.A. Council meeting . . . *and*

If it says "Why don't you buy a new dress? I'm tired of that old one," then doesn't notice when I appear in a new purchase . . . *and*

If my hair looks like last year's haystack and I smell like afternoon-in-the-hog-barn (which is where I've been), and it says, "Gee, you look pretty today" . . . *then*

It's my husband.

BONNIE WADEWITZ

Hoarding's his thing

Help me face up to this—I married a pack-rat.

Anything you need, just ask my Jon. He has it. Not that he could put a finger on it right away (give him six months and he could).

See those hundreds of boxes in assorted sizes and shapes, stashed away on the top shelves of the garage? What's in them? Goodness, how would Jon know—he put them there because it might come in handy some day.

See those cans on the next shelf? In them are interred the remains of all the paint, varnish and shingle stain that have been used on these premises in the last 30 years. Why doesn't Jon throw out the old stuff? You've got to be kidding. Under one of those dried-on lids may be a bit of the exact paint or varnish or shingle stain he'll need some day!

So what does he do when he needs a nail or a right-hand glove or a wornout electric plug? Well, you certainly wouldn't expect him to search in all that junk, would you? He simply hies himself to the nearest hardware store and—move over, boxes and cartons and jars, you are going to have company.

ELIZABETH ZERBEL

Dog's best friend?

When I married, I didn't realize I was also accepting the role of care-taker for dogs, though my husband had casually mentioned he liked to hunt.

On our first anniversary, instead of bringing me roses or some other gift, he surprised me with a young beagle. The pup was given the name Big Dog and was endowed with an appetite of the same proportion.

Many dogs with royal names, if not royal pedigrees, have graced our home. There was a Queen, a Prince and three Dukes. After them we had commoners, Nell, Peggy, Cindy, Mike and Rin Tin, who was the most persistent at bringing in the cows. (If barking did not get them going, he would pull their tails—so once he brought in a bob-tail cow.)

My husband is not particular about breeds—we have had collies, police dogs, bird dogs and mixtures. Whenever our dog family got too large, my mother-in-law would catch the overflow.

For 34 years I have given dogs first aid, deloused and bathed them, prepared their special diets, house-broken them. And I feel sure when I get to heaven, I'll be caring for Queens, Princes and Dukes.

BERNICE BELL

Love and marriage . . . . contentment

CONTENTMENT IN MARRIAGE MIGHT BE DEFINED AS A KIND OF SERENE OPTIMISM. ON MY LAST BIRTHDAY, HUSBAND BROUGHT ME A BOX FROM THE BAKERY. INSIDE WAS A CAKE, DEC-ORATED LIKE A SUNDIAL, WITH THE WORDS "WE COUNT NONE BUT THE SUNNY HOURS"

OLETA NAYLOR

OUR marriage started like a fiction story. Boy meets girl. He soon whispers soft words of love and so they marry.

Now some years and three children later, he still speaks sweet words. But he is a natural born farmer so can he help it if they sound like this?

"Darling, can you spare a few minutes to help me line these front brakes?" . . . "Honey, will you help me string this roll of wire on the lower fence?"

I remember the first day I tried to plow with our new diesel tractor and let it run away with me. The thing was flying through the field. I couldn't reach the brake pedals, so I just turned the beautiful red monster around and started back up hill. My hero came quickly to the rescue. He jumped aboard the tractor and stopped it. Scared and white as he was, I was ashamed of myself for laughing, when suddenly he burst out, "Hon, don't ever do that again—you could wreck the tractor."

Sometimes he even sounds like this: "This pineapple cake is tops, sweetie," adding irrelevantly, "Let's you and I clean out the workshop sometime tomorrow."

All these endearments mean much to me, but the big reward comes after the work is done. My bashful six-foot farmer ruffles my hair and says, "Brat" (his pet name for me), "you were wonderful today. Thanks for your help."

I ask you: With a romantic guy like mine, a home and three little farmers, what more could any wife want?

VIRNELL BANKS

Is he brave?

Tonight my husband asked me if I thought the astronauts were the bravest men in the world. He sounded wistful.

"No, I don't," I answered firmly.

As a boy, my husband yearned to be teacher, engineer, politician, pilot. But to farm was his final choice. I wondered if he was thinking that he himself might have encircled the globe.

To control the grasping jaws of a corn picker, use the whirling, whining power-take-off or to dislodge a clot of hay bales at the top of an elevator—isn't this danger? Don't these jobs take nerve? A space flight can be postponed until the weather cooperates. My husband is at the mercy of nature's whims—drought, floods in bottom land, row-crop blight, doubtful pig average.

Heroes' tours are spacemen's just due. Similar honors for my husband? Well, no. Yesterday he drove the pick-up to town for feed and accepted a neighbor's invitation to "Come on, I'll treat you to coffee."

My farmer probably will never address a joint session of Congress, but he speaks with conviction at farm meetings and talks humbly with God. I think he is a brave and valuable man, and he's my hero.

MARYLOU BAUM

Profile of the man I married

My husband is a person who can't find his socks, though they've been kept in the same drawer for 12 years . . . awakens me at 3 a.m. to ask the time, though the clock stays on his side of the bed . . . insists the bank people are right when I've overdrawn (they are and he is);

Who doesn't put away his tools and is exasperated when I can't tell him where I left the hammer . . . can't understand how I could forget that payment due on the 15th, or where the money went;

Who wonders why I can't keep the kids quiet, but promises he'll take them fishing Sunday when I'll be cleaning house for company . . . fails to comprehend that a woman prefers being given a hat or flowers rather than an electric frypan;

Who, just when I'm sure he forgot our anniversary, announces with a grin that it seems more like 20 years than 12, but how about us going out to celebrate . . . is bewildered by feminine tears, but is the most comforting, lovable man I know, and I wouldn't change him if I could (and I couldn't).

GARNET MILLWARD

Part of myself

What I love most about my husband is that he seems to enjoy having me around. With him, I feel comfortable—free to be myself, to express my thoughts and dreams without being afraid he'll laugh or criticize. He seems to understand me when I hardly understand myself; in fact, he seems to be a part of myself that was missing until I met him.

And he appreciates me—lets me know he needs me. He usually compliments me when I look nice or cook something special. (The other day he thanked me for being me.)

Our marriage is not always a bed of roses! I have to control jealousy in myself. The cure is trust, I believe. I don't just sit back and say "I trust him," though, but try to be a wife to whom it's worthwhile being faithful. I stay as attractive as I can, and try to put a little bit of surprise into our everyday living.

NORMA DUNCAN

Tokens of his affection

A few hours ago my husband walked into the kitchen where I was putting dinner together. He wore a big smile and proffered a bouquet of wildflowers he had brought from the timber. It is true that the man I married hasn't given me a corsage since our wedding, 11 years ago. But every spring there comes a day when he walks in with his special springtime gift.

And he expresses his devotion in other ways (so what if they are on the practical side?):

Sometimes he gets breakfast before he calls me. . . . He's not above washing a dish or changing a didy. . . . He is friendly with my relatives —loves to visit my parents. . . . He spends time with the children and me.

These ways of saying "I love you" are more substantial than the box of candy which he always forgets.

MILDRED L. DRIVDAHL

Statistics notwithstanding

I have always read with interest every article I could find about couples marrying when they are very young. Most marriage specialists seem to frown on teen-age marriages.

My husband and I were both eighteen when we were married. Neither of us had gone to college; we had a two-day honeymoon, and then moved in with my husband's parents. We had about $75 in cash, an old car and a bedroom suite. That doesn't sound like an ideal start for a good marriage, does it?

This year, in spite of many dire predictions, we celebrated our 11th anniversary. We own an 80-acre farm, have a nice new home nearly paid for, and have three wonderful children—a girl, eight, and two boys, six and two.

The other night, I had tucked the children in bed, and my husband and I were sitting in front of the fireplace when he said: "You know, if I had it to do over again, I wouldn't have married you when we were eighteen."

My heart did a quick flip, and slowly sank toward my shoes. I hazarded a weak question: "Why?"

He grinned. "Because I would have married you even sooner!"

Gee, it's wonderful to hear your husband say that, after being married more than eleven years! We've had our share of measles, mumps, and mortgages, since that hot August afternoon in 1943 when we were two nervous, very much in love kids, standing in front of the preacher in the little parsonage, but we wouldn't have missed a minute of it!

MRS. JEANNE TOBIAS

To hold a husband

After having read many articles on how to hold a husband, I decided I'd better take heed. So one morning I got up earlier than usual, closed the windows, bathed, dressed, and started breakfast before I called my husband—the way the magazines say.

Hubby didn't say much. But I kept it up.

After one very late night, I thought, oh, what I'd give for five minutes more sleep. So I shut off the alarm, and turned over in bed. I overslept. No time to dress. I just slipped on my housecoat and slippers.

At breakfast, I said to hubby: "I bet you think I look like a witch." To my surprise, he took me in his arms, and said: "Honey, I think you look kind of sweet this way."

Now, I don't advise slopping around half asleep every morning. But this did happen to me—once.

Our values and how they grew

When John and I were first married, we were young and strong and times were good, so we went all out in getting ourselves set up.

As we looked at the years ahead, our possibilities seemed unlimited. I dreamed of a handsome home, closets of pretty clothes, a car of my own. My husband foresaw pastures full of fat cattle, barns full of hay, and sheds full of the latest machinery. When our first baby came we began to plan to send her to college. Nothing was out of reach.

Now, only a few years later, we are coming down to earth. We have found that a farmer can't work all the time, that he must prepare for inevitable streaks of bad weather and bad luck, and that it costs plenty to raise a family.

But coming to earth has felt good, too. We have learned that happiness is not measured by what you have, and that joy in a new possession is in proportion to how skillfully you had to manage to get it.

And we have learned that it would be unfair to cheat our children out of their right to earn the things that seem important to them. Now we believe that faith in God and faith in himself are much more precious gifts to a child than to hand him possessions.

LOIS NEWMAN

Love story

This afternoon I climbed from the tractor-trailer and ran to turn my mud-spotted face up to my husband and asked teasingly: "Don't I look kissable?" I was astonished at his reply: "You sure do."

This incident brought to mind many more such incidents in our 11 years together. At times I've been far from lovable, but he still goes on loving me. I've been tired and temperamental at times; sloppy and not-so-feminine on other occasions; sometimes absent-minded or unsympathetic.

There are hundreds of amazing things about my husband. One is the fact that he fell in love with me; another is how hard and uncomplainingly he works to support us although he has a serious back injury. I think it's most wonderful how he blossomed into a devoted father to our two children.

So many women have written of their shock and hurt when their marriages have not withstood the years. Is it not more amazing that marriages—started on merely a golden, slender thread of love—survive? Why do we take human goodness for granted, and become perplexed at human weakness?

GENE WOODRUFF PEPPER

I love you because . . .

A famous poem begins, *How do I love thee? Let me count the ways.* My husband is not likely to ask me that question; but if he ever does, I'm ready with answers. I'd say, I love you because—

You always consult me before making major decisions. This considerate practice somehow establishes your position as head of the house more firmly than if you insisted on being boss.

You like raisin pie—especially the raisin pie I bake. . . . You thriftily save every scrap of junk to clutter up the place. . . . You don't snore.

I love you because you're a family sort of person. You work your head off, accept responsibilities, overcome setbacks, all to make our future secure.

You don't just plan for the future of our sons and daughters; you spend time being a father to them *now*. You give them fun and understanding, yet don't shirk your share of the discipline.

I love you because you haven't forced me to accept your opinions; you have leaned toward mine, to help us find a meeting place.

You have learned not to bring up touchy subjects before breakfast, when I'm likely to be at odds with the world anyhow. You have put up with bad habits, bad disposition, and occasionally bad cooking, with tolerance and good humor.

But most of all, because you openly show your affection for me, I love you.

CLAIRE T. JOHNSTON

Unexpected dividends

When my husband and I married, we moved into the farmhouse where his family had lived. As I was moving things to make room for my own belongings, I often wished we could start out in a new home. But as soon as I found time to search the house, I discovered there were many compensations.

I rummaged through storage areas and found pretty vases and woven baskets. In the attic were beautiful picture frames. Hiding under a sheet of plastic was a lovely walnut drop-leaf table.

A small box revealed the most treasured item I have yet to find— a diary my husband began when he was 9. It gave me insight into the little boy who was to grow up and marry me. One of the first entries said: "I was very bad today. I got into Mother and Daddy's love letters." And with all the confidence of a 9-year-old, he wrote, "We played basketball today. I made the most points, as usual."

We have been married almost three years now, and occasionally I still make new discoveries. It's like receiving an unexpected gift. True, it would have been more convenient to move into an empty house—but how much I would have missed.

JUDITH KALLENBACH

Before you can say "paperhanger"

Long ago I used to approach my husband and ask in my meekest tones, "Could you possibly help me hang wallpaper one day this week?"

Usually he couldn't. The waiting to get a room papered seemed endless—comparable to the waiting to have a baby.

But not anymore! After 22 years I've learned that being a farmer's wife has its advantages if you use the right strategy. Now I secretly select, cut and hide the wallpaper. Then, on the first cold, snowy day The Man is marooned in the house, I ask casually, "What have you planned for today?"

Before his procrastinating imagination has time to go to work, I've whisked out my materials and paper hanging is under way.

I'd like to point out that any couple who can live through a siege of amateur paper hanging and still wear the gleam of love in their eyes can be proud of a marriage built on solid rock!

LENA BRAUN

A marriage grows rich through shared memories

After we had filled the Christmas stockings and relaxed over "Santa's tea" (left for him by our children), my husband said, "Let's go see the animals."

When we opened the barn door, the cows lumbered to their feet and the goats came bleating to be petted. We had brought apples for all; and for the pony Trinket an extra bonus—two lumps of sugar.

As we walked back to the house through the starlight, a blessed peace fell upon us. It seemed fitting that the Child Jesus should have been born in just such a friendly, serene place as our stable.

GLADNESS W. LUCE

Adjustment

My wedding ring was worn too thin; so, the day before Christmas, Douglas took me to the jeweler's and we selected matching bands. He had never worn a wedding ring; now the whole world will know he is mine!

LOIS ROSEBROOK

Surprise item

Today I was doing my weekly grocery shopping and I glanced down my grocery list. It read "lettuce, soup, sugar, milk, black tea,"—then I stopped short.

Below the list were four little words in my husband's handwriting. "I love you, dear."

He's told me this in many ways during our 22 years of marriage, but never like this.

SARA ELLEN PETERS

Love with lunch

Like many rural couples today, my husband and I both work away from home. To make matters even more complex, I work days and he works a night shift.

On a recent evening I was jotting down some things I wanted to mention to him. On impulse, I added a P.S.: "You're wonderful and I love you."

I slipped the note into his lunch pail. My husband came home from work, bursting with pride. In fact, he was so pleased with his "love letter" that he carries it in his wallet. What's more, I've found a love note from him!

MARY ELLIS

Children

How to describe a small boy's laughter?
Gay and sudden, defying capture—
It's spring, it's boy, it's bees in clover,
It's joy welling up and bubbling over.
It's mother's bonus, especially
When the small boy laughing belongs to me.

MARTHA NELSON

Children

Children . . . born free

I PERCEIVE THAT CHILDREN, BORN FREE, ARE TOO OFTEN HEIR TO HANGUPS AND BARRIERS. HEAVEN RESTRAIN US GROWN-UPS FROM TOO-ZEALOUS "MOLDING OF CHARACTER"

EVERY week our six-year-old Dan gives up his pony ride for a car-pool trip to the nearest town. There, in a studio, he exchanges his cowboy boots for tap shoes, mat and a 30-minute tap-and-tumbling session in dancing class.

The idea of taking lessons in the dance was Dan's own entirely; in fact his dad at first opposed it. Argued Jim, "There isn't another boy in our county who'd take lessons like that. Dancing's for girls!"

Dan had watched male dancers on TV with increasing interest. He even gave up a chance to accompany his dad and older brother to a basketball game in order to watch *The Nutcracker* on TV. That convinced us that he really wanted to dance!

When my husband's brother Tom returned from Vietnam, we told him of Dan's wish to dance. "Well, you'll let him, won't you?" said Tom matter-of-factly. Apparently it takes a 6'4" battle-tried Marine to get a boy into dancing class.

Dan's teacher admits that most fathers go into a flap over the idea of dancing lessons for their sons. How unfortunate; for dancing improves boys' physical coordination, helps them develop balance and rhythm.

Dan holds one reservation about his lessons: His carpool companions are all girls. "But I guess I can stand them long enough to get to lessons and back."

We parents have learned something from Dan's lessons, too. We are becoming more aware of our children's real needs, and less prone to be over influenced by a public attitude.

SUE MULLINS

Freedom to try

Yesterday, while I was doing the laundry, our young daughter came in and showed me a can containing a remnant of blue-green paint.

"Mother, may I use this?"

Automatically I replied, "No."

"Why not? I want to paint a table I just made."

I shook my head, but she persisted. "Just tell me one reason why I can't use it!"

Cornered, I couldn't think of one really good "because." Well, I can own up to a mistake now and then, so I reconsidered and let her have the paint.

Later, she called me to see the dressing table she had made herself *and* painted. The paint was streaked, and the whole thing wobbled a bit; perfection eludes all of us. But there has to be a first effort; and there has to be the freedom to try.

EVELYN P. HAMILTON

Kindred

It was such perfect, larkspur-colored weather!
The sun had poured its pail of gold light over
The maple-tassels, and each tall, grassy plume
And shining head of jewel-weed and clover.
It was the kind of morning to be out
Making friends with a colt. The small boy stood
And stroked the silky mane, the velvet flank.
Oh, they were of the same, bright brotherhood
Of young fleet-footed creatures, born to run
Across a sunny meadow in sheer joy.
Tenderness lit up the boy's proud eyes;
The brown colt whinnied, and then colt and boy
Sped out of sight, but leaving on their way
Their shining signature upon the day.

PAULINE HAVARD

With thanks to 4-H

Let me tell you about Little Sis. That's what we called her when she came into the world 12 years ago, because she *was* little—and sort of sissy.

Maybe days in the incubator do mark a tiny piece of humanity. Anyway, Little Sis seemed to build her own "incubator" and shut herself away. We worked to draw her out; but it looked as if she'd never get any spunk.

Enter, 4-H. Little Sis muddled through sewing and cooking, because

—well, because the other girls took sewing and cooking. During her third year she joined her brother and sister in a baby beef project. A calf named Hertha became her charge, and thereupon began a transformation!

The bigger her calf grew, the more determined Little Sis was to show her who was boss. She even got so she could back Hertha; it's no small thing to put a 900-pound hunk of beef in reverse. Came show time at County Fair, how proud Little Sis was when the judge had her back Hertha into the purple ribbon class! From then on, we could see her self-confidence grow.

Eventually the calf had to be sold. I'll never forget Little Sis's somber dignity as she led Hertha into the sale ring. Bidding over, Hertha was shoved into a waiting pen. . . .

Little Sis stood there, holding the halter. For her this was the end. But in a way it was the beginning, too. Many victories and many defeats lie ahead of her, but she'll cope.

THELMA RODEKOHR

Analysis of hangups

These are the things my 15-year-old city brother is afraid of:
1. Cows (any kind or size)
2. The swimming hole
3. Roosters
4. Setting hens
5. Snakes (I am too)
6. The dark
7. Work

Things our 3-year-old farm boy is afraid of:
1. Nothing

PATRICIA SCHMID

Promising protégée

We have an art gallery, right in our home. This year we are showing kindergarten art exclusively. Each day, when our little girl (the artist) comes home from school, she comes rushing to the kitchen where our gallery is. Work stops while we take time out to examine her latest masterpieces.

The daily offerings are nearly always colorful—or "blatant" might more accurately describe that square of paper aflame with orange, red, blue and green. Our young exhibitor has shown paintings made from patterns: autumn leaves, pumpkins, goblins, valentines, bunnies. However our favorites are the freehand pictures created from the child's imagination and daring.

We no longer jump to hasty conclusions about such pictures. Once I made the mistake of saying "Oh, what a lovely sun!" when, to the artist, the picture was of an egg, sunny side up. So now I say, "I like that. Tell me about it."

To exhibit the works of art, we tape them on refrigerator, bulletin board, or any likely space. When a display area becomes overcrowded, we take down some pictures and put them away for safekeeping. Or we may send some enclosed with letters to relatives. Grandparents especially are receptive—always happy to help us clear the gallery for new masterpieces.

RAINEY HEARD WILLIAMS

Never too early

An exciting "let's read" experiment has highlighted this past year at our house. Our preschool sons are the main participants. After only six months, four-year-old Trey could recognize 40 words, two-year-old Joe 10. They also began quickly to point out the big letters on signs, as these symbols began to mean something to them.

All of us have enjoyed this prelude to the boys' more formal learning. We parents aren't trying to raise geniuses, or to compete with the school, or to force-feed our children's minds before they are ready. But why deny our fellows the adventure of learning while eagerness is at peak? At this stage of development, their minds "soak up" like little sponges.

For Teacher (Mama) our brief reading times are better than a coffee break—a short rest from the work for a special kind of rapport with our young learners. Large bonus: the satisfaction of seeing the boys started in a skill they will use and enjoy all their lives.

We began with the word Mommy, progressed to Daddy, then moved on to parts of the body. Even before little Joe could talk well, he'd point to whatever object a word meant. His older brother couldn't wait to learn words about the ranch. He helped me make a list: tractor, plow, barn, horse . . . and soon we were on action words: jump, run, hop, sing. . . .

For a teaching guide I use Glenn Doman's book *How to Teach Your Baby to Read* (Random House, 201 E. 50th St., New York, N.Y. 10022). We don't read every day, but when the boys ask me to read, I try to do it *right then*. It's remarkable how the work still seems to get done.

SANDRA YARBROUGH

Facts of life

Last week was a red-letter time for our four children. They "helped born" five baby pigs.

Preparation for this began a year ago, when our oldest son bought a weaner pig for his 4-H project. Bertha, as we named her, developed the healthy, long, slender body that means a good brood sow; so we kept her. And was she spoiled! Always at the kids for back scratchings and hand-fed ears of corn.

After her breeding, the boys kept a close watch on the calendar. All must be ready for the blessed event. They prepared a clean, sterile pen, and got Bertha moved in. On the birthday eve, the boys settled down beside the pen. They watched all evening as Bertha arranged and rearranged her bedding, never quite satisfied.

At 2:30 a.m. boys and pig were dozing. But at 6:30 things began to happen. The boys flew into action, gathering clean cloths and awakening little sister so she could watch.

Pig psychology reared its head; Bertha was so wise to us humans that she started playing on our sympathy. As she labored, she insisted on the petting she had come to expect as her due.

When the first piglet arrived, one boy took it, dried it off and put it to sleep in a box warmed by an electric light. And so on till all five were born.

What a happy, satisfied family we were after these hours of working together. And how better could our three boys and one little daughter learn about the miracle of birth than by actually witnessing it?

MRS. M. W. WISE

Himself at last

Our small fellow spends the day being bits and pieces of various people—cowboy, Indian, fireman, doctor and astronaut. But at night the pieces all go together, and the completed jigsaw puzzle pictures a normal, rosy-cheeked four-year-old—sound asleep.

BETTE KILLION

Children and fantasy

I hadn't realized how much talk about the world's trouble spots was seeping into our children's minds from newspapers, radio, TV and meal-time conversations. It was brought home to me one day last week.

My husband had thrown about 50 bales of hay down from the mow, and the kids had used them to build a "Berlin Wall." Lynn was attempting a dramatic "escape" over the wall, only to be shot down by brother Joe, the "Communist guard."

I didn't interrupt their game. In fact, I wished we grownups could play out our anxieties like that!

LORRAINE KINSTETTER

Children . . . teen grow-years

HERE THEY COME, YOUR TEEN-AGERS, YOUR HOPE FOR THE FUTURE, WITH LONG STRAGGLY HAIR

To Linda, at 16

Once, even on tiptoe, you weren't quite able
To reach all the treasures on my dressing table.
But that was long since when your mother was known
To have one good slip she could claim for her own.

My jewelry box once blinked bright as I'd dress
But now it reveals a bleak emptiness!
And almost as deftly, you've worked to deposit
My favorite garb in your very own closet.

The sweet aroma that about you does drift
Is entirely the essence of my Christmas gift,
And the cream that you use on your velvety cheek
I bought for my own skin one day last week.
Small wonder that people are telling each other,
"Linda is the very image of her mother!"

ALICE BOYD STOCKDALE

Why the label?

My husband clicked off the TV set after we had watched another program about juvenile delinquency. He said, "There must have been something wrong with my family and with society when I was young. I never even realized that I was a 'teen-ager.'"

I knew what he meant. Our national preoccupation with the customs, morals and hangups of teen-agers has long been more than I can understand. I can't help feeling that this special labeling of our young people is harmful to them.

Since I work with young people in 4-H and church groups, I have learned that they resent being lumped together under a label that too often carries derogatory implications. "I hate being called a teen-ager," one girl burst out. "We're people, like anyone else!"

It is true that adolescents have problems peculiar to their age, but so do other age groups. How about the familiar "I won't" of two- and three-year-olds and the obdurate ways of elder citizens?

I believe that my husband's family had the right idea a generation ago. No one was a "preschooler" or a "teen-ager" or a "young married," but each was recognized for what he was—a *person*.

FRANCES WOLD

Happiness sans hippiness

With all the fuss being made about rioters, hippies and flower children, I would like to tell about six boys from our high school whom I can whole-heartedly describe as valuable citizens.

154

These fellows fixed a deserted neighborhood barn into a Halloween playland for the children of our county.

They made half the barn into a "spook house," complete with cardboard skeletons, weird noises and twisted passages. The rest of the barn was fixed up as a baby-sitting center for the benefit of parents who would take older children trick-or-treating. There was a 10¢ charge to go through the spook house, and baby-sitting cost a quarter a head. These fees paid for refreshments and materials.

It was a relief for us adults to share in the spirit of happiness generated by these wonderful teens. We are looking forward to their event next year, because this one seemed to bring the entire county together.

GINNY REED

Independent or sorority?

To pledge a sorority or not to pledge: That is one of the most dramatic issues for a teen who goes to college (or to a high school that allows sororities).

I chose to be an independent. Last year, as an incoming freshman, I investigated the sororities and their qualifications, requirements and activity plans. But, once on campus, and having compared what's emphasized in that dream sorority house with what's emphasized in my 4-H club at home, I was disappointed and angry. Maybe I just wasn't prepared for the idea of girls being tried, judged and sentenced by other girls who only know them by brief acquaintance.

Often the hurt to those who are not chosen for any sorority is senseless and brutal. Such a girl may think she is a social outcast for life. With all the furor that college students raise about human equality, how can sororities continue to attract them?

NADINE MEIER

Boy, Dad and gun

Our 14-year-old son wants a rifle. We have a small wooded area where he could hunt, under his father's supervision. But my husband says no—he never had a gun himself, a gun is dangerous and besides he doesn't have time to take the boy hunting.

I wonder: If we deny our son permission to buy a rifle, will he in turn be too busy to go hunting with his son of the future?

Hot-rod phase

We gave our 18-year-old son Ken $25 for his birthday. And what do you think he did with it? Bought a Model A Ford body and frame. A piece of junk? Not to Ken. It was a potential hot rod.

155

A year later, after hundreds of hours of work, the hot rod was taking shape little by little. Ken spent days and hours searching junk yards for the right parts. He made many trips to the library hunting for books to give him the answers to his problems in mechanics. Other boys come from miles around to exchange ideas on building cars. And all the time Ken was getting valuable experience.

We still feel that our $25 birthday present drew 100% interest.

JEANNE DREYER

How much trust?

Do you agree with me that too many parents have gone overboard in trusting their teen-agers? I have done a right-about-face on this since I was a teen, because I was so sure then that my mother was wrong. She made it her business to know exactly where I was going and when I would be home. Sometimes she checked on me.

A few years ago when I was teaching, I thought it was my duty to tell a teen-ager that her behavior with a boy on the school bus was unbecoming and suggestive. "What would your mother say if I told her about this?" I asked.

The young girl looked me in the eye and laughed. "She would call you a liar, because I would deny it. My mother trusts me. If you don't believe it, ask what happened to my seventh grade teacher." (It turned out that the teacher had lost her job because she'd reported the girl to the principal for similar behavior.)

It was no surprise when the girl married in a hurry and gave birth to a very premature baby.

Not long ago a boy begged a local policeman not to report him for drag racing. His parents trusted him, and he had sworn never to speed, much less race.

Aren't we asking too much of our teen-agers when we give them cars, plenty of spending money and complete freedom, and then expect them not to be reckless? It seems about as safe as handing a child a loaded gun for a toy and asking him not to point it at anyone.

Will our young people blame us in later years for not giving them guidance and discipline as well as trust?

ANN DICKINSON

Film Development

Small boys like movies with gunplay and gore,
With riders and robbers to fill them with bliss.
They look upon love as an absolute bore—
They sicken when hero and heroine kiss.

Small girls like movies with peaceable plot,
Dancing, romancing and costumes, of course.

They seldom like gunmen, the guy who gets shot,
The ranger, the stranger, or even the horse.

But little girls ripen and little boys calm;
At teen-age they're prone to agree,
When shoulder to shoulder, and palm against palm,
They like any movie they see!

ANITA RASKIN

They "had to get married"

Rural communities are often very cruel. Not because the moral code is more strictly enforced in them, but because there's very little privacy. In our community everyone can remember who your grandmother was before she was married and what year you graduated from high school. If a young couple really has a premature baby, or if an unmarried girl has an emergency appendectomy, people do talk; and rarely do they give the victims the benefit of a doubt.

Knowing all this, I was simply overwhelmed when our oldest boy managed to tell us that his girl was pregnant. They were still in high school and had been going steady for over a year. For a time, the distraught young girl couldn't bring herself to tell her parents who were facing another tragedy—a beloved grandson was incurably ill.

From those days of our deep despair, one thing stands out. That is the wonderful help of our young minister. His response to us was immediate, understanding and helpful. Within an hour he had encouraged the desperate kids. He saw that they were basically sound youngsters and could build a good future with help. There has never been a word of blame for anyone, including our boy and his girl. I do feel that parents' attitudes at a time like this can make or break these children for the rest of their lives. Why load them with guilt? They are sorry enough.

And God bless our friends. They may not approve of the way the kids started out (neither do we!), but they are standing by. We parents arranged a quiet beautiful church wedding and asked a few close friends. We sent no invitations, but useful presents keep arriving. Our new daughter has found a temporary job, because her family and ours are in moderate financial circumstances and she realizes her responsibility.

We don't know what the future will bring. But when our young folks went to church service together a week after the wedding, I felt that they were accepting their new life responsibly.

Discount for quantity

Having six boys in school at one time requires a lot of things in wholesale amounts—shirts, shoes, school supplies, hair oil, peanut butter, and patience.

ALICE COCKRELL

We pair up children too early

Most of us parents bewail steady dating at 13 and premature marriage at 16 or 17; but don't we close our eyes to the fact that these customs begin in grade school? And that we parents help them along?

Our 10-year-old Joe was highly disgusted with the school valentine party. The boys were given half a pasteboard heart and girls the other half so they could match up. Next the boys had to escort their "valentines" to the cafeteria and bring them refreshments.

Facing this, Joe was in favor of pouring lemonade down his little partner's charming neck, and I secretly sympathized.

Little girls take to this pairing off, for folk dancing and for skating by moonlight, where the right boy for a partner is highly important. But to boys of 10, it's poison.

Let's give children time to be children, without prematurely thrusting the opposite sex at them from all sides.

MARIE MICHAUD

They speak up and out

Last winter our 15-year-old son announced that he wanted to take public speaking, an evening course sponsored by the county's 4-H Clubs and our local REA.

As far as I could tell, his only speaking abilities ran to debate; he often had heated arguments with his brother over who hogged the bathroom and who should get the larger piece of cake.

Through 4-H, I knew most of the teen-agers in the class. At least I was acquainted with their dancing contortions, far-out discussions and insatiable appetites. I enjoyed these young people, but at times I wondered what kind of human beings we were raising to take over the world.

The classes were held in a small town several miles away. Since there was no place for us chauffeur-parents to spend time profitably, we were allowed to sit in the back row and listen.

I was amazed. The budding speakers covered many topics. They showed broad knowledge, depth of thought, great concern for our nation and our world—and a remarkably solid sense of values.

This insight into their thoughts was a pleasure and a morale builder for me. I'd like to voice my confidence in today's teens.

LOIS FIRMIN

Surprise

Something is wrong. How can this be?
My teen-ager agreed with me!
LAVONNE MATHISON

WE PARENTS GET UP-TIGHT ON WHAT WE OUGHT TO TEACH OUR CHILDREN, BUT DO WE EVER CONSIDER WHAT WE MIGHT LEARN FROM THEM?

FAYE WILLARD

The Pay-off

I toiled for years attempting
To make ladies of my daughters;
With "don'ts" and "do's" I taught them
Their "must not's" and their "ought-ters."
At last I am rewarded
And my heart should be singing,
For now I have two mentors
To see to my upbringing.

ELOISE WADE HACKETT

Just "being"

My three-year-old had disappeared from view. Frantically, I called, "Paul, Paul, where are you?" No answer. "Paul!" again. I rushed out to hunt him.

There he sat on our huge porch. "What are you *doing?*" I said exasperated.

"Being," Paul said.

That didn't sound right, so I sharply asked him to repeat.

"Being. Just being!" (At three, Paul could imitate my own irritability.)

I went back into the kitchen. Being! Of all things. But the word stuck. My three-year-old had suggested something: Why must a boy always be "doing" something. It was time I myself had a little less doing—busyness for busyness sake—and allowed myself a little more being. The pine on the lawn no longer whispers unheard. The Johnny jump-ups don't flower unseen. The wild cherries don't ripen untasted. I'm "being."

LAVERNE HASSE

Grace note

On one of our infrequent trips to the city, my husband and our little son Tony went to a popular, crowded cafeteria for lunch. When we'd passed through the line, the only seats left were at a table for four, where an elegantly dressed stranger occupied one chair.

When I asked, "May we join you?" he nodded agreeably. So we unloaded our trays and sat down. Whereupon Tony, as he always does at home, folded hands, bowed head and in his penetrating voice proclaimed clearly: "Our Father, we thank Thee for this food . . ."

I heard slight, napkin-muffled sounds of choking; but when I opened my eyes, the debonair gentleman beside me had his head bowed, too. I was a little embarrassed, for I discovered that many others were looking at us. Then suddenly I felt a warm glow. Every face wore a smile!

I thought, "And a child shall lead them," and smiled at our not-very-saintly little towhead.

WILLIA C. STONE

My Little Collector

My son's a collector of stones and things,
Of chunks of cement and butterfly wings,
Vessels of sand he has brought me to see;
Interesting twigs and a fly and a bee.
Anything new or old . . .
The roots of a weed, a flower of gold.
Numerous treasures his bright eyes can see
At one and a half. So what will it be
When my little collector's the old age of three?

RITA ALTOFT

Forgotten commandment

In our son's home the custom is to ask a blessing before meals. The turn came for five-year-old Pat to say grace. He ended his prayer with "Bless the Viet Cong."

After we began to eat, Pat's dad remarked, "Son, you know the Viet Cong are our enemies."

Pat didn't hesitate a second to reply, "The Bible says we are to pray for our enemies."

STELLA ELMORE

Be wise with wishes

Last year before Christmas, I told my classes (in our state school for the deaf) the fable of the poor fisherman and his wife who were granted three magic wishes. The wife hastily wished for a pudding as large as a tub. Her husband, angered at her stupidity, wished the pudding stuck on the end of her nose. They had to spend their precious third wish to remove the pudding; so they were no better off than before.

I asked my pupils to make some Christmas wishes, and challenged them to make wiser choices than the pair in the fable. Here are some of the youngsters' replies:

I wish teachers would smile more (Ouch! Could he mean me?)

I wish Mommy and Daddy wouldn't argue. (Their deaf child can't hear the words, but she's sensitive to anger in the air. How much more aware of family discord hearing children must be.)

I wish I could travel all over the world and see everything we study about. (And would that I could go along, atuning all my senses to a keener awareness.)

I wish I could have more time by myself. (Only one who has experienced group or dormitory living can appreciate the depths of this wish.)

I wish we had no war, so my brother could come home. (Amen, amen to that wish.)

EMMYLOU KROHN

Thank-you to whom?

My husband and I were laughing one morning about a letter he'd read in the newspaper's advice column. A man had written, objecting to his son's saying thank-you to God at mealtime. The father felt that he himself should be thanked, since he earned the wherewith to buy the food!

We joked about this point of view, and then forgot it. But not our five-year-old Donny. At supper, he looked at his father and said, "Thank-you, Daddy, for my food." Then he bowed his head, continuing: "And thank You, God, for my daddy."

LOLA JANES

Family theater

All of us become actors when I play with my two small ones, son Jackie and his little sister. When I'm the doctor, it doesn't take long to give the ailing doll a shot (with a fork since I'm usually in the kitchen). When I'm Grandma, I call on the play telephone and invite the children to dinner. At the play-pretend eating place, I switch roles and become a waitress or a carhop.

ROENA SUDIK

I'd rather *not* do it myself

It took an illness to make me realize how much we mothers cheat our children by insisting "It's easier to do it myself."

Since I was confined to a couch, able only to issue instructions, the household chores fell to my three young sons. Instead of the makeshift meals and shoddy house keeping I expected, the boys fried chicken and made pot roast (our nine-year-old even surprised me with a triumph of coconut pie), and cleaned the kitchen, laundry and bathrooms as well as I could.

The biggest thrill to me was their change in attitude. The usual bickering was replaced by sincere joint efforts to get things done. I realized that *my* former attitude of "I'd rather do it myself" had robbed my boys of their due: the pride of accomplishment and satisfaction of usefulness. I also realized that responsibility makes happy children, not rebellious ones.

BETTY HEAD

To stop a quarrel

One night while I was preparing supper, I was giving our two older sons a good tongue lashing. Indeed, I had been scolding them most of the day. Evidently I was carrying things too far, because the four-year-old stopped playing, walked over to me with outstretched arms, and upturned cheek, and cheerfully but firmly declared: "It's *kissing* time!"

Needless to say, we all laughed. Now, those words are magic when one of us gets a little too carried away.

BARBARA MUECK

Land of little people

For days our son Johnny, four, talked of the things he would show his older brother who was soon to return home on service leave. The day and the brother finally arrived. Dinner table conversation among adults, snapped around like rubber bands—flipping from places visited to community happenings, job problems and memories of summers on the farm.

During the meal, I became aware of Johnny's solemn-eyed face and his untouched plate. "Don't you feel well?" I asked. His answer startled and shamed us: "No, I don't. Nobody talks to me in my little world!"

How easy it is to forget the very small—the young citizens of a mini-world.

JANE COLESCOTT

Children . . . the cord that binds

HOW SHARP THE EMOTIONAL SHEARS REQUIRED TO SEVER APRON STRINGS!

First Day of School

My thoughts go with you on the bus,
I see the brightness of your hair,
How small your hands are and, to us,
How wide with trust your eyes. I dare

162

Not think too far beyond this day,
But work away with cloth and brooms.
Your daddy went to load the hay;

He could not stand these quiet rooms.
We lunch in silence, wait and watch
The hours go inching like a year.
We'll soon adjust to this, but now
You seem so young. What's this I hear?
As proud as when you came to us,
Your daddy shouts, "Here comes the bus!"

CONSTANCE FRALEY

I'll not compete

I'm playing second fiddle to three women, and I love it. They are my six-year-old son's teacher and the two school-lunch cooks. Since they have come into his life, my prestige has fallen rapidly. No longer am I queen of his universe, nor am I even his best cook anymore.

But I don't mind; I know that this means that my son is a well-adjusted child, happily moving on away from Mother and finding a new and challenging world at school.

IRIS JUST

Bride-to-be

Shall she wear traditional satin,
With a veil to frame her face?
Will she choose a seed pearl tiara

And grandmother's heirloom lace?
Will she want to be real modern,
Gowned in shimmery pastel blue?
Well, we've lots of time to think yet,
Janie's turning half-past-two!

KAY GERRISH

Ponderings of a soldier's mother

It seems only yesterday they handed him to me, our first-born—dependent on me for all his needs. Today—teen, tall and muscular—he waved as he started for training camp to learn about war.

Yesterday he was sighting wood-chucks along the barrel of his .22. Tomorrow he'll learn how to rain machine-gun bullets at the "enemy."

Yesterday he was playing football (would the coach let him start the game?). Next week he'll be on maneuvers, learning battlefield survival.

Yesterday he was wondering if a certain girl would go to the dance with him (was his white shirt clean and ironed?). Tomorrow night he'll be washing his socks in his helmet.

Yesterday he got his first job—with a good company, at a good salary. Today he made out his insurance to Dad and me.

Before he left today, he talked to me about aggressors, invaders, atomic warfare. I don't understand; I only wonder: What will my son's tomorrows bring? Will I ever hold grandchildren in my arms?

MARGUERITE STANDHART

Monster

There it was! Its distant shape was vague but the color was distinguishable. The Orange Monster was on the prowl again—headed our way!

I drew my child close and remembered how a neighbor had warned me that one day this demon would come to my door. "You'll fight back pools of tears, but after the shock of the first days, you will come to accept the inevitable," she had said.

As the Monster loomed over the hill, I could see the black ribs along its side. I clung protectively to the small figure beside me and searched our son's face for signs of fear. In disbelief I watched a wide smile cross an expanse of freckles. The boy was not afraid!

The Orange Monster stopped at our gate and swung an orange arm out to summon my child. As it left our gate, its black ribs became letters: B-U-S.

I kicked at something in the grass—an apple—then picked it up and ate the tear-salted fruit. No, Teacher, you shall not have this one! I've already yielded you a treasure—the apple of my eye.

NAN ALEXANDER

Growing Up

For two sweet years I was his world;
I diapered, bathed and fed him.
And down each strange and unknown path
With my own hand I led him.

Then he grew up, as babies do,
To be a charming lad,
But when he spoke, his words were these,
"I want to go with Dad."

BEVERLEE SWANSON

Earthy symbol

I guess it's the man-he-is-to-be in a little boy that makes him love worms. He may sense that these wriggly creatures are meant to per-

164

form some important function.

So long as our little boy continues to stuff worms in his pockets, I know he is still part mine. But on the day he appears with a tin can half-filled with dirt and an old cane pole, I shall know that he has embarked on manhood.

And I approve, knowing that the lowly earthworm, like the psychiatrist's couch, helps preserve the sanity of man.

MARY V. BACHMAN

Two-way traffic

I sat alone and the house pushed its silence about me. The rooms were so much larger now. Even so, they seemed unable to hold all the quiet inside them. As I went into the yard, the cloud followed and settled on my shoulders.

Bags packed, goodbyes said, my last child had gone to another part of the country in search of tomorrow.

I choked on dust, only then realizing that my husband had just come up the drive. "Why don't you go with me to get the cows? Bring some bread along; we'll stop at the pond and feed the fish."

The cloud was lifting, the sun sifting through. I walked briskly to the barn toward my waiting husband. As I looked down the gravelled lane, I suddenly realized: That road doesn't only run away from the house. It runs back, too. We will be here, waiting for our child's first visit home.

LETA FULMER

Individual Differences

My husband's relatives agree
    our baby's physiognomy
resembles in each small detail,
    though yet, quite miniature in scale,
someone of their own family.

But I just smile with sweet restraint,
    display the patience of a saint,
and quote authoritative books:
    "Each infant has distinctive looks ...
his own identity ..."

(Besides, it's very plain to see
    he looks just like my family.)

MILDRED R. BENSMILLER

OUR CHILDREN ENJOY CROSSING THE MANY AND VARIED BRIDGES THAT LEAD OVER INTO ADULTHOOD

O NE of my friends believes that children are more self-confident and become more valuable assets to a community if they grow up learning to express themselves well. So she started a Word-a Day Club to encourage her youngsters to build large vocabularies.

Each day she writes a new word on a card and tacks the card on the kitchen bulletin board. Once a week the family has Word Night when they test each other on what these new words mean and how to use them fluently. Mom provides little treats and surprises to make Word Night an occasion.

I have been impressed at how easily the children converse; they are not show-offs, but enjoy talking—and listening. And their mother tells me that their school work has improved.

MRS. J. R. DAVIS

We discovered riches

We were in a hurry to finish chores the other morning and I wondered why Jack, 14, hadn't brought in the cows. He was standing on a tree stump, reciting Shakespeare to a dozen Holsteins!

There was a time when my husband Rex and I would have said that such works as Shakespeare's were for the intellectuals, not for us. Then one evening we were invited to a concert. The symphonic music was strange to our ears. But as we observed how utterly absorbed the audience was, we felt cheated and apart. We talked about this sense of isolation and agreed that in the future we would seek more cultural experiences.

We began by listening to music. I'd put waltzes on the record player as our children went to bed. Then we graduated to Beethoven, Verdi, Chopin and Wagner.

Reading had been part of our life from way back. Lately we've read aloud, this year "Macbeth." That classic play has changed our conversation. The children no longer "turn off" the lights; they say, "Out, out, brief candle!" And when Rex comes in from the barn, someone is sure to pronounce, "All the perfumes of Arabia will not sweeten this little hand!"

Our public library also lends art—reproductions of great paintings. So we change our pictures often and read up on the artists. The children hang their favorites.

The world we live in is alive with creative translations—in music, color and words. We are glad we discovered that all this is for us to enjoy—right here on the farm.

LUCILLE CAMPBELL

Keeping up with kin

Both my husband and I come from large families, but we're scattered; the nearest relatives live 1,000 miles away. We seldom shared their letters with our children, reasoning that the youngsters wouldn't be interested in Hazel's rheumatism or the soybean crop in Minnesota.

But the day when I mentioned Cousin Joanie getting married and our nine-year-old asked, "Who's Joanie?" I decided we had to put some effort into keeping them acquainted with their uncles and aunts and cousins. There is a wonderful sense of "belonging" in a big clan, and we wanted our children to experience it even without the family reunions we attended as children.

So I dug out all the pictures that had been sent us through the years —weddings, babies, graduations, family get-togethers. I arranged in family groups both sets of grandparents, our brothers and sisters and their children, mounted the pictures on green burlap in a frame. Now when I receive snapshots or school pictures or nieces' and nephews' wedding pictures, I add them in the proper places.

We read aloud letters from relatives and encourage the children to write to their cousins. Now when relatives visit, they are real folks and not strangers.

FLORENCE EKSTRAND

Savings Account

Though they don't save for rainy days
(They spend it when it's sunny),
Eventually my children learn
The value of their money.
To speed the process I have found
A method that's a gem:
As soon as they've amassed a bit,
I borrow it from them!

HELEN GORN SUTIN

Our worship center

The favorite corner in our living room is the spot where our children are learning reverence. We have an improvised altar on top of a 4' high bookcase where we place our Bible, beside a tall white candle. A drapery of green cloth provides the background.

At Christmas the Bible is open to Luke 2: 8–20. To the left is a reproduction of Madonna of The Chair, with sprigs of evergreen before it.

The children change the setting according to the season. Our six-year-old brought a beautiful winter bouquet from the woods. As he showed me branches of red berries, I explained that in this way God cares for the birds through the winter and that He loves His human children, too. In spring we gather the first buds and flowers to remind us of the Resurrection as we get ready for Easter.

ESTELLE GRINDE

Courtesy and communication

Our children needed training to improve their manners at mealtime. They not only interrupted each other, but older people, too.

So we started a game. Every day on the way to and from school, each of the children was to look for something interesting to tell about that night—without interruption.

The children liked the idea, and it was surprising how soon they learned to tell their daily experiences with poise, and to listen. They have become closer observers and are always ready with something to relate.

This exercise in narration has been a great help to them at school, and I'm sure it will be an asset in many ways. Anyhow, they no longer interrupt often, and their table manners have improved.

JULIA R. DAVIS

Teacher came for supper

Our eight-year-old son Dennis asked us if he could invite his new teacher to supper. My husband thought that was a grand idea; but sixth-grader Gordon said he saw enough teachers at school without bringing one home. Ann, 5, who can hardly wait to start school, begged, "Please, Mommy!"

When the invitation had been accepted, I began to worry. Mealtimes at our house can be pretty hectic. Usually I am like an octopus on springs; the boys tease Ann and pester me with "How many cookies each, Mom?" And their father must too often remind: "Dennis, take your elbows off the table."

When our guest arrived on the big evening, Dennis proudly introduced his teacher and took her coat. At the table, he solemnly asked the blessing.

I was proud of my family and, my, was the teacher impressed! It was written all over her face. Gordon intelligently discussed a school project, and Dennis manfully helped with the serving. Usually a chatterbox, Ann kept politely quiet. She did lean over once to ask in a stage whisper, "Am I being a good girl?"

When I went to the kitchen to dish up dessert, Dennis brought out the dinner plates. I couldn't resist asking him if it seemed fair to let his teacher think we were always so well-behaved. He answered, "Don't worry, Mom. She has me in school all the time; she knows I'm not really this good."

So I returned to the table to enjoy my perfectly-brought-up family, resolving to invite teacher more often!

ELMA LANG

Special Days

The smoke of dusk curls softly round a world
Of stars and candles. Now the splinter set
Aside so carefully last Yule shall light
A new log. Thus by custom have we met
Again in memory; for hearts, too, hold
Their guarded spark—from warm,
      bright hours reclaim
A cherished brand of friendship to ignite
Each coming year with gold and crimson flame.

DOROTHY P. ALBAUGH

Special Days

NEW YEAR WISHES

Now where shall I begin, to send you
New Year wishes, when a veritable store
Of good may very well be waiting you
Without my words? I wish you health, but more:
An added zest for living; happiness,
With all the dear, innumerable delights
In little things that never fail to bless.
As well as peace of valleys, peace of heights
I wish you; song and laughter, plus a deep
Clear pool of quiet never far removed.
I wish that you be generously loved.
Yet more: your heart have love it cannot keep.
And not only along strange ways, and dim,
But through the sunlight may you walk with Him.
                                        ELAINE V. EMANS

Inexpert prophets

Last New Year's Eve, both my husband and I wrote down our predictions for the coming months. Each tried to foresee what would happen in politics, world events, personal and family affairs, including finances.

Half in fun, half seriously, we sealed away our predictions in an envelope. All too soon the busy year had slipped by and as we again discussed plans for New Year's Eve, we remembered the envelope. We had about forgotten what we'd foretold, so we were curious to break the seal!

Neither of us had been gifted with prophecy, it turned out. Only about half of our predictions had been correct. But something else was instantly apparent: My husband was an optimist. Nearly all his predictions were for improvements and better times to come. Almost all of mine were gloomy, foretelling the worst. I hadn't realized that I was developing such a negative attitude!

Both of us were surprised at the events that had concerned us just one year ago. They seemed trivial in view of all that has happened since, in the family and in the world. (We made the most wrong guesses about our families.)

So, on the basis of last year's inefficient, but self-revealing, predictions, I feel I can profitably make some resolutions:

For one thing, I resolve to borrow some of my husband's optimism; I shall refuse to get wrought up about the world or its people, unless there's some constructive action I can take. And I resolve to be more tolerant and relaxed with those dear ones I *thought* I knew so well until my prophesies proved otherwise.

WILMA PERRY

Resolved not to resolve

As New Year's Day approaches, I'm deciding I'll not resolve to "turn a new leaf." By now I know I *will* sometimes lose my temper, run short of patience and find myself being critical. A leopard can't change its spots! If I can correct a mistake, I will do it. If not, I shall forget it and not let the past becloud the future.

FLORENCE L. WOODEN

Start the new year

When January dawns, I look forward to getting a new calendar to catalog the new year's events. Preferably, this calendar is one of the big, old-fashioned kind with a separate page for each month and about an inch of space for each date.

First I mark the birth dates of family members and friends. These dates remind me of parties to give, gifts and cards to buy and send.

Next I mark dates on which money must be paid out: interest on a loan, installments on land, cattle or machinery; dates on which insurance premiums are due; renewal dates for magazine subscriptions; deadlines on local, state and federal taxes: Keeping those dates in mind helps me manage to have money on hand when it's needed.

Now happier dates: when we're due to receive income—from rent or matured government bonds, for instance. Knowing when money is coming in helps us plan our purchases better.

As time goes on I add dates for business meetings, parties, doctor's appointments and so on. Anytime we want to know when an important thing was done—or is to be done—we "look it up" on our calendar. It's a wonderful help and timesaver.

MATTIE PATTERSON

THE CALENDAR REMINDS US OF HOLI-
DAYS AND DATES FOR CELEBRATION. IT
DOESN'T TELL US WHICH WILL BE OUR
BEST-EVER DAYS — THERE WE'RE ON OUR
OWN TO MAKE THE DAY SPECIAL IN
MEMORY

Easter

Within my hand I held a bulb,
Brown, wrinkled, lifeless—so it seemed.
I placed it deep within the earth,
And trustfully, I hoped and dreamed
As others did, who through the years
Have watched for Resurrection morn
When flowers bloom, warm breezes blow,
Birds sing, and earth's reborn.

FLOSSIE HAMBRECHT

New Easter outfit

Five-year-old Teri Anne helped color Easter eggs for the first time.
When the fascinating job was finished and the mess cleared away, Teri
Anne went to the bathroom to clean up. She stayed such a long time
her mother tapped at the door.

"Honey, aren't you through yet?"

"Wait, Mommy, I want to surprise you." And she did. The opening
door revealed a bare but colorful Teri Anne —here blue, there pink,
elsewhere yellow and violet. She had poured Easter egg dye into the
bath water, and emerged a miniature rainbow.

"I wanted to be pretty for you," was her explanation. Teri Anne's
mother accepted the gesture gracefully.

"Probably the most unusual Easter outfit she'll ever have—splotchy
but beautiful."

EVELYN L. CALDWELL

Angel for a Day

Our Ginger's friends have ringlets,
*   Which frame angelic faces;*
While Ginger's butchered stringlets
*   Suit black eyes, bumps, and braces.*

173

To a son on Mother's Day

Once I lay in labor clutching friendly hands and breathing deeply and yearning for the end; when the fog lifted a small form lay in my arms and it was mother's day.

A hundred nights I asked myself in panic "Is he breathing?" and ran to a cradle and touched your warm body.

On sunny afternoons you stood in your crib and reached for a sunbeam; and you have grasped for tangible things, baubles I cherished that broke at your touch, and I have wept a mother's tears.

I have heard your screams and have run to stop your flowing blood, and sat in emergency rooms stroking your head and holding your hand and praying . . . on mother's day.

I have looked at school pictures of dishevelled children and seen only one face—yours; I have sat in auditoriums where among a hundred performing children only you stood out.

I have watched you at play with strange children and you stood aside shy and frightened; and again I have watched you lead a charge on the haymow with all the neighborhood kids in pursuit. I have gone at the tug of your hand to inspect tree houses, tent houses, caves, leaf piles, forts and snow men. Always it was mother's day.

I have scolded and chastised and paddled; I have cajoled, laughed, applauded, advised. I have untangled fish lines, tied tails for kites, sewed bags for marbles, laced ice skates; I have made milk shakes, baked cookies, packed picnics, performed the many small joys for you that complicate and enrich a mother's day.

I have screamed at you in my impatience over unimportant things, and gone to you in your hurt and apologized. I have recoiled at words or deeds "good" children do not inflict on their mothers, and been overwhelmed with forgiveness when you said, "I'm sorry." Then it was mother's day.

Your father and I have shared you and delighted in the sharing. There were times of arbitration when I explained you to each other and times you drew apart from me for father's days I could not share. Best of all were days of unity and harmony we enjoyed together—family days.

You have come clattering into the house with the smell of school rooms heavy upon you and shouted, "Mama! Guess what?" And I have guessed a thousand times, and known the only truth was that you wanted me there.

From the window I have watched you at play and at work, developing strength and independence, and I have felt the tug of the "silver cord."

174

I have given you over to other mentors—to teachers, ministers, 4-H leaders, coaches—and been grateful to them for what they gave you of themselves and proud to share my mother's days. Sometimes I have been jealous that always you show them your best face while at home you bare your other faces (realizing, of course, that this is as it should be).

The world claims you more and more, and I go to bed not always knowing where you are, but loving you and trying to trust you always.

You bring me a plant for Mother's Day, or a handmade card, a handkerchief, or a bottle of cologne; or you bring me nothing more than you have already given, and certainly you need not. I gave you life, and every fulfilling day since you have given me back something wonderful of yourself on a succession of endless mother's days.

PATRICIA P. LEIMBACH

Mother-in-law Day

With Mother's Day approaching, I can't help but think what a wonderful person my husband's mother is. I am thankful that my children have the opportunity to know this older woman who does creative and interesting things.

Come spring, she's watching for a hot sunshiny day following a rain. She'll give her two sisters-in-law and three special friends (they call themselves the Sociable Six) a "mushroom ring" on the phone: "Come on out! I'll fix the hamburgers."

They used to walk, but now they all pile in the car. Generally it's noon when they get to the woods, so they find wood for the fire. Mother starts the hamburgers, then out come salads, potato chips, cookies. Each fills her plate and finds a log to sit on to enjoy the exhibit presented by Nature. The leaves are coming out, the birds are in tune and Dutchman's Britches and violets are appearing.

Then out for mushrooms! Shrieks fill the air as each gatherer finds her first one. When their eyes become accustomed to searching, the mushrooms are easier to find and identify.

Later they look for wildflowers, and may select some for their own gardens. Then they head homeward.

For these hardy oldsters, it's mushrooming in the spring, nutting in the fall and quilting in the winter. They celebrate each of their birthdays, too. Mother-in-law and her friends set an amazing example of sheer enjoyment of living!

VIRGINIA GRAY

What Mother yearned for

"Happy Birthday, Mom! Bet we got just what you wanted."

What I wanted? New gutters . . . whole day at home alone . . .no more late departures for the school bus . . . gates to replace sagging gaps . . . health for the children, and peace in their time. . . .

"Go on, open the package."

"Lovely! A nylon nightie. How could you have guessed it was *just what I wanted!*"

SUE GERARD

Happy anniversary

One year when bills were overdue and the bank balance read precariously close to zero, I knew there would be no gift exchange on our wedding anniversary.

During the afternoon my husband drove off in the car without a word of explanation. Soon he returned and walked silently into the kitchen where I was working.

"For a happy anniversary, Sweetheart!" he whispered and held out a red plastic tulip he had brought from the dime store.

I immediately remembered the ad, "One tulip says, 'I love you!' " I was so touched, I burst into tears.

Days are better now and the anniversary gifts are more expensive, but the flower that graces our table on anniversaries is that same red plastic tulip.

JEANE CAMPBELL

To Husband, with love

It's difficult for me to come up with a birthday gift my husband can appreciate. So, this year I'm keeping a record of the tools he borrows from friends. I'll select his gifts from that list. I hope both he and his friends will be pleased!

RUBY LAWSON

Mother's Day

She mended a dolly, and the washing waited.
The dust lay thick while a fish hook was baited.
When Injuns attacked, her dinner burned up.
She provided a bed for a straying pup.
A two-year-old helped with the cookie dough.
The ironing dried out while she romped in the snow.
Her neighbors whispered to one another,
But her children laughed and adored their mother.

CAROLYN BEAUCHAMP

Hit gift

A corsage with spendable foliage is sure to make a hit with Mother on a birthday or Mother's Day. Buy a real or artificial flower, trim it with several bright, new bills for leaves and deliver it in a gift box. It will buy some luxury Mother has secretly wanted; and it's an easy way for her grown children, who may live too far apart for a family confab, to agree on what to get.

VERA LUND PRAAST

Financing a family reunion

Many families are not able to get together because one member is located far from home. This was the case with my husband's youngest brother. Getting his education after World War II and supporting a family of five, left little for a cross-country trip. He hadn't been home in 14 years. We felt that seeing him and his family would be a real vacation for all of us. So his parents and each of his three brothers contributed $50.

The trip was assured. How the old homestead rocked with fun those short weeks. The dozen grandchildren, ranging in age from 4 to 19, were together for the first time.

This plan didn't work a hardship on any of us and paid off in real pleasure. We recommend others consider the idea.

MARIE PAGE

Commencing commencement

My husband and I buy each of our children a high school graduation present as soon as he enters second grade. The gift is a $37.50 Savings Bond. By the time he graduates, it will be a nice round $50.

Since graduation is the time when there are a good many extra expenses, it is nice to know that there is a substantial present already bought. Meanwhile we are helping Uncle Sam!

LETA DUNN

Vacation from family

Fun though it is to bring up children, child-rearing years are very confining. Everyone needs a vacation *away* from the children occasionally. So, we worked out a vacation-from-kids scheme with friends of ours. We "borrowed" each other's children.

My husband and I were the first vacationers. Our daughters took a few treasured possessions to their temporary home to make them feel secure. And in the excitement of their own "vacation" they forgot to wail.

When we returned from our trip our girls had been happy and well-behaved. Their temporary mother vowed that visitors in the house had provided so much fun that brother-sister squabbles in her own family had disappeared.

I wasn't so confident of my ability to manage. But when my turn came I discovered what it does for a household when its children have guest playmates—and learn the art of being guests in other homes.

ANNE PAYNE

Winter vacation— free!

Most of us, up our way, tire of our northern winter long before it is over. But not too many of us can give the cows sleeping pills, and then take off for Florida or California when we're bored with snow and ice. But last winter our family had a real vacation 1,000 miles south—without ever leaving home.

For our "visit" we picked a small city in the southwest, and subscribed to its daily paper. At first we were chiefly interested in the weather report. We warmed up every time the temperature at our vacation spot was 20 or 30 degrees higher than our own. That felt so good we started combing the real estate ads for farm bargains.

Were we in for a shock! Our 80-acre Wisconsin farm would hardly buy a small house with three to ten acres of irrigated land. Home looked pretty good, after all.

Then, we went grocery and furniture shopping by way of the ads. Those prices were on a par with ours.

We read the local news, and learned lots about the life in our El Dorado that the travel booklets never mentioned. We found out what went on in the churches, what kind of parties people had, how the local high school team was doing in basketball. People were worried about a drought, there—and we worried, too.

When our three months' subscription ran out, spring in Wisconsin was just around the corner. We returned to here and now, considerably set up over our newspaper "vacation" in the South—but quite willing to settle down at home again.

LUCINDA OAKLAND MORKEN

It was a lovely day

Today I did two things that I had forgotten I could do—and brought laughter to my children.

First, I rode a bicycle. Unsteadily and shakily I reached the top of the hill, and as I sped down the other side, completely missing the turn at the foot and careening up the lawn, I realized I had no brakes. I can still hear my son's laughter, and my own.

The other thing I did was to go after the cows with our five-year-old Susan. Susie and I started down the lane to find the cows in the cool of the woods. When we came to the pasture, we stopped and called the cows. They slowly got up and came to us, switching their tails.

I remembered how I jumped happily from bog to bog when I went to call the cows when I was a youngster. "I'll jump bogs with you," I said. We laughed and jumped.

As we reached the house, Susan said, "Didn't we have fun?"

Well, that's what I did today. Not much. But the joy my two children had, and have as they retell these experiences, makes me realize how it's the little, seemingly unimportant things that add up to happiness or the reverse in childhood.

SHIRLEY FREDERICK

Children need change of pace

Just before mid-winter school recess, our daughter, who's in the third grade, brought home a paper she'd written on "What I'll Do During Vacation." Reading it, I was stunned to realize how dull home can be for farm children sometimes.

Lois had written: "I don't think we will go any place. We will do the same thing we always do."

Her words inspired me to plan something pleasant for the children to do every day during vacation—nothing expensive or even very time-consuming.

One day, for example, we just built a fire in the fireplace and sat on the floor in front of it, eating popcorn. Another day we took them to see a puppet show. The children's own animated chatter about their vacation assured me that it had been far from dull!

SELMA GRANT

Special Days . . . Thanksgiving

THE GRATITUDE SEASON REMINDS ME OF PRIVILEGES I SOMETIMES FORGET TO APPRECIATE

WATCHING baby calves grow into cows . . . having a sun-darkened little boy yell "Mom!" from atop his own pony . . . being praised for the chicken I've served fried to a golden brown . . . having homemade butter that melts over homemade rolls . . . received a coffee-break kiss from a grease-smudged husband. We farm women are the most blessed of all—I am sure of it.

BERNICE M. GRIFFITH

Preferred stock

A wonderful thing happened to our family about Thanksgiving time last year. We met a plane from the Orient and received our two newly adopted sons. Brian four, and Billy, two, were born of Korean mothers; their fathers were American soldiers. Social outcasts in their native country, the boys were precious additions to our home.

That first night Billy soon fell asleep in his crib. Brian, fresh from his bath, curled up in his new father's lap and they rocked in front of the fire. I don't know whose face showed the most contentment, Brian's or Daddy's.

179

Seeing how our boys have responded to love and care makes our hearts ache for the thousands of orphans overseas who will never know the warmth of belonging in a family. Our three older children, in high school and college, love their adopted brothers devotedly and are the boys' self-appointed teachers.

As for my husband—he calls these dark-eyed adoptees our "preferred stock in the Orient." Surely Brian and Billy have brought us dividends far more worthwhile than we'd ever realize from a purely financial investment.

MAXINE DeVILBISS

Symbolic place-cards

Thanksgiving at our house used to be mostly a matter of loading ourselves with food—a far cry from the Pilgrims' first winter in the New World, when they were stalked by starvation, freezing weather, Indians and disease.

Legend has it that at one time there was just enough corn to give each Pilgrim only five grains. So, to remind us of our forefathers' hardships and their spirit of gratitude, we started the custom of placing five grains of corn for each person at our Thanksgiving table.

We place the grains in tiny cellophane bags, tie the bags with ribbon and pin on name cards. Before we carve the turkey, each person tells of the five things he has been most thankful for during the year.

When we seriously count our blessings, remembering what hardship really is, we are truly thankful for the good things that are ours.

MILDRED DOOLEY CATHCART

Thanksgiving Table

How joyously I offer praise for all
These dear hands folded now in thankfulness
In their familiar places; large and small
Well knowing in their own way how to bless.
Square little-boy hands; butterfly-deft ones
Of little girls; old hands whose touch instills
Quiet wisdom; strong hands warm with many suns,
And mother-hands adept in tender skills—

Oh, I am thankful for the touch of these
Loved hands on mine, for all the wealth they hold
Of gentleness, and love, and healing ease;
And thankful, most of all, that all who fold
Their hands in reverential, thankful prayers
May feel the hand of God enfolding theirs.

JANE H. MERCHANT

Gratitude summary

Thanksgiving is around the corner again. Here is my parade of little blessings for which I want to say "Thank-you, God":

The baby's napping, so I could get the wash done without interruption ... The roast I almost burned, which turned out tender after all ... the rain coming down from the south the day I'd left the *north* windows open when we went to town ... My baking a cake at exactly the right time—just before guests arrived unexpectedly.

Mom's bringing us bath towels when we were about to hit bottom in the linen cupboard ... Having the baby's photo turn out real cute, though she was grouchy as all get-out during the photography ... The head of the house dropping a raw egg—in the sink, not on the floor!

SYLVIA HEKEN

A farm wife reflects on abundance

Here on our Pennsylvania farm, Thanksgiving climaxes what I call our season of abundance. It begins in late summer when flowers bloom continuously and, though we give away vegetables galore, the garden has a surplus. As the season progresses, orchard trees become heavy with fruit, vines with melons.

By mid-November our barn is brimful of hay, wheat bins overflow and great golden loads of corn are stored. If we've had a good year! An extra generous harvest provides a lovely chord in our symphony of abundance.

Every farmer knows that all this didn't just happen. Only by clear planning, hard decisions, proven procedures and bold new techniques —and a measure of luck—does he reap an abundant harvest. Even then he cannot always be certain of reaping richly. There are dry spells, drastic drouths, sometimes too much rain and always the danger of hail or early frost. On the other hand, a super harvest or a drop in exports may send prices to rock-bottom.

The dyed-in-the-wool farmer finds a particular abundance in his partnership with nature—the seasons, the soil, the sun and rain and snow, the seeds he plants, the creatures he breeds and feeds. He knows with a quiet certainty that—good times or bad—nothing could induce him to exchange the way he has chosen to make a living. He uses this slack season at the end of the crop year to restore his perspective. He has a little time now—to reflect on his values, to look for possibilities he has missed. He has time to balance the rewards against the frustrations. He may consider how, in the foreseeable future, the food which farmers produce might be more skillfully distributed, to eliminate hunger throughout the world. He values himself anew; for it's his business to feed the hungry, and his business is indispensable.

Gradually he regains a sense of order, of faith that he can weather a hard year as well as exult in a year of ample yield and profit.

As a farmer's wife, I have been impressed with the analogy between cultivation of the soil and cultivation of the soul. Abundance of the spirit doesn't just happen either. As when growing crops, one must make difficult decisions, follow proven procedures, explore new horizons.

It isn't easy for one's soul to "yield"—the spirit, too, has its dry spells and destructive storms. Nor can we be sure of the compensations. Most of us escape real, material want; but we all inevitably suffer sadness, anxiety, frustration and disappointment. Disasters on the national and international scene remind us that tragedy, also, is no respecter of persons; it visits the rich, the poor and the in-between.

A special abundance results, though, when we can begin to see adversity as an ordered part of total experience and look for ways we can use an unhappy time to advantage. In much the same way a farmer takes stormy weather to make his machinery repairs, we may use a troubled interval for repairing and renewing the spirit.

We may, for the time, simply be still and know that God is God. The skeptics say that He is dead; but I have no other name for the very alive force which moves me to keep seeking and working toward spiritual fulfillment . . . toward the inner abundance for which we humans yearn.

BLANCHE PERKINS ZIMMERMAN

An extra day for thanks

As a young family, we wanted to have a tradition of our own for our immediate family.

Christmas and Thanksgiving are big family affairs, so we decided to have an extra Thanksgiving Day on July 4th. Our wheat harvest is always over before the Fourth; so what better time to give thanks?

We've done this for seven years and our children really look forward to it. I cook a regular Thanksgiving dinner, from turkey to pumpkin pie. Our one concession to the season is corn on the cob!

Even if the crop should turn out to be a poor one and I'd have to serve baked hen, we would still have much for which to be thankful.

MURIEL STAUTH

Horn of plenty

What a year! Each harvest in its turn seemed the most abundant. Our rains began in mid-July; after that, you should have seen our garden and fruit crops! Plus the wild fruits the kids kept bringing me; we put up chokecherries, blackberries . . . I don't remember a year *ever* with as much of everything.

October even brought us another baby. The family voted in advance for a boy. I "thought pink," but the only hint of pink was *his* hair!

LORRAINE KINSTETTER

Christmas

Christmas is loving,
Is giving and receiving,
Is God come to earth.

RUTH DUERKSEN

Christmas

I REMEMBER CHRISTMAS—THE SEASON'S
EXCITEMENTS AND STARRY-EYED WON-
DER, ITS SPECIAL HAPPENINGS, ITS PER-
VADING JOLLITY AND LOVE

C HRISTMAS has a way of bringing long thoughts. Busy as you
are, you'll recall from the past a special Christmas day, an unforgettable hour or moment, and hold it in reverie.

What is there about a particular memory that makes Christmas
mean more forever after? Childhood delights—the suspense, the
smells, the sounds, the shine of Christmas. The special doll or toy.
The first Christmas you spent among strangers or welcomed a new-
comer to your circle. A time when your thoughts blended with another's—a spiritual sharing.

Remember the Christmas when somebody (you?) smoothed life's
seamy side for someone, or when a little miracle turned sadness into
joy?

Such memory standouts emphasize the good-will theme: Heaven
and earth are not far apart. The ways in which we reflect God's love
bring us closer to him—Christmas and every day.

Heaven, I think, is a place where you'll feel as you did on
Christmas morning when you were eight

For weeks before Christmas, the large double door between our living
room and parlor was kept mysteriously closed. We children weren't
allowed in the parlor; but such beautiful sounds came from in there—
rustlings of paper, squeakings of nails being pulled out of wooden
boxes. . . . Evenings we'd sit in front of the hard-coal burner and string
popcorn and cranberries. For every grain or berry we strung, we ate

two of course!... Christmas Eve was so exciting, we could scarcely eat our supper; for soon Santa would rap on the parlor side of that door.

When the rap came, we had to wait until Santa could get away across the front porch. (He never stayed—he had other visits to make.) Then Mother opened the door, and there was the most beautiful tree in the world. Sniffing its fragrance was like taking a walk through a pine forest.

How much children miss today, not seeing lighted candles on the Christmas tree. Our parents had to watch out for fire, but we saw only the breath-taking beauty of countless dancing flames.

About that time Father would come in—always just too late to hear Santa rap on the door!

GLADYS BURNS

I specially remember that Mother had sent away for a box of six angels. They were four or five inches tall, had yellow hair and spun-glass wings and robes. They cost 25¢ a box! In childhood there's none of that "anticipation is better than realization" logic. Christmas, no matter how simple, is pure Paradise.

VERA LUND PRAAST

How vividly I recall a Christmas when snow fell and we children awoke to find "reindeer tracks" and sled marks leading from driveway to brick chimney. Thence the trail led out to the calf barn—old Santa must have taken off from there. He had really come down our chimney! To prove it there was a big sooty boot print on the hearth. We young ones were almost teen-age before we caught on to older brother's loving deception.

LUCILLE THOMPSON

The message of the cactus

Grandma's Christmas cactus! It just *had* to bloom by Christmas. Along in October, each year, Grandma began her anxious hovering watching for buds.

Then came the day when she called to us excitedly, "Daddy! Celia! Come here quick! The cactus is budded!"

Sure enough there were the microscopic buds. A quick calculation confirmed Grandma's heart's desire. "Yes, it'll make it by Christmas!"

The Christmas cactus was typical of Grandma. Money was scarce, life was simple and frugal, but she knew that souls need feeding too. So, though blizzards might rage, hens stop laying, the pump freeze and mail be delayed by snow-blocked roads, still there would be fragrant gingerbread baking, and the Christmas cactus blooming in rosy radiance during our stark Iowa winter.

Many times in the years that followed, I would have been destitute had it not been for the soul-food that Grandma taught me to appreciate so long ago: the red flash of a cardinal . . . a crusty heel of warm fresh bread . . . or a Christmas cactus against the snow.

CECELIA STANLEY DERRY

At that very moment Santa might be downstairs

When I was small, I received a lovely doll every Christmas. But one year I heard Mother and Dad agree that now I was too old for a doll. I couldn't bear that!

I thought of all the dolls Santa had brought me—mama dolls, baby dolls, special ones like Shirley Temple and Snow White. To my parents I said nothing; but when we went shopping Christmas Eve, I secretly bought a tiny dime-store doll. She had pigtails and dimples, and was "just my age." After grownups were in bed, I placed her under the tree —along with all my doll family, as was my custom.

That Christmas present to myself, at age 10, is the gift I remember best. I think this dolly helped me over a hard "first step" in my growing up.

RUTH SCHAEFFER

Unforgettable journey

My husband and I were traveling by train from Omaha, Nebraska, to San Bernardino, California. We were due to arrive in time for breakfast on Christmas morning; this meant we'd spend Christmas Eve aboard The Challenger. It was a long holiday-train; those in our car ranged from young families to grandparents.

What a congenial group! Toward evening someone suggested that we celebrate the season by singing carols and sharing some Christmas treats. Immediately to my mind came the thought, and why not also share the Nativity Story?

No sooner did I make the suggestion than I was pressed to perform. In my travel case I had a beautiful, red leather Bible. I had read the Story often—from St. Luke, the second chapter; but never before had I read it aloud while streaking through a star-studded night across the plains of Wyoming!

The reverent hush that followed was at last ended, as someone began to sing, and we all joined in: *Silent night, holy night . . .*

VIOLET M. GEARY

My memory is of Dad . . .

When I was nine, we had an especially severe winter. Since we lived two miles out in the country, my folks agreed that I'd stay overnight with my girl friend if a big storm should come up on a school day. And storm it did—a real blizzard—the day of our evening Christmas program at the church.

My parents had anticipated bad weather and sent my best dress. The roads were practically impassable—few farm families would get in.

When it came my turn on the program I was close to tears because none of my family was there. But suddenly the door opened quietly and in walked my dad! He couldn't take the horses out, but he walked two miles through the storm to hear me "say my piece."

BLANCHE HOLMES

Christmas . . . gifts

FOR THE FIRST TIME I UNDERSTOOD THE TRUTH—THAT IT'S MORE BLESSED TO GIVE THAN TO RECEIVE

I was 19 and teaching my first school. It was a depression Christmas. My father was a farmer, and that year there was no money at all. We teachers hadn't even been paid; but a few days before Christmas I received my first salary check!

On the way home for the holidays, I stayed overnight with my aunt in town, and did the first real Christmas shopping of my life. I got dolls for my two youngest sisters; a red wagon for my little brother; balls, books, dishes and tops for the older children; a rattle for the baby.

What excitement when I showed up, gift-laden, at the old farmhouse! We had no tree that year, but we surely did have Christmas in in our hearts.

CARMA LEE WALKER

Picture story

Our farm is all things to my husband, his vocation and his hobby. So, January before last, I started a picture-and-caption book about the farm—for his gift the next Christmas.

Camera in hand, I recorded the new farrowing stalls, sows and litters, porkers at regular intervals. I placed selected snapshots chronologically in a scrapbook, each appropriately captioned: *You tried barley on this bunch. . . . This gilt's performance was impressive.*

The scrapbook also had a sheep section and one for crops. Plus miscellaneous: *You set those cedar posts in September. I argued for oak, remember?*

Bill was delighted with his picture story. So I added a notation, "To be continued."

EVELYN WITTER

Giving with purpose

A couple of Christmases ago, after we had opened our numerous and beautiful gifts to one another, our grown daughter sat silent and thoughtful. Finally she burst out: "Ridiculous! We don't need all this!"

Every one of us agreed. And last Christmas was different. Each of our three families—son's, daughter's, my husband and I—gave $30 and Grandmother gave $6, for a total of $96 to help send one student to the Hwalien Girls School for a year of nurse's training. It takes three years for our student to graduate, so we will repeat our gift each year until that is accomplished.

Needless to add, we cut down on our gifts to the children and their grandmother. The remaining six of us drew names for a $1.50 gift. Now Christmas has a new and deeper meaning for us all—because the girl we are helping will, in turn, give of herself by serving her people on Taiwan.

MRS. EDWIN THIEMANN

Gift exhausts itself in giving joy

Today I made a candle for a friend. I asked her not to save this gift but to use it right away. One must burn a candle in order to enjoy its whole beauty and meaning. It is a symbol of faith, a gift from the heart. . . . A gift candle carries the giver's hope that the one who lights it will have long-lasting health, harmony, happiness and prosperity.

DOROTHY ENGLERT

Miracle of sharing

I had the afternoon before Christmas off from my job as Star Route mail lady; so I visited my new next-door neighbor. She was young—with three small children, and a husband at work for the first day since their arrival. Through her bright shield of pride I could see she was distressed over how to explain "no Christmas" to her anticipating youngsters.

Back home, I pondered how I might help without offending. I could hear the children "playing Christmas." . . . My reverie was interrupted by two farmers who lived on my mail route. They were delivering a huge pine—their Christmas gift to me.

But those children came running. "Santa gave you the wrong address! We live over there!"

Our grownup eyes met above the youngsters' heads—then my friends delivered the tree to the "right" place. That broke the ice! Now a shopping trip was imperative; then, after their children slept, our neighbors joined in the fun of trimming and wrapping.

Christmas morning that tree shimmered over packages bunched forward to look plenteous. My husband and I, basking in the children's happiness, forgot our own unopened packages.

THELMA DOHERTY

Christmas every month

Last Christmas I gave my mother a gift of my time in the form of day-long trips. The trips were to be of her choosing. To make the gift tangible at the appropriate time, I made a booklet containing 13 "tickets" —one for each month and extra for the immediate holiday week. The tickets, bright and varicolored, read: *Present this ticket in* (name of month) *for a trip of your choice with Margaret* (me) *and Sunbeam* (the car). *Up to two guests may be invited.*

Our trips have included picnics, an afternoon of gathering wild-flowers, several visits with friends or relatives, a nut-gathering outing in the fall and a shopping trip to a nearby city.

My gift to Mother has been a gift to myself also—one I hope to repeat each Christmas for many years.

MARGARET POST

For Mothers at Christmas

For all the mothers, Lord, who lift
Their prayers with love which never tires
That every child may have the gift
At Christmas, which his heart desires—
O teach the anxious ones, dear Lord,
Children are wiser than we know,
And it is not the shining hoard
Of presents to admire and show
That matters most to them, but being
Together with the ones they love
And knowing they are glad, and seeing
Thy glory in the stars above,
And sharing the wonder, still and bright,
That came to earth one holy night.

JANE MERCHANT

Christmas in July

Years ago a friend of my mother's came to call while my husband and I were working in the garden one early spring evening. She gave us a packet of globe amaranth seeds and told my husband to plant them— not too close together, and in a sunny location in the yard.

They became strong plants and produced beautiful flowers—we even won a blue ribbon at the State Fair the following summer. Later that year, I saved the seeds from the flower heads for the next season's garden plantings.

I thought about those seeds as Christmas drew near. For different greeting cards that year, I bought plain folded notepaper and some small waxed-paper envelopes that stamp collectors use. On the front of

190

the paper I sketched the globe amaranth blossom, stem and leaf. Inside the fold, I enclosed the envelope containing enough seeds for a garden border, planting instructions plus the message, "from my garden to yours."

The following summer a friend living in Georgia wrote of a new friendship she gained because of the globe amaranth seeds I'd sent her. Others too, have written of the pleasure they've received from these lovely flowers. Another year, I'll try orange cosmos.

CAMILLA KNOX

Gift for Small Boy

When buying a gift for the modern boy
This formula can't be beaten:
Always select an object that can
Be blown or smashed or eaten!

GRACE V. WATKINS

Our wear-forever gifts

It used to be that our children received too many Christmas toys, most of which were lost or scattered, broken or forgotten by February. My husband and I decided there must be a more rewarding way to spend for gifts.

We hit upon a great idea: Each Christmas we'd start a year-round hobby for the whole family. Last Christmas it was an aquarium. We have spent the year since, learning about breeds of small fish (we're even raising a brood of little ones), and types of plants that grow well in aquariums. The better informed we become, the more interested.

This Yule, our gift to ourselves will be a camera; the new project, photography. By the end of another year we expect to be developing and printing our own snapshots.

Other projects in view are stamp-collecting, painting, camping, maybe even glass blowing!

The most important part of a family hobby is to involve everyone; to read together about the new interest, to work at it and enjoy it together. We can honestly say that now we have a new rapport within our family of eight.

ANNEMARIE DIRKMAN

Gift extraordinary

My Christmas present this year is the 160-acre woodland farm my husband and I bought early this year, after living in town for 35 years and rearing our family there. As I look out the window, I see white-frosted trees sparkling in the sun. The evergreens are more beautiful than any decorated tree, there are so many of them.

Yesterday eight deer walked across the field, single file, heads up, white tails bobbing. In the fall we had a coon visitor; our dog had chased him from the cornfield and treed him in the big elm near the back door.

All summer I enjoyed picking wild fruits—raspberries, chokecherries, high-bush cranberries, gooseberries. They made wonderful table treats, and there were plenty left over to preserve. My husband hunts in our woods and fishes in the lake nearby. But he is a good farmer, too; right now he is down by the barn, feeding the sheep.

Not all retired couples should take to the land; but for us it was right. We are happier and in better health than we were 10 years ago. With what enjoyment we will welcome our children and grandchildren to share this first Christmas on the farm!

ANNA KERTSCHER

Christmas puzzlement

Why does a money gift offend some people? Money is one thing that can't be criticized for inferior quality or poor workmanship.

FLORENCE ANDERSON

Heirloom gift

My daughter's first Christmas present to her baby was the little red chair which had been *her* first Christmas gift, years ago, from a favorite uncle.

EFFIE MONDS

The angel smiled

When our second son came home from college for the holidays, he insisted that Dad and I take a trip to Florida—he'd stay home and look after his invalid brother. At our first motel, we were across from a little church. Carols and spotlights proclaimed that services were beginning, so we hurried over.

Outside the church we saw the most beautiful and realistic Nativity scene. There was a temporary lean-to, its earth floor covered with straw. Mary and Joseph moved about caring for the Baby, a life-size doll. A cow, with newborn calf beside her, calmly munched hay. Shepherds carried real lambs, and were accompanied by a white dog.

Three angels "hovered" on a high platform. They had an ethereal look—accomplished, we learned later, by imaginative stagecraft. Yards and yards of pale green nylon net veiled the heavenly scene. The angels were so motionless that my husband insisted that they were not real people. But when he peered up at them, one smiled. . . .

Thus did we commemorate the birth of God's Son. The experience was enriched by the knowledge that our own son had given up his holidays so that his parents might have a treasured adventure.

MRS. HERMAN L. ROBERTSON

Traditional mystery

When I was small and asked curiously what Grandmother was doing behind closed doors at Christmas time, she'd reply mysteriously, "I am making a coat for a green elephant." This has become a familiar expression in our family. (I told it to my godchild last year and he kept looking, literally, for a gift-coated green elephant!)

It is a nonsensical way to reaffirm that Christmas is giving—of the heart as well as of things. We deliver many gifts from our farm. For our city relatives we make up boxes of walnut meats, dried fruits. We give quart jars of honey to the children's music teacher, our retired minister, the man who drives the milk truck. Then, for a couple of shut-ins in retirement homes, I make foot-high cone trees. (These really make a hit!)

It would be simpler to go out and buy all our presents. But that would defeat the concept. For Christmas is extra thoughtfulness. It's whispered consultations with each child about the others. It's "a coat for a green elephant."

DOROTHY KENNEDY

Of the spirit

My gift to a busy young mother: two days during the holiday season to spend as she wishes—to shop, rest or visit. I keep her children at my home and enjoy that as well as the mother does. We both regard this as a "gift of the spirit," tailored to her special need.

MRS. C. FURNER CAIRNS

Christmas . . . and Santa, please

DEAR SANTA: PLEASE BRING TO THE WORLD—AND TO MY FAMILY—AN IRRESISTIBLE URGE TO PRACTICE THE GOLDEN RULE. BUT FOR A STARTER, AND MOSTLY FOR ME, HOW ABOUT A PACKET OF GIFTS EVERY HARASSED MOTHER NEEDS?

COULD you bring me a calm voice to replace my frenzied one? I could do with a big supply of patience, too. My stock was rather small to begin with, and it dwindled alarmingly what with teen-age phone calls, daily battles over home work and the pet turtle getting loose.

What do you have that would help me keep order among our family bulletin boards, scrap books, unfiled clippings and articles? Every family needs handy information on dinosaurs, atomic research, and the culture of Ancient Rome; my husband looks at me strangely when he opens a closet door and a box of clippings falls on his head. (Maybe you could bring *him* a crash helmet.)

In fact, if you could spare a fourth-dimension closet, it might solve our storage problems. Our passion for geology has resulted in a half-ton collection of rocks. I also need a Handy-Dandy Mind Reader's Magic Menu and Meal Maker guaranteed to put a stop to cries like "But we already had that spaghetti glop at school!"

And Santa, dear, if you have any leftover hours, please drop them down our chimney. It would be wonderful to have some time every day for thinking deep thoughts, reading Shakespeare and making myself pretty.

Now, in case you think I don't want to give as well as receive, I'd like you to know that I'll gladly give you 30 or 40 nice chubby pounds I've managed to pick up along the way.

Merry Christmas!

VERNA SMITH TRESTRAIL

Help wanted

I would like a chance for my dairy farmer husband and me to get away from children and cows for a week or so.

This involves a reliable baby-sitter—one whom our three children like, and who knows that the odd chirring sound in the kitchen wall is only young chimney swifts. Also, we'd need a substitute farm manager; there's too much for our hired man to do alone, even for a week.

If you can't possibly give us that second honeymoon, see what you can do to help me develop a this-too-shall-pass perspective about drouth, a 3-year-old's phases and the pressure of time.

JOANNE PASSMORE

My very own want list

My wants for Christmas fall into two categories: Intangibles—world peace, a healthy family, good crops; and real, solid, touchable *things.* Such as:

1. A kitchen-desk for me. A large one with room on top for my cookbooks, a lid to cover whatever current disorganization I'm involved in, and drawers that are mine alone—free of old spelling workbooks, defunct clocks, obsolete *Popular Mechanics,* loose bird shot. (Note: I specify No Telephone here. A telephone makes a desk everyone's—and this one is for *me.* Exclusively!)

2. A lovely, extravagant perfume—my annual request. Despite my shirttails, sneakers, and drill-instructor voice, I want my family never to forget Mother is a girl.

MARJORIE EATOCK

Christmas by the foot

We have nine children, and my fondest yearning is for a year's supply of footwear, both for Sunday and everyday.

Oh, to be relieved for one whole year of driving 40 miles to the only store I've found with shoes that fit the high-arched, extra-wide feet of our 12-year-old. Or of wrestling to fit shoes on the chubby feet of the littlest preschooler.

I dread the indecision of our high school daughter who trails from store to store. I wince at the wallet-deflating bill after buying the two oldest girls their "career" shoes. But how proud our boys are when they graduate into men's sizes (and prices).

Now for boots. In our snowy climate, my year's supply would include: low mud rubbers, stadium boots, four-buckle arctics, zipper boots for the kids, not to mention insulated hunting boots for the men of the family.

We always need bedroom slippers, though there is a certain amount of handing down in this department. You may bring sneakers by the carload—all sizes and any color.

One piece of footwear you need not bother about: my Christmas stocking. My old one will do fine!

LORRAINE KINSTETTER

Lock of hair enclosed

My wish takes some advance ordering to be just right. I'd like to have a glamorous wiglet—a hairpiece to perch atop this utilitarian clipped-in-the-back and flat-curl-over-the-ear hairdo.

Then when that wonderful year-round Santa of 20 years standing says: "Let's eat out tonight and see what's going on among the other half," I can be up-to-date for the occasion.

BETTY KING

Equipment for living color

I want a camera, the kind used by professionals. They're so expensive I've never dared to whisper this wish.

How I'd love to match the gleam of anticipation in my pet ewe's golden eyes, as she gallops towards me for a cookie. With a telephoto lens I'd catch the self-satisfied smirk on an old sow's face as, rhythmically grunting, she lines up her pigs for lunch.

How I would treasure a picture of the man in my life in after-supper contentment. Chores done and lawn freshly mowed, dogs and cats gathered in a circle of adoration—His Majesty in a lawn chair, king of all he surveys.

My farm home and its surroundings are lush with photographic material, but with my make-do camera I get a blob of color here and a what's-that shadow there. I guess I really want to show others the simple magic that delights me as I go about my daily duties.

LETA FULMER

NOW MORE THAN EVER, FAMILIES SHOULD OBSERVE AT LEAST ONE CHERISHED CHRISTMAS CUSTOM, TO OFFSET THE IMPERMANENCES OF THESE TIMES

OUR family's day in the mountains getting a Christmas tree is the highlight of our Yule preparations. We enjoy that trek every year. A family of neighbors goes along; one year my diary recorded nine children, from tots to age 10.

For us, the tradition of finding and cutting our own tree began when I was a little girl living on the West Coast. The woods weren't far from home; our excursions were brief and usually without the excitement of snow. Now my husband and I must take our gang much farther and higher, through snow that invites a lot of frolicking.

We always take along sleds and skis. We don't have a regular ski run, so we use the natural hills. My husband is building a "sno-cat" to tow us uphill after a slide. (It will also be handy for getting feed to the cattle when the snow is deep on our range.)

We build a fire—for warming and drying out, and for cooking our meal. The men are our campfire cooks; for the menu they rely on hamburgers, wieners, coffee and cocoa.

We plan to build a camper for our pickup so we can snow-picnic overnight and get in more skiing. In summer, our outings are limited because of much ranch work. We like winter picnics even better— especially that all-day one for bringing in the Christmas tree.

LOUISE MORSE

Family communion

On Christmas Eve we have a traditional Polish celebration handed down by my grandparents. Our children will inherit the custom.

We have a special supper table, with seven to nine simple, meatless courses. Before sitting down, we break a wafer called Oplatek (available from a priest in a Polish parish), and exchange good wishes. The wafer is thin and unleavened, like altar bread, and it is stamped with figures of the Christ Child, the Virgin Mother and Christmas angels.

We send the wafers, known as the "bread of love," to any members of the family who are away from home. We also share them with our animals, since animals are said to have been present in the stable when Christ was born.

MARY A. FIGURA

We are in favor of tradition, but not a slave to it. Here's my Ode to Our Nevergreen Tree

I love our silver, shimmering tree;/ From great frustration I'm set free—/ From shopping, shivering, finding not,/ Then settling for what they've got./ From crooked trunk to portions bare./ From needles dropping everywhere./ Now conflagration can't ensue/ Or watering cause a spot or two./ Aluminum is neat and snug,/ Worth its keep—so light to lug./ Bought at after-Christmas sale./ Saves us dough—no waste or wail./ No need to buy a fir or pine/ To have tree glee that's genuine!

JEAN AUGSBURGER

Wonder unlimited

If you've wondered how to get supreme satisfaction from Christmas, I suggest that you borrow an orphan.

Not just for the day itself. Your visitor will be dazzle-eyed over advance holiday preparations; to a child who has no family of his own, helping bake cookies is big excitement. He'll love to shop with you in a suburban center or city department store. His delight will delight *you* if you give him a small money gift so that he can choose a present for himself, or to give someone.

It shouldn't be hard to find a child who needs you this Christmas. Your church or the county Welfare Department can direct you to homes for orphans in your area. Be sure to apply well in advance.

Your date with a youngster will be a gift you can't wrap up and tie with ribbons; but it will live long in your memory, and in the child's.

ELIZABETH CARSON

Milestones in miniature

A tradition in our family is to add to the Christmas tree an ornament significant of something that has happened during the past year. A toy drum and microscopic "gold" saxophone reminded us of the beginning music lessons; a tiny baby doll in its cradle honored the last child to arrive; pine-cone figures and china bells recalled a trip abroad.

A small teddy bear hailed the birth of the first grandchild; a little plastic house stood for our new home; and miniature silver bells symbolized a wedding—our first giving of a daughter in marriage.

We purchase our selected ornament of the year, or make it in quantity, and tie it on special gifts to a grandmother and other relatives, or to friends who know of our custom. Providing the ornaments in quantity also ensures each child a set of "heirloom" ornaments for his own family's Christmas trees of the future.

MRS. ARDEN SHERF

Party-pretty custom

Once when the children were small, I was dressing for an unaccustomed evening party—a formal. One of the youngsters asked, "Why don't you ever dress up pretty like that for us?"

A good question! We were nearing the holidays and my husband and I decided we would really dress up for our family's Christmas Eve at home.

The children were so pleased, and what mother doesn't thrive on flattery? Over the years, dressing up for Christmas Eve has become our firm tradition—for each other, and for ourselves.

PRISCILLA B. MORSE

Great Expectations

Kiss them softly, hearts atremble,
Gently touch each flannel sleeve,
In small heads what dreams assemble—
Children sleeping Christmas Eve.

KAY GERRISH

Pre and post

Nicest things in the world: a Christmas tree when it's first put up, and the living room when you finally take the tree down.

LOIS REED

Christmas . . . unforgettable

THE ESSENCE OF CHRISTMAS IS HELD TO BE CHANGELESS. WHY, THEN, I WONDER, DOES ONE CHRISTMAS ALWAYS SEEM SO SPECIAL—AND SO SPECIALLY UNFOR- GETTABLE?

ON Christmas Eve our family, satisfied with its traditional oyster-stew supper, sat and watched the unbelievable pictures sent back by our country's orbiting astronauts. When from outer space came those words from Genesis—*in the beginning God created the heaven and the earth* . . . lumps came to our throats, and none of us could express our awe and reverence.

MARJORIE KOPF

That wonderful rush

Two years ago, worn out with hectic preparations for Christmas, I vowed that next year I would get everything done ahead of time.

So I shopped in summer for gifts, addressed our cards by Thanksgiving, did Christmas cooking and shined the house well ahead of the big day.

The week before Christmas, everyone but me was caught in that happy whirl. I was missing one of the main ingredients of Christmas. This year will find me back in the crowded, pushing, wonderful rush!

HAZEL DIAZ PUMARA

Strange passenger

Last Christmas one of our church members was assigned the job of getting a tree for the Sunday School. She and a helper cut one on her sister's farm and hauled it to the church in a truck. They had to drag the tree quite a distance through snow, then beat the snow out of its branches before mooring the tree to the platform.

Later on that evening, some of us went to the church to trim the tree. We heard a strange rustling sound and, to our amazement, there was an owl looking out at us from its evergreen perch. Apparently the bird had been an unsuspected, silent passenger since before the tree was cut down!

ELIZABETH FREDERICK

Christmas privilege

For years I resented our cows every Christmas. Why? Because that was the hired man's day off, hence my day to get up before sunrise and take his place in the milking barn. This always seemed just too much on a festive morning.

Last year on Christmas morning the barn was extra quiet. One of our cows licked lovingly at a newborn calf. The stars glimmered down on fresh snow. . . .

Then gladness dawned. Who but the farmer and his family has the privilege of beginning Christmas as it began long ago—in a stable?

BERNICE YUNKER

Turnabout stockings

Christmas morning two unusual stockings appeared along our mantel. One was labeled HIS, the other HERS. For us parents! Our teenagers said it was our turn to receive little gifts.

The stockings were nylons—each a pair, one inside the other for extra strength. Each double stocking was stuffed with small articles that showed through.

The gifts carried appropriate sentiments. Our daughters had inscribed a set of mixing spoons for me, *From your three woodenheads.* When I found *This old rag?* on a very new washcloth, I knew Son was ribbing me about my customary rejoinder when someone compliments me on a dress. For husband John, the message on a green plastic fly-swatter was *Dadsville, you'll slay 'em!* (John stalks flies as if they were big game.)

The turnabout stockings gave us extra merriment. And the thoughtful gesture on the part of our children reminded John and me that they are making commendable progress toward maturity.

LUCILLE ANDERSON

Atop the heights

Last year my husband's Christmas enthusiasm took him to the top of the silo with a decorated tree. I wasn't too keen on the project—Elmer's no spring rooster. But now that the tree is planted high and lighted at night, I must admit it is beautiful.

LORRAINE KINSTETTER

Without equal

Christmas Eve was special because we'd just brought our baby Eric home from the hospital after double pneumonia. We had dinner and presents by candlelight, then I suggested that each of us mention the gift he liked best. Laurie, 4, climbed on Daddy's lap and said, "I like best that God helped you find all us children." The miracle that their adoption has been to us parents is no secret to our trio.

ERLENE UNRUH

Santas in miniature

Our two 11-year-old adopted boys are always coming up with ideas. Last Christmas we especially enjoyed one of their brain storms.

On the Sunday before Christmas we called Grandma and Grandpa to come to see our tree. Bob asked if he could wear my red hat and jacket and make a beard to look like Santa. Fred wanted to join in, too.

Then on the day before Christmas, I was busy getting all the cookies in canisters which, along with other gifts, we take to relatives and friends. But I took time to iron for the boys the red parkas which my husband and I usually wear only for deer hunting. I sewed strips of white cloth around the rolled up sleeves and hood, and I made beards. The boys padded their tummies with pillows, donned the parkas, cinched them with black belts and each boy filled a pillow case with our gifts. By four o'clock we were on our way to deliver. At each stop, we parents sat in the car, while our miniature Santas went in to deliver the gifts.

That night the boys were pretty tired Santas, but they felt they had helped spread Christmas cheer. I'm sure they'll want to do it again.

GLENNA LEET

200

CHRISTMAS IS BECOMING A MORE THOUGHTFUL SEASON. FULL OF GLITTER, YES, BUT BENEATH IT ALL THERE IS A CURRENT OF SOMETHING THAT DOES NOT GLITTER

MERCHANTS say the flow of dollars increases; yet in the future, looking back to the Sixties and Seventies, we may call these Yule seasons Christmases of Anxious Affluence.

The poor, whose very silence used to be a reproach to human indifference and neglect, are now raising insistent voices requiring an end to injustice. We are reminded often that hunger and disease walk the world, that men still struggle to be free, that nations still rely vainly on force to settle their differences.

We worry, and we challenge the injustices. But we continue to celebrate peace and good will even if we break bread with only one lonely person.

For Christmas remains Christmas, though for some it may narrow down until it is just one candle burning.

FAITH PRIOR

Seek and ye shall find

The hurry-scurry of the holiday season was at its height. As shoppers jostled each other in the stores, I wondered: Has the real meaning of Christ's birthday been lost in the jingle of cash registers?

Then I attended the Christmas pageant in our small rural church. Hushed reverence pervaded the sanctuary. The light from the rostrum reflected on the front pews where the little shepherds and angels waited their turn.

Choral readers told the story. *There was no room in the inn. . . .* Could it be that our tensions and frivolities leave no room in our hearts for the Christ spirit?

All eyes were on the Star as it guided richly robed Wise Men. That the star's radiance came from a tiny flashlight, and that it was pulled by a boy backstage with a fishing reel, did not dim its symbolic beauty.

As we drove home through thickly falling snow, the blond girl angel beside me (cherishing her costume) looked back at the boy angel (spectacles and butch cut), and with feminine wisdom of her six years told him: "You know, there really *are* boy angels!"

Suddenly I realized that relaxation had replaced tension. An island of peace is to be found each Christmas, by those who seek it among the distractions.

PAULINE HARLAND

The irony of progress

Around the holidays we had a beautiful snowfall in our southern community. We seldom see snow; the kids had a ball playing in that white stuff. And eating it! Then the Weather Bureau announced cautiously that the snow held "a certain amount" of radioactivity. I couldn't get over the irony: Nature's wonderful gift contaminated, and a population's future threatened by man's craze for destruction.

MAGGIE DAVIS

Indulgent cheating

As our family took a pre-Christmas tour of toy departments, our four children stood, open-mouthed and shining eyed, gazing at all the new marvels including "space ships" equipped for a journey to Mars.

Dolls . . . what a variety! Modern dolls wriggle, talk, walk, nurse the bottle and wet their didies. Some have wardrobes fit for a Hollywood star. Old Raggedy Ann would drop her head in such company!

Nowadays, for a boy to "hunt tigers," he must have a pith helmet, a toy hunting rifle with telescopic sights, and binoculars.

I wonder: Are we truly helping our youngsters to mature into the inquisitive, inventive adults they have a right to become? Maybe we cheat them some, with too many toys that leave nothing to the imagination.

Many a tiger has been stalked and shot in our spirea bushes, and the hunter's only equipment was a stick rifle, a loud voice for hollering *Bang!*—and a vivid imagination.

Without imagination, the world would never have had a Columbus, a Marconi, Doctors Einstein and Salk, or the astronauts. Creativity is God-given; let's "deprive" our children just a little so they'll be free to develop it.

HAZEL C. MILLER

Christmas . . . peace

PEACE ON EARTH, GOOD WILL AMONG MEN . . . WAS THE ANGELS' SONG A PROMISE? A COMMAND? AN IDEAL? OR SIMPLY A LYRICAL CHANT? IS IT FUTILE TO TALK OF PEACE ON EARTH?

NO! If for one season, or one month, or even one day, we can—more perfectly than usual—practice good will and harmony, we are closer to universal peace.

Christmas is that season, that month, that day. It's a time for extra friendliness with neighbors, kinfolks, newcomers and overworked store clerks. It's a time for remembering those in need, both near and abroad.

At no time of year do we need Christmas so much. How easy it is for a farm family to hole up and see no farther than the end of a snow-blocked driveway. Only an excuse as good as Christmas could persuade a man who has battled snow and wind all day to go out again, to shop or visit.

The true preparation for Christmas is not in the baking, cleaning, or gift-shopping, but in preparing the heart. A Christmas heart is extra loving, extra patient, extra sensitive to the needs and problems of others. Such a heart is peaceful, and from the peaceful hearts of millions will eventually come peace on earth.

JULIA GAMON

Reflections on peace

In our country's tapestry of cultures, each with its own manner of marking Christ's birthday, custom has merged with custom and the result is a confusion of festivities—religious, frivolous, commercial. Yet underneath it all there is a core of good will and renewal of faith which promises a gradual fulfillment of the peace ideal.

ANNE HADLEY

Perhaps peace on earth is not more important than other ideals: honor, integrity, equality and freedom over the world. Peace is our hope, but it must be a just peace, not a spineless yielding.

BETTY MAIWALD

My gesture toward peace is to write our family's "December Story" to my 10 pen pals in that many countries. I describe everything we enjoy, from Advent to the last holiday candle's final flicker.

LORRAINE KINSTETTER

The story of Jesus' birth has become a universal symbol of God's love for man. Many followers of non-Christian faiths revere the Nazarene as a great spiritual leader. Hence I believe that each Christmas brings the brotherhood of all humanity closer to an ultimate fulfillment.

BARBARA JONES

203

I have an uneasy feeling that we all, especially our leaders, could work with less threat and prejudice—and more understanding—toward some kind of agreement between nations.

MRS. EDNA DUNKIN

Christmas reminds me that too many of us are not practicing the philosophy of the Man whose birthday we celebrate. How can we expect nations to do any better than the individuals who compose them?

MRS. G. S. JOHNSON

The peace proclaimed by herald angels did not mean between nations, but men's individual relationship with God. Christmas is the Christian's act of faith—that hearts all over the world may experience this "peace that passeth understanding."

RUTH O. PATTERSON

To the multi-megaton exploders it may seem that we are hiding behind scriptural slogans such as Peace on Earth. Yet here I am, and there you are, too, I dare say. We are not running scared; fact is, we are prepared to rise up if blasts should threaten our cherished maple trees! They shaded us in our childhood and we want them to shade our children and our children's children.

JEAN BELL MOSLEY

Good will is growing

There never has been a time when there were no grievances, no hates. Longfellow, during the Civil War, expressed doubts about peace, in a poem beginning "I heard the bells on Christmas Day."

> *And in despair I bowed my head;*
> *"There is no peace on earth," I said,*
> *"For hate is strong, And mocks the song*
> *Of peace on earth, good will to men!"*

But there is more to the poem—a reassuring reflection for our times as well as the poet's:

> *Then pealed the bells more loud and deep:*
> *"God is not dead, nor doth he sleep!*
> *The Wrong shall fail, The Right prevail,*
> *With peace on earth, good will to men!"*

Today violent acts are in the news: man against man, nation against nation. Unmentioned are the neighbors who sit with sick friends, the people who help the orphaned.

A nation perched on the edge of time must search for an inner peace. Hence we see a return to the old traditions; there are new faces in church. We see more generosity for the handicapped. We see there *is* a growth of good will among men!

EILEEN M. HAASE

Good Idea

Try borrowing someone's pet adventure, project or discovery. You are welcome! You don't have to pay it back, but you may wish to pass it along.

Good Idea

Good Idea . . . bringing up kids

A SCHOOL PRINCIPAL ONCE TOLD ME:
"THERE ARE SOME KIDS YOU CAN
TEACH ONLY THROUGH THE SEAT OF
THE PANTS." WHAT A SAD THEORY!
I'D RATHER BORROW THE SUCCESSFUL
TECHNIQUES OF OTHER PARENTS

I have always been careful to keep matches out of reach, so I was surprised to discover several unused ones in my four-year-old son's room. I put them away. When he went to his room and came out disappointed, I spoke to him about the danger of playing with matches, but what I said made no impression.

A day or so later, I noticed him running straight from the kitchen to the barn. I followed, and when I questioned him, he reluctantly led me to where he had lit a match. Luckily no damage was done.

Realizing that fascination often comes from things that are unknown or forbidden, I taught him to use matches properly. He became my chief assistant for burning waste paper—under close supervision, of course.

Since then, I have not caught him sneaking or lighting matches. They are still on a shelf he can't reach.

This method may not work with every child, but it's worth a try. Teaching a child to use matches properly may save his life—and buildings, too.

RITA SCHLOEGEL

A happier crew

With all our chickens, cows, sheep, rabbits, pigs and ducks, chores seem never-ending. To make them less of a drudgery, our family uses a "job jar." On slips of paper, I write jobs that need doing each day and they're drawn from a hat.

Since some jobs are more tedious than others, I put in a few surprise slips: "have a candy bar," "watch a TV program," or "1¢ for each fly killed." Each person gets one trade.

Signed slips are returned to me so I'll know who is responsible if any job isn't done well. The children like this system better than assigned chores. They even help each other after doing their own jobs!

REATHEL KINGSBURY

Private enterprise

Our cookie jar used to go empty before the sun set on our twice-a-week baking day. Now Mark and Dorothy have individual jars and space out their snacks.

GEORGIA PARKER

I take my toddlers shopping

When I see a mother wrestling with irritated youngsters while she tries to shop, I want to pass on to her some tips to ease her job.

When I take our two (ages one and three), I make a list in two parts —"musts" and "possibles." I get the "possibles" done if the boys behave well and I can shop an extra half-hour.

I simplify our expeditions in advance by ordering some things by phone or mail, from newspaper ads or catalogues. Blue jeans, towels, sheets and hardware—all are ordered without my leaving home.

Comes shopping day, I pack an oversize pocketbook with list, a bottle of water, hard cookies, a lollipop. Also a carrot or chunk of apple for the baby to chew on and not have crumbs all over him. For "big brother" I take a small toy.

We do our weekly food shopping in one grand swing around the store. I'm familiar with the market's layout, so usually I finish in 30 to 45 minutes. I don't mind opening the package of cookies for the boys; a treat makes the trip pleasanter for them, so they are more likely to be cooperative.

Most of the time I limit trips to about an hour and a half. When the baby starts to squirm, I stop the stroller out of the line of store traffic and give him some water. This calls for a short wait; I never give him the bottle and keep going—not since the time he broke the bottle in the store's busiest aisle!

Our children really seem to enjoy shopping. The trick is to keep the trip short and interesting, so their dispositions will stay sweet.

DORIS MEYER

And milk to match

Like all mothers, I want my children to drink milk, but they simply wouldn't touch it—until I had an idea.

One day, my 3-year-old came into the kitchen to ask for a soda. I told her to go back to the den, and I'd bring a surprise drink.

She was wearing a pink dress, so I put two drops of red food coloring in a glass of milk. Presto, pink milk! I added a red striped plastic straw, and she loved it.

Now, each morning she has milk colored to match her dress. Our other children caught the idea, too, so our table is always a rainbow of colors.

MARION HEEB

Young money-managers

Allowance day used to be a terrible time at our house. Either the kids didn't have quite enough money for what they wanted, or they spent it all on the first day and then found something they *had* to have. Since we feel learning to budget and spend money wisely is important, we decided to try a new system.

The children still receive their allowance once a week—but if one finds something he can't afford, we decide on one of three methods.

He saves *part* of his weekly allowance until he has accumulated enough for what he wants; he buys the item on the layaway plan; or he borrows the money from me and pays it back in weekly installments. This is a last resort, but no one has the misguided idea of not paying.

The children are learning that if they really want something, they may have to sacrifice a little to get it. Best of all, our plan is teaching them to make wiser choices, and to be more sure of them.

BETTY TURNER

Merchants in miniature

At our house we've found an entertaining and educational answer to the plaintive question "What can we do now, Mom?"

I use extra care in opening small packages of foods like jello, cereal, instant pudding; then reseal the boxes with colorless tape. A supply of these, plus small empty cans, jars and paper bags, stocks a play store for our children. Add dime-store equipment—a toy cash register, play money, toy phone for " orders"—and the children are in business.

ANNA USREY

"Oops, I'm sorry!"

Our three teen-age sons suddenly became unreasonably sensitive about any comments made by one about the other. When we sat down to what had always been pleasant meals with a good-natured exchange of conversation, remarks about school, haircuts, clothes or friends would be interpreted as criticism.

The inevitable result was a sarcastic reply or challenge to "do something about it." Our meals began to taste like sawdust!

209

To promote peace, I made three cards and put them by the boys' places at meals. One card said "joke," another said "compliment" and the third—"Oops, I'm sorry!" When a remark was made that could possibly be misinterpreted, the speaker quickly raised the most appropriate card.

The cards made us all laugh, forgetting the previous remark. Our meals together are now pleasant, and the cards no longer necessary.

ELEANOR MILLS

Monarch for the day

To cut down on quarreling, we have two turn-about kings in our family, their respective reigns designated by the big calendar in the kitchen.

I've marked each day of the calendar with a child's initial, alternating *H* and *J*. On *H* days Howard, the older boy, is king; he chooses the games, gets first look at the comics, and so on. Since privileges and responsibilities go hand in hand, His Majesty also feeds the chickens and gathers the eggs.

The next day, Howard abdicates in favor of brother John. Under our royal system, a glance at the calendar quickly settles a dispute before it can happen.

MERLE L. KLINE

Filed away for winter

In winter when cold weather keeps lively little guests inside the house, a birthday party can be a nerve-wracking ordeal for Mama.

I solved the problem last year by taking movies at a summer party, making certain that every child was there who would be invited to our winter birthday party.

Before the winter party, I rented a movie cartoon. That was the first film featured. Next came the surprise home-talent reel, and you should have heard the squeals of delight as each "actor" was recognized. The children begged for a second run, after which there was barely time for refreshments. Those movies made the winter party our most successful one—with no aftermath of jangled nerves!

GLENNA THOMAS

Tots and baby brother

When our fourth child arrived, I discovered more than added physical labor on my part was needed to keep our home running smoothly.

Caring for the baby consumed most of my time, so I was unable to spend many minutes with our other preschoolers. While I was occupied, they would busy themselves with mischief—covering themselves and the surroundings with hand lotion or powder, dumping cereal throughout the house. After days of this confusion, the baby developed colic from my yelling and the interruptions of his feedings, and my nerves were jangled. Changes were needed!

210

My solution was to invite the three mischief-makers to gather around while I fed the baby. I then taught them songs, verses and rhymes or told Bible stories. Sometimes I would ask one to bring me something for the baby or hold his bottle. This not only kept them occupied, but helped them know their brother better and increased their interest in helping care for him.

A potential disaster thus became a wonderful opportunity to teach and train my three little girls. Looking back, I realize that all of us greatly benefited from those months.

RAMONA DIGGS

Barrels of fun

The most versatile toys our children have ever had are three empty gasoline drums which they found and rolled into our backyard.

With each child mounted on a barrel, continual raids are made into "enemy territory"; the barrels have endless possibilities for balancing games; add a board and there's a see-saw; add more boards and the barrels become the core of an interesting construction project such as a house or car.

Barrel games are inexpensive. They encourage lively exercise, they spark imagination, and they are seasonable most months of the year.

LUCINDA OAKLAND

Birds like cookies, too

Most cookies don't last long at our house, but every fall we make one kind to enjoy all winter. It's a special recipe for the birds.

On one of those rainy Saturdays when you can't do much outside, we mix, in a large container, leftover flower seeds, bits of suet, small grains, various cereals, raisins, birdseed and cracked corn. We like to include some watermelon seeds, too, because they are a favorite with cardinals.

I render some suet and pour it over the dry ingredients, stirring well. When the mixture is cool enough to handle, the children—all six of them—form it into "cookies." Some of these we place in our bird feeder; others we wrap in pieces of plastic mesh from onion bags, to hang on tree branches. Another method we use for hanging the treats is to pack the mixture into old jar lids, through which we first punch holes for wire.

MARY WILSON

Ingenious remedy

Sprays have been developed for control of almost every mildew and insect, but not for the control of two male pests, ages three and six. With great persistence they "molted" Tinkertoys, puzzle parts, blocks, guns, trucks and cars—all over the premises.

An unused walker came to my rescue. I removed the cloth seat and attached to the frame a large square denim bag, making it a portable toy collector. I embroidered a simple design of an engine with two cars on the front.

With a little prodding, my two engineers soon became adept at using their "train" to pick up passengers (scattered toys) and return them to their "depot," otherwise called the toy chest.

MARIE MITCHELL

Recipes for reluctant eaters

While going through magazines one day with my two preschool children, I discovered their interest in the colorful food photographs. Since they were such picky eaters, this came as a surprise.

When I suggested that we try the recipe under a particular picture, they could hardly wait. Making a fuss over the preparation of the recipe and discussing it with them seemed to sharpen their appetites. They cleaned their plates!

Since then, we often try recipes selected by the children. Their new interest in food has encouraged me to be more creative in the kitchen; I can be reasonably certain of appreciation at the table!

CHARLOTTE TOBIN

Perfect pumpkins

I wanted to control the weeds between my raspberries and strawberries, so when son Gerry was 10, I gave him three pumpkin seeds to plant there. He really took care of his little plot, and from those three seeds he sold 35 beautiful pumpkins!

The business has grown until now, eight years later, the goal is at least 500 well-shaped, bright orange pumpkins by Halloween.

Gerry's brothers—Mike, Jim and Charles, ages 10 to 19—share in the enterprise. The year's work begins before Easter, when the seeds are sprouted in flats. Then come transplanting, weeding, spraying for squash beetles.

A local supermarket manager likes the boys' work and takes all the pumpkins they can produce. He also likes the unusual pumpkin faces the boys sculpt; so for a while in October our basement looks like a Halloween project in Santa's basement. The pumpkin's shape dictates its face: an Indian, a clown, a kitten.

The boys have other garden projects which pay their school expenses; but pumpkin money (about $20 for each boy) goes for pleasure, Christmas shopping and hobbies.

Worth even more is the good feeling the boys have when they pass out their pumpkin-face originals to the children in a hospital. In fact, we call pumpkin raising our happiness project; because whether you make, buy, sell or are given a homegrown jack-o'-lantern, you are the happier for it.

MARGARET SCHMITZ

Good-bye box

When relatives with small children come for a visit, I like to give the children gifts. I put a few things in a box to be handed into the car just as the family leaves: It's my good-bye box. A sturdy cardboard box will do—sometimes wrapped as a present, sometimes not.

The idea is to have a lot of little things suitable for car play. The surprise of digging into the treasure is worth more than expensive toys. I save things like plastic or cardboard containers, lots of cast off jewelry, dolls I've made from sewing-thread spools. Sometimes I pick up a storybook, coloring book and box of crayons, when I'm shopping.

At the last minute I tuck in a packet of homemade cookies or individual packages of raisins. The good-bye box saves tears at parting, and parents appreciate my helping keep the children interested while they're in the car.

VINNA MIDDLETON

Good Idea . . . for smoother days

IT'S AMAZING HOW A GADGET, A PSYCHOLOGICAL GIMMICK OR A CREATIVE BRAIN-THROB ACTED UPON CAN OIL THE GEARS OF LIVING

IN April I'm usually trying frantically to cope with farm chores, gardening and house cleaning while still not neglecting the children. When I was especially frustrated I consulted the four other young mothers in our area who were also at home with young children.

To free up some time, we agreed that each mother would take all the children (seven) one day a week during the month of April. This has allowed each of us to have 16 *free* days during the month—time to plant the garden, paint, clean, sew, shop and even spend a few hours relaxing or reading.

Our system has worked so well that we have tried it in winter, too. Now we can have some time to spend with our husbands when they're not quite so busy with field work.

LOU GREENLEE

Swap of chores

Every Sunday my husband and I trade places—I do his chores, he feeds the baby and prepares the meals. After I've finished feeding the cattle, I realize why my husband is so tired and hungry when he grumbles: "Isn't dinner ready yet?" At the same time, he realizes why I sometimes find my routine boring and frustrating. Since the switch we've become more tolerant and appreciative of each other.

JEANNE DANIELSON

Farm office—homemade and handy

Like many young farm wives, I look enviously at magazine pictures of handsome offices. We plan to add an office someday. Meanwhile the farm's business goes on.

Before our marriage I had acquired a typewriter, and just lately we bought an adding machine with money saved by my barbering for my husband and our sons. But we needed better storage.

My husband built a "business board" to go in unused wall space (2' wide) between a door and a corner in the kitchen. The telephone is there and the directory hangs nearby. Next to the phone I have my own typed list of numbers I call frequently or might need in an emergency. The list is thumb-tacked to a bulletin board made by cementing four cork floor tiles to the pegboard bulletin board. Above the phone hangs an appointment calendar with pencil and pad—always handy.

A hanging shoe-pocket file has compartments for receipts and expenses to be entered in our records, and other slots for "pending" and "miscellaneous." Below is the children's bulletin board and a blackboard. (The phone, message center and calendar are beyond our preschoolers' reach.)

My husband also built a portable bookcase to fit on top of a base cabinet in the kitchen. Its compartments keep books, magazines and papers neat. Shelves are adjustable with metal strips and clips. Anyone can build these two inexpensive "organizers," and how they do smooth and speed our farm and home business.

EILEEN BAHR

Rideabye baby

I've always enjoyed taking walks to pick autumn leaves, listen to the squirrels chatter, observe the migrating birds and watch crops and animals. When our baby came, I was afraid I could no longer get out whenever the mood struck me, and I envied American Indian women who carry babies on their backs.

I did some scouting, found a firm that sells papoose-type baby carriers, and sent for one. I used it from the time Mark learned to hold up his head. Most of my walking was up and down hills, so I could carry him this way for half an hour (until he weighed about 20 pounds) without becoming really tired. My hands were free, and I could even climb fences. What's more, I didn't feel any strain in my back. Mark seemed to enjoy the trips, too, especially when we stopped and I set him down in a drift of fallen leaves.

The carrier proved a boon when I shopped for groceries. Mark could see things, but not get into them. Although he weighs about 25 pounds now, I still take him in the carrier for short walks.

ARLEEN HERRING

Giant hunt

I've been caught off guard many times when people phone to give five minutes' notice before dropping in. Often I'm in the midst of ironing or baking and have let my house go, and there's not enough time for me to tackle the disorder alone.

Recently I found a solution that saves embarrassment and provides an exciting game for my youngsters. When someone gives me five minutes' notice, I shout, "Giant hunt!" and my children come running. I hand out "weapons"—brooms, wastebaskets and dust cloths. We charge through the house in search of "giants"—anything that's out of place.

With five heroes attacking together, we make short work of the giants, and our kingdom is soon in order. I'm able to relax when our guests arrive, and I feel a glow of pride that my children willingly make my peace of mind possible.

PATRICIA MULLETT

Camper's slick trick

On our first camping trip to the mountains we discovered the nights were damp and cool. We were so grateful to a friendly camper who gave our youngsters this idea reminiscent of the ancestral warming paw: Heat a rock in the evening campfire for a half-hour; wrap it in aluminum foil, then in an old towel. Put the warm rock at the foot of your sleeping bag.

This was great incentive for getting our youngsters to bed, and the warmth seemed to relax muscles tired from mountain climbing.

IRENE KUEHN

Blessed quiet

Our family doctor was here on a house call. After making his careful diagnosis of our six-year-old's complaints, he remarked: "It's a pleasure to examine someone in a quiet house for a change."

As concerned parents of a sick child, we had silenced the radio and TV and settled the three other children before the doctor's arrival. His comment reminded me of a discovery I'd made when our first two were babies.

I had often turned the radio on for news and left it on all morning, thinking it necessary for me to maintain contact with the outside world. Or I enjoyed a favorite television program for a half-hour, then neglected to turn off the set.

But one day I decided to reduce the tension-producing noise. "Reducing the noise" meant turning off radio and TV, since babies aren't equipped with off-on switches!

Except for something special like an election or rocket launching, I've stuck to that decision. The resulting comparative quiet has in turn seemed to quiet the children. I know it has improved my working environment, and my state of mind.

RUTH PETERSON

Personalized reading

Family albums probably are as old as cameras themselves. I'm an ardent "paster-inner," but our family does something extra to multiply the enjoyment.

From each set of new snapshots, we select one or two, identify and date them and place them in books—books we read for pleasure, reference or account books, the Bible.

What a pleasant surprise to flip a page while reading and find a picture of a favorite person or happy occasion. It might show a youngster's first tractor ride, an ox-pulling at the fair, relatives home for Christmas, a school happening or vacation scene. We take only a moment to look at the picture, but the memory lingers on. At dinner someone will mention his picture-bookmark find, and we'll all "remember when."

PRISCILLA SMITH BOTTI

Money-maker on the farm

One of my neighbors has turned her interest in cooking into a paying business. She ran a newspaper ad: Spend Sunday on a farm. The idea seemed to appeal to town people, because out they came.

The guests wander around and look at the animals or sit under the trees while they wait for dinner. The hostess serves real country meals —her own garden-grown vegetables, home made bread and butter, fresh fruit pies and a special angel cake six inches high. Of course, the farmhouse is clean and neat as a pin, and pretty—the kind of place people feel at home in.

There are no other attractions—not even horseshoes! But guests say, what could be more attractive than plenty of scenery, broad skies, sunshine, pure air, and a good country meal?

ETHEL ROUSSEAU

Have table, will travel

Farming often interferes with vacations, but family picnics are our favorite pastime. For these outings our family of six joins a couple with one child—too many people for one car. Last summer we found a unique solution.

We loaded an 8' picnic table into our panel truck and stashed the food under the table. The sideboards made perfect backrests. Children sat on benches with parents behind. Our traveling picnic table made quite a sight—but it was handy.

BARBARA BAKER

Fantasy to fight gloom

When the skies are drippy and we feel gloomy, we play a game at our house. Pop comes into the kitchen and says in a dismal voice: "Tell me why I shouldn't stop the world and jump off."

That's my cue to tell him, "Why, you have this fine place, a bank account, a few government bonds—and a gorgeous wife."

Now, actually the place is mortgaged, our financial assets are frighteningly small, and I'm not Marilyn Monroe. But we both get a good laugh and the day is less melancholy. And also we are reminded of our real values.

A dash of imagination as we go about our daily chores gives life a touch of glamor. When I plant seeds, I imagine the flowers. See some in an arrangement on the communion table at church. I see cheerful bouquets I can take to friends who are ill, or to well ones just to show that I care. I am a long way from childhood, but grownups, too, thrive on fun and make-believe.

GLADSIA RUSSELL

Expediter unaware

I have a hero—my knight, I call him. He drives a white station wagon and carries the mail.

He doesn't know it, but he is my greatest inducement for getting the work done. Each day I bargain with myself to complete a number of tasks before allowing myself the pleasure of reading the mail!

MAE ARNOLD

Anger in the garden

What do you do when you're angry? Me? I grab my old straw hat and head for the garden. With each pesky weed I yank out of the ground, a small amount of my anger ebbs away. By the time my garden's shipshape, I'm calm again.

I often pause at the gate to ask, "Now, why did I come out here?" My most violent thoughts are soothed as I work the soil and coax the young, tender plants to maturity.

LILLIAN BOOS

I use psychology on me

My Achievement of The Year was to start a work diary. I used to keep a list of things I must do. Some of the jobs on the list got very old.

My new diary mentions work that did get done—*finally cleaned the bookcase upstairs*—and that spurs me on.

MARCELENE BELL

"Eating out" at home

At our house the question is not "When do we eat?" as often as it is "Where do we eat?" If my husband comes in from chores and finds no supper table set in the kitchen, he isn't worried; he knows his wife is satisfying her need of variety by moving the meal to whatever spot suits her fancy.

Nothing adds more pleasure to the routine than putting our dining table on wheels. In winter we like to eat from a card table in front of the living room fireplace. If I am feeling festive, it's the regular dining room complete with best silver and dishes *and* candle glow! In summer we choose among three picnic areas; pondsite, backyard, front porch.

Luckily I have a husband who enters into the spirit of things. No grumbling if I suggest clean slacks. He even clears the table!

ADELIA CROLEY

Good Idea . . . problem solvers

LIVES THERE A WOMAN WHO HASN'T BEEN BUGGED BY A PROBLEM UNTIL SHE GOT IT SOLVED? IF YOU HAVE MY BOTHERATION, YOU MIGHT BE IMPELLED TO TRY THE SOLUTION

B ECAUSE our kindergartner attends school only afternoon sessions, it is impossible for her to ride the school bus with the older children. So I've found myself in the role of chauffeur at one o'clock and 3:45 each weekday.

At first this was a great frustration. I had to drop everything to haul her to and from; and, because parent picker-uppers must be prompt, I'd have to wait 10 minutes or more in the car every afternoon.

After just sitting, tense and waiting, the first week I took a new look at the situation. I decided those 10-minute intervals could be a gift.

Since then I have used waiting minutes to complete a needlepoint bag I thought I'd never finish; embroider two cross-stitch aprons for gifts; put the hem in a new dress I'd made. What's more, I've learned I can "spare time" when I have to—so why not when I *want* to?

LEONA HAMMOND

Office on the farm

I guess no farm can really do without an office—whether it be a separate room fully equipped, or a counter top and a few kitchen drawers.

When my farmer-husband also took on a community job which requires lots of paper work we converted a corner of our dining room into an "office."

We started with a sturdy old oak desk we unearthed in a neighbor's barn ($15), refinished it, and got a typewriter and a 4-drawer army-surplus filing cabinet. We bought a second-hand mimeograph machine from our church for $20. I used it constantly to make out pedigree papers when we sell our registered cattle, and to earn some extra money doing work for our creamery.

To cut down on cost, we have personal stationery printed in large quantities and buy plain paper by the ream. Manila file folders, gummed labels and a rubber name stamp are big efficiencies. I file carbons of all business letters and use a telephone credit card so business calls will show separately on our bill, for tax records.

IRIS MYRON

Emergency measures

The introduction of dial phones in our community presented the problem of what to do in case of emergencies. We have four pre-school children. Our oldest can read numbers, but can't read names in the phone book. This is what we did:

On 3 x 5 file cards we pasted pictures representing the doctor, fire department, police, our nearest neighbor, our employer, and the children's grandmothers. We used some actual pictures of individuals, and an old catalog provided pictures of a fire engine, doctor with kit and policeman in uniform. On each card, in large figures, is the number to be dialed. The cards are pinned on a bulletin board above our phone—waiting for an emergency we hope will never arise.

Sometimes we adults are not so calm, so the cards may even help us keep our cool in a crisis.

HAZEL MILLER

Variety at breakfast

It's easy to get into a rut with breakfast, and when my husband announced he just couldn't face eggs in the morning any more, I realized that I had. We always had some kind of meat and fruit or juice which I varied, but fried eggs—produced by our own hens—were my standby.

Determined to remedy the situation, I taped breakfast menus—planned ahead—inside a cupboard door. Two months have passed. We've had pancakes, waffles, spoon bread, rice, muffins, hot cereals, cold cereals, French toast, mush, coffee cake. Sometimes I have had to get up a bit earlier to get something started, but it's been worth it; we enjoy breakfast more now. We still have eggs fairly often; but now I serve them in a variety of ways, and not only at breakfast, but at other meals, too.

RHODA BARNHART

Scarecrow, scarecrow

Every year the birds used to harvest the crop of apricots from our little tree in the backyard. Then my husband placed our transistor radio underneath the tree and let it run from morning until night. His idea really worked.

What a comical sight to watch the bewilderment of those birds when they flew in for a feast. They'd perch nearby, apparently deciding to make a try for the fruit, and—bam!—a station break with The Big Voice, and away they'd fly.

Now I'm sure some commercials are "for the birds."

MIMA PRATER

Come on bake day

Where to go and what to do? That was the subject under discussion by a group of teen-agers who gathered at our house. No one seemed to have any inspired answers that night.

About that time I walked in with a tray of fresh bread, butter and knives. The bread was so hot it couldn't be sliced, so I suggested that the young people break bread with us.

In no time at all, the gang had settled down before our fireplace. Surely someone would turn on the TV, I thought. No one did. Conversation started, and Dad drew up a chair. Everyone talked. There were some logical, friendly arguments. Eventually someone began to sing. Hours passed unnoticed—Dad and I had stayed up past our bedtime.

Often when the phone rings, a young voice inquires if it's baking day at our house. My invitation is quickly accepted. Other groups we've heard of have followed our idea.

Wouldn't it be nice if people the wide world over broke hot, home-made bread together?

MYRTLE BATSON

Gardener's slick trick

We economically solved our problem of slugs in the garden by buying a pair of hardy Pekin ducks. Then, since we have no lake or stream, we faced the problem of devising a place for the ducks to swim.

Finally, I bought a child's medium-sized wading pool with sides about a foot high. We laid a board on one side to act as a ramp.

The pool is easily cared for. We just lift one side to empty it, and an occasional hosing keeps it clean.

Our waddling slug-eaters provide entertainment for everyone. To add to the fun, we put two decoy ducks in the pool. The drake repeatedly attacked the decoys until he had triumphantly sunk them both.

PATRICIA BARTHOLOMEW

Chain parties for funds

Our community has found one of the most promising fund raising stunts devised in recent years:

Each member of the sponsoring organization agrees to invite five friends to her home for coffee, telling the guests in advance that the coffee will be 50 cents a cup and the money used for such-and-such a project. They are also told that they will be expected to hold a similar coffee, inviting four different friends. This process continues until the last hostess invites only two guests. A group with 30 members can raise more than $3,000, providing you have 3600 people to draw from.

A word of warning: The technique can easily run in the ground if every club pounces on it. We find it works best for a one-shot fund raising—in behalf of a valuable cause that the whole community will want to support.

DONNIE C. RUSSELL

Is this antique necessary?

When we bought a spacious farm home, I thought at last I could indulge at auctions—buying antiques.

But how fast this hobby led to the clutters! All my treasures must be dusted, polished and cleaned.

Now I discipline myself and ask: Is this a working antique? Can it pay its way? My rules don't apply to a lovely piece of Sandwich glass —that has a known value.

My charming little trunk justifies its position in the living room by holding my son's toys and tools. The old Bennington crock is a magazine holder; the huge bowl decorated with cabbage roses is ideal for soaking tired feet.

Sometimes the beauty of an object is sufficient reason for owning it. Each collector must set her own standards. But if you feel more like a museum curator than a mother, as I did, it's time to do some re-evaluating. Retire that uncomfortable chair and rusty breadmaker. Sell them —at an auction.

FAYE SMITH

For benevolent buyers

At bazaars and charity events in our community, some people (particularly the men) are willing to spend money for a good cause, but they can't find anything they really want to buy.

To solve the problem, I knit sweaters and caps in children's sizes and hung a sign over my booth: *Buy a garment for a refugee child.* The

221

idea proved popular. At the end of the day I had an empty booth and a large package for CARE.

VIOLET PAULSON

Whirly curls

Why can't I keep my hair looking nice like other women do? When I've just had it done, no matter how carefully I tie and fasten a net to my head, the next morning the net's missing and I always look as if I've been sleeping under a helicopter.

Once I tried the advice of a friend, and wound my head in toilet paper. To this day I'm still picking up bits of paper!

One night, as I examined laundered stockings for runs, I thought of winding a nylon discard around my head. I pinned my topless turban in place—and awoke the next morning to find my hairdo as pretty and unmussed as it had been the night before!

ANNA MAY MEYER

Jaunt money available!

Our strictly non-elastic budget never seems able to permit one big vacation per year. In fact, our dearth of cash and time continually limits us to a few modest afternoon jaunts.

Finally, I got an idea of how to save for an afternoon or weekend blowout. I took one large envelope and labeled it $10, and labeled a smaller one $5. We work on them, one at a time, and when the money goal is reached, we seal the envelope.

Into the envelopes goes every bit of extra money we earn. If Daddy works at night on an off-the-farm job, he puts this pay in an envelope. When Junior is paid for mowing lawns and Sis for baby-sitting both donate half of their earnings to the vacation envelope. Me? Well, I make and sell Christmas gifts. And last summer, I boarded two children while their parents were away.

Each envelope is laid away as soon is it is filled. Then, some great day, Dad says: "Let's take the afternoon off." We grab up a packaged vacation and are on our way, bound for a wonderful afternoon including hot dogs and ice cream, or for a weekend at Grandma's.

Time capsule

When our son reached the age where he lost interest in toys, we cleaned out the closet to make room for sports equipment.

The contents of the closet told the story of his childhood. There was the yellow rabbit he had held as a baby, a collection of make-believe hats, a battered electric train and some well-worn books.

Rather than discard his favorites, I decided to pack a "time capsule" for my future grandchildren. I chose the things he loved the most for his children to treasure.

LOUISE PETERS

...ked magic

...igerator I keep a batch of refrigerator rolls and often they
...speak my thoughts when words fail me.
...to-earth language they say "Welcome, neighbor" to an out-
...ple moving nearby. Thus begins a lasting friendship.
...neighbor brings home a new baby. A pan of hot, fluffy rolls
...ratulations, Mom and Dad."
...end develops an appetite when taste-tempting rolls express
...shes. An 86-year-old is cheered because hot rolls tell her
...bor cares."
...have welcomed new pastors, consoled bereaved families and
...grandchildren. When the need arises, I don't worry and
...t I can do to help—instead, I roll out the rolls.

EVELYN PICKERING

...hand

...r shame-facedly asked our public health nurse if she could
...some unmatched dishes. She said: "You have no idea how
...I go into that don't have enough dishes to set a table."
...ollecting nightgowns, bed linens, tray cloths, juice glasses,
...les, books and pictures. When I have a box full, I take it
...health office. It is really appreciated.

STELLA M. MATTHEWS

...loveliness

...yra is the wife of our sheriff. One of our favorite pastimes
...n sales and antique shops.
...an auction she bought a basketful of goblets for only 50¢.
...he world do you do with all those unmatched glasses?"
...as driving her home, and she said, "Come in and I'll

...dining table I saw four goblets. Two were ready to take
...d friends: a lovely blue one of pressed glass containing
...tephanotis and another, larger, one half-filled with water
...ed a pink carnation and a sprig of fern. Myra explained
...lmost always find enough garden flowers for a goblet
...h requires little space on a bedside table.
...vo fancy goblets were for a shut-in friend, Myra told me.
...ave some extra fruit on hand, I make a little jam or jelly,
...et, wrap the glass with saran and add a bow. Now let me
...favorite, which I use for a different purpose."
...me a slender goblet of sparkling cut glass.
...le who are in trouble come here to see my husband, and
...eone will ask for a drink of water. It gives me pleasure
...of those to whom I serve it in this lovely goblet. They
...ft out of being offered such beauty."

ELSIE LEE

Neighbors

Country neighbors seem to know
Your need at such or such an hour;
Come to your fence, and smiling, show
Their gift; and, be it fruit or flower
Or cutting you had coveted,
Your country neighbor is wise in the ways
Of loving help. Though little's said
In words, perhaps through work-filled days,
Friendship in the deepest sense
Is passed across a neighbor's fence.

PAULINE HAVARD

Neig

Neighbors . . . we care

A THOUGHTFUL
SIGNIFICANT TO
YOUR NEIGHBO
IS MORE IMPOF
YOU HAVE A F

Heartglow

My neighbor
My time is
But yesterday
She stoppe

Second thoughts at the

I've always thought when
prefer a minimum of visitor

Recently, I found this is
for some long-delayed su
was positively elated the d

But oh, the next bleak d
my husband not to broad
to worry about me. Then
me complex. When my hu
and a small gift from our

My hospital stay was
cards, offers of help and
certain amount of self-pit
taught me to be more thou

Fresh-ba

In my refi
rise up and
In down
of-state co
Another
says "Cong
A sick fr
get-well wi
"Your neig
My rolls
delighted 1
wonder wha

Lending a

Once I rathe
find use for
many homes
I started c
jig-saw puzz
to the public

Goblets of

My friend M
is visiting far
Recently at
"What in
I asked. I w
show you."
On Myra's
to hospitalize
tea roses and
on which floa
that she can
bouquet, whic
The other t
"Whenever I
put it in a gob
show you my
She handed
"Many peop
frequently som
to see the face
seem to get a li

Barter system is alive and well

In recent years farm hands have become a novelty in this part of the country. Machinery has eliminated the need in part, but we truck farmers still need hands to pick the fruits and vegetables.

Here's how we get the job done: When the produce is ready, we pass the word to local townspeople. Those who want stuff to freeze or can pick their own; we charge them less per pound. Some people pick on the shares. We appoint one person to supervise the picking, weigh the produce and instruct the pickers on proper harvesting methods.

We also swap services. My husband services farm equipment for a poultryman in return for all the eggs we need. A woman I know gives me permanents and hair-dos in exchange for fresh peas, beans and cucumbers. Neighboring farmers swap the use of a tractor for air-conditioner or machinery servicing.

All this may not sound very businesslike, but in our area people help each other, and we've proved that to be "good business."

FRANCES CRAWFORD

You meet the nicest people

As we left the Badlands and headed for the State Fair in Minneapolis, our vacation route took us across South Dakota. It was evening when we came to the small town of Gettysburg, and we noticed a police car following us. As we were leaving town, the officer flashed his red light to halt us, and four men introduced themselves as Jaycees. They invited us to be overnight guests of the town.

Our first stop was the Sage Motel. While we changed clothes, our car was completely serviced. Several Jaycee couples joined us for supper at the Medicine Rock Cafe and a tour of the town, which included a visit to the big radar base. Last stop was the Legion Hall where we danced past midnight.

Next morning after breakfast, we enjoyed a visit to the Nagel Brothers Ranch and saw a type of farming much like our own. As a final highlight, our picture made the front page of the Gettysburg paper.

We drove away recounting all the people we had met: a banker, two teachers, a newspaper woman, nurse, supermarket manager and rancher. Now they seemed like lifetime friends, reminding us that there are genuine, down-to-earth people all through our great land.

JOAN GUNDRY

Who hath ears—and heart

Last year I spent Christmas Eve with 350 youngsters who had never heard the Christmas Story; yet they told it on their program. For me this was a high point in my first year as a teacher-in-training at the Iowa State School for the Deaf.

Have you ever watched a chorus of deaf children? Their faces are extra expressive, their gestures eloquent. Seeing them "sign" instead of "sing" a song is an emotional experience.

But our program was not all silent. *The deaf are not mute*—they can, and do, learn to speak. Some can sing, to a degree; a program may feature a duet—one child singing and one interpreting in sign language. For the program last year our speech therapist had worked out a simple speaking version of "Amahl and the Night Visitors," geared to the cast's varying abilities.

These children are country pupils. Their school is surrounded by farms; they have woods to explore, slopes for sledding.

In fact, this rural community has taken the school to its heart. A wonderful farm couple on the staff gives the children hayrides and weekends, entertains the faculty at many a backyard steak fry. An instructor in shop often takes the boys out to his father's farm. A farming newspaper editor and his wife have some pupils on their own place for summer vacations.

A group of rural homemakers considers the school as one of their permanent projects—helps finance students' trips to Gallaudet College in Washington, D.C. (only college for the deaf in the U.S.). This year the women are creating costumes for our holiday fetes.

Perhaps God has a missionary purpose for children with handicaps. Certainly our deaf youngsters bring out the best in the people of our community—and not just at Christmas.

EMMYLOU KROHN

Brightness for a grim need

My neighbor has everything—including, lately, a broken arm. What could I give her that would help? Then I remembered an idea from an acquaintance of old.

I visited a fabric shop and bought an assortment of remnants at a small cost. From these I styled attractive arm slings, one of each remnant: a pink-striped denim for housewear, print terry cloth for gardening, pale blue linen for trips to town.

My neighbor was delighted. And her eagerness to show off her smart slings made the giving of them a delight to me.

CLYDIA STEENSON

Someone to remember

An elderly patient in a mental hospital recently received a postcard—the first bit of mail he'd had in months. It came from the friend of a hospital aide. The old gentleman carried the card about, showing it to everyone who would look, until the card was too crumpled to read.

A friend told me about this "forgotten patient"—someone literally abandoned by relatives and friends. I thought about him when I walked to my mailbox, and wondered if he'd receive another card.

My interest led me to inquire, and I found that his story could be repeated about 6,100 times among mental patients in our state alone. I also found I can do something about these forgotten people: I can become a part of the Adopt-a-Patient plan in my state by contacting the Local Mental Health Association, or by writing the mental hospital nearest me. When I'm assigned a patient, I can write to her and send her a gift if I like—even visit her. However, I'm under no obligation to do more than write, and so be her friend.

It's a lovely morning. The sun is shining and the trees are beginning to change into beautiful fall colors. I have my home, family, friends and health. I'd like to share my world with a "forgotten patient."

BETTE KILLION

Neighbors

Across the road, white napkin-spread,
Goes Mrs. Brown's banana bread;
And back, within a week at most—
Croquettes from Mrs. Johnson's roast.

Like clockwork, past the picket gate,
(And always on the same blue plate)
Corn fritters, corn sticks, corn pone vie
With apple fritters—jelly—pie.

For twenty years the plate has passed;
For twenty more the game will last—
Which one would stop it? For that matter,
Who knows who owns the Passing Platter?

PHILENE HAMMER

Get-well garden

Since I am tied down with small children and can't visit sick friends, I've always sent get-well cards to friends and neighbors who are ill. This year, though, I got an idea that I believe is better—a get-well garden.

My husband spaded up an additional flower plot for me, and we are planting bright, quick-growing flowers there, to cut for sick-beds and shut-ins.

I'll deliver flowers through courtesy of the coffee man who makes his rounds weekly; or my husband will take them to our grocery, which is pretty much a community meeting place. When Jim Smith stops in for a loaf of bread, he will carry home my flowers to his sick wife.

RUTH MUNDY

Shower by mail

I planned to surprise my nephew's wife with a baby shower, but she surprised me first by going to Texas to be with her husband who was in pilot training school there.

I fretted for a while, then decided to have a surprise shower-by-mail.

My invitations gave the couple's address and suggested a date on which to mail the gifts. A bonus: I was able to "invite" friends from other states.

When the mailman began delivering packages, the parents-to-be were truly surprised. It meant a lot to them to be remembered while they were far from home.

JOYCE PENN

Any day a special day

A neighbor and I felt a need to do something constructive for patients in a meagerly-endowed home for the elderly in our town. After a bit of telephoning, the woman in charge gave us permission to bake a monthly cake for those patients having their birthdays within a given month.

Our birthday cakes are not expertly decorated, but we can offer a little variety by taking turns with the baking. When one of us bakes, the other supplies birthday cards and colorful napkins. To make the cake more personal, we top it with candles and plastic numerals to show ages and change the numbers for each person with a birthday.

The honored person's eyes light up with the sound of the "Happy Birthday" song, and we take a snapshot of each celebrant with "his" cake. After the film is developed we give each person a print and the negative as lasting mementos; a print is something to share with distant relatives or friends.

What might have been just another day becomes a special one—for the birthday people and for us.

LOLA MAE SCHAFFERT

Salute to a neighbor

"Flowers leave part of their fragrance in the hand that bestows them." That old Chinese saying reminds me of a neighbor who made it possible for me to see my own garden bloom though I spent many weeks of spring in a hospital.

My neighbor could not come to visit me, since she was in ill health herself. But often she would walk over, pick a flower in my yard, seal it in saran and mail the flower to me with a note telling how my garden grew.

I saw the first snowdrop; a lily-of-the-valley; a violet from my patch; a graceful spray of bleeding heart that blossomed along our white picket fence and purple clematis that twined on the trellis by the garage.

This spring I am at home to enjoy my garden, and my thankfulness grows for a neighbor with a loving heart and a fragrant hand.

GRATIA SCHNEIDER

A day for baskets

When I was in grade school, mother sewed pretty May baskets of crepe paper with braided handles. We filled them with homemade fudge and corn that we popped. Then the real fun began—setting down baskets, ringing doorbells and running.

Years passed but I still missed the thoughtfulness of that day. So I started an adult version of May Day several years ago. I make baskets for all my neighboring farm wives and fill them with popcorn, candy and gum. Instead of running away, I visit 15 minutes or so at each stop. I have been surprised at how many women, some older than I, have never received a May basket. This revived custom makes them happy and gives me a chance to make good my intention to visit more often.

ARLENE TAYLOR

Neighbors ... so do ye also

IF YOU ASK ME, GOOD MANNERS ARE SIMPLY ONE WAY TO PRACTICE THE GOLDEN RULE—AS OPPOSED TO THOUGHTLESS DISREGARD FOR ONE'S FELLOW HUMANS

TODAY for the umpteenth time a car pulled into our driveway and honked. I stopped my work, set the baby in her playpen and went to see what was wanted.

This driver did get out of the car (lots of them don't make even that effort) and asked, "Where does Mrs. Hercules Jones live?"

We are the first house off a county highway on a road that goes back 12 miles past many farms. I know only two of these families.

We are asked directions to homes needing phone service, homes awaiting delivery of goods, to farms advertising livestock for sale.

Now why don't people give directions clearly when they expect visitors? It would save the driver's time, and my time and temper. I've partly solved the problem of carsitters; if they stay in the car I stay on the porch and we holler.

ANN KIRCHNER

Don't ask me

Larry, our son's buddy, was spending the summer with us on the farm. At lunch one day, my husband and I began arguing about a store in Spokane. This was Larry's home city, so I turned to him and said, "I'm right, don't you think?"

He looked at me for a moment, then replied, "Don't ask me. I came to stay all summer!"

Larry went on to explain a family joke—about a woman who used to visit his home and who always gave her opinions, asked for or not. She quickly wore out her welcome.

I suddenly realized how often my husband and I disagreed on unimportant topics. Any guests present were inevitably drawn into the conflict.

Now we have a rule to save all arguments until we are alone. This assures a more pleasant atmosphere for everyone. Besides, by the time we are alone, we often have forgotten the disagreement or no longer care about it.

CORRINE BURKE

Junk or treasure?

Years ago, city visitors left the farm happily carrying a dozen fresh eggs. Nowadays he (or usually she) is likely to direct quick glances around the farmstead. Nothing is sacred—or maybe everything is. He spots the little rose-sprigged pitcher (long used for battery water) on a tractor shed shelf. Or—on the back step—the large earthenware pitcher we use to water plants. Dusty cups holding assorted bolts in the tool shed, jugs in the garage, empty bottles on the barn window sill. Nothing eludes the seasoned antique seeker—not even the dog dish.

It's no different inside the house. A sugar bowl that survived the growing up of five lively children is ogled, and I am advised that if it is not for sale, I should at least put it away. The same goes for saucers under flower pots and the everyday meat platter.

We've wised up—removed all these coveted objects from sight. We are using our best set of china for everyday, rather than the usual odds and ends. Who knows what *they* may be worth some day!

DORIS BRECKA

Telephone soul-searching

What is our greatest time saver *and* time waster? We could hardly get along without it, yet sometimes we can hardly live with it.

That's right—the telephone! Friends call to chat endlessly when you are racing to finish ironing before supper, or hurrying to an appointment.

I wonder if I am guilty of telephone irritation? I'm checking myself on these points:

Will my call be welcome? . . . Is this an appropriate time for it? . . . Do I keep the conversation brief, but friendly?

I put myself in my friend's place. She will appreciate the call if she hasn't heard from me too recently, or if there's a reason for my calling —to give or request information, to offer help or congratulations.

Considering her family and her usual work schedule, I can judge the time of day when she can take a minute to chat. Nevertheless I tell her, "If you're bogged down, call me back when you have time."

SADIE M. GETZ

Valentine of gratitude

When I sent a thank-you note to a childhood teacher, she called to tell me how much this pleased her and said I was the only pupil who had ever taken time to write.

I told my Sunday School class of teen-agers about this, and they decided to write thank-you letters to people who were important to them. (Since the time was early February, the letters served as valentines!)

Words of appreciation came back from aunts, uncles, grandparents, teachers and neighbors. A stamp will deliver a written message sure to be treasured long after an audible one is forgotten.

ETHEL STANCIL

Cooperation on a party line

Visiting via party line for hours shows extreme lack of consideration.

We've developed a "gentleman's agreement" in our neighborhood which has helped to promote good social relations. We talk no longer than 15 minutes and wait between 15 and 30 minutes before placing another call. This allows the operator to call in on the line.

Our system also makes it easy to ask a long-winded caller (in a diplomatic way) to end the call quickly and relinquish the line to other phone users.

Neighborly limit

We all admire the farmer who can fix anything and is always ready to give of his time and himself. In our neighborhood, my better half is the one who's called.

He gets dirty crawling under machinery while onlookers stand and relax. He adjusts the knotter on a baler so it ties instead of turning out loose bales. He sets the spark plugs on a motor or welds a piece on a potato planter. His time, tools and electricity are given free. Family plans are often sacrificed because of these "emergency" calls.

Helping others makes for happiness, I know, and I want my husband to be well-liked. But he, too, needs a few hours of relaxation to rest tired arms, aching legs, raveled disposition—and for just plain sittin'. Without being called a battleaxe, I would like to wrangle a few leisure hours somewhere along the line to protect his health. I wish he would learn to say no, and I wish neighbors would realize how their many requests mount up. Operating a repair service is not my husband's main business.

Thank you for calling

In this age of wonderful freeways that take us to distant places, I'd like to get one message across to relatives and friends: Please let us know you're coming. We are weary of drop-in guests.

We do love you. We do want you to come. But when we have an important meeting we've promised to attend, we find it embarrassing to call and beg off—especially in front of you. We do have extra bedrooms, but often they're helter-skelter with hobby supplies or fixings for a wedding. It takes valuable time from our visiting to clean out the mess.

You are always welcome; but do give us a call first and we will both enjoy the visit more.

A rented place is home

Have you ever heard farmers say, "We just rent the place" as a reason why they can't make improvements? I have.

We rent, too, but we believe that although the farm may belong to someone else, it is *our* home. Renting imposes limitations, but we've found that owners are often willing to make major improvements if we show we're willing to put out elbow grease and small expenditures, too. It doesn't cost a penny to rake and remove trash around buildings; it costs few pennies to plant flowers.

We sanded and refinished floors in our home without much expense. The results aren't professional, but they are gratifying. New ceilings and linoleum have been installed with our labor and the landlord's money.

I believe there would be fewer moves and less dissatisfaction if renting people took more interest in the property they live on; I'm sure this is one reason we've had successful dealings with our landlord for eight years now.

PAT CHRISLER

No time for amateurs

Have we become so accustomed to professional talent on TV, radio and records that we can no longer be courteous to amateur talent?

Recently, at a local teacher's talent show, while a teacher played a piano solo, members of the audience visited with each other and left their seats.

Shouldn't we appreciate the time and work a person devotes to developing his talent?

If we want to leave the room during a TV show in our own home, well, that is our privilege. But when we are part of a live audience, inattention is discourteous.

MARY ELLEN BELL

WE LOVE OUR NEIGHBORS; WHILE WITH THEM, WE HAVE A FEELING OF KINSHIP AND ASSURANCE THAT EVERYONE HAS A CHERISHED PLACE IN THE SCHEME OF THINGS

GRANT and I and six other couples in our neighborhood take turns having a supper party once a month—on our patios, weather permitting. Menus range from hamburgers to fancy south-of-the-border suppers.

We have a leisurely meal and talk of many things. Relaxing this way in open air, we find beauty in our way of life—in the whitening boll of cotton, clusters of grapes, fragrance of newly cut hay, the distant bawl of a calf.

We find our club evenings a respite from the hustle and bustle of wresting a living from the earth.

EDITH DOWNING

Just what they've needed

For Christmas I am buying each one of my grandchildren a sleeping bag, like the ones woodsmen use.

I got this idea last summer when friends visited us with their three youngsters.

The guests arrived unexpectedly, and my heart sank. The parents would be comfortable in our guest room, but where would we put the children?

When bedtime came, I sighed with relief. No problem! Each child produced a comfortable sleeping bag, and in a matter of minutes all were asleep on the floor.

A family that brings its own beds is welcome almost anywhere—but do write or phone ahead.

LAURA TARDIFF

Our forest for friendship

Come fair weather, gray skies or storm, the first Sunday in every December finds us Fosters, with numerous kinfolks and neighbors, picnicking and Christmas-tree hunting on our evergreen farm.

The event is a friendship harvest as well as a tree hunt; one peak year there were 140 of us, from various and sundry tots to Aunt Ella Taylor in her 90s. By tradition, our festival opens the Christmas season in our community.

These 40 acres of sandy soil used to be wasteland, like a good share of the land was in this Kinnickinnic Valley. We started evergreens back in '41, as a family reforestation project. We were the first around here to plant conifers, but others quickly followed suit. Our county forester loves to brag about how many acres have been rescued from uselessness in this way; and how many farmers are building ponds in the wooded areas, to help sustain the wild life.

Everything was snow-blanketed at last year's tree-and-friendship fete. Our little travel trailer, with gas heater to take the chill off, was a popular haven. So was the outdoor fire where there were wieners to roast and all kinds of picnic food up for grabs. Visible harvest: a tree for every family, and several others—for the library, the church, rest homes. Actually this is our Foster festival number two; early in May we have a picnic-style jamboree for *planting*—plus pruning and clearing. I must own that it is not as well attended as the Yule event, for who wouldn't rather play than work? But even those who just "help thin 'em out" in December have absorbed to some extent our Valley philosophy: that the land is ours only in trust—we have a duty to the families of the future who follow us here. We are glad we'll leave them forested acres instead of blow sand.

LETHA FOSTER

Just his dish

Recently our Future Homemakers club tried a new kind of buffet supper. Each girl brought a foreign food identified with her ancestral country, along with a bona fide ancestor—her dad!

VERLYN SCHLAGEL

Dubious glory

When a woman turns fortyish (both by the calendar and around the hips) people begin taking her for granted. She's too old to be glamorous, too young to be mellow.

That was my predicament. To my children I was just plain Mom. My husband loves me, but he thinks the smartest thing I ever did was marry him (and it was). To the neighbors I was just plain Bernice.

That was before I won the contest and became the owner of a brand new Chevrolet plus a thousand dollar bonus, by filling out the 25 words in "I'd like a new Chevrolet because . . . "

Well, now, the neighbors say, maybe the old girl knows something besides the best remedy for green cabbage worms. I even had my picture in the paper with my new car.

Now when I go to town I have a purely awful time trying to get from the grocery on one corner to the variety store on the next. Everybody stops me, from those who ask, "How much income tax will you have to pay" to the Ford dealer: "What's the matter with our competitors? They giving Chevvies away these days?"

By now I'd give anything to have someone glad to see me just because I'm me, ask how I got over my poison ivy and what to do for tomato blight.

BERNICE JAMISON

Friends indeed

This is to say thank-you to (and for) three people who help make life on the farm the satisfying life it is.

My first bouquet goes to Central. Sometimes after cranking the daylights out of our wall phone, I confess to a hankering for the efficiency of a dial system. But when Central finally says "Hello" I forget my vexation in a hurry.

What dial phone could tell you whether the drug store is open, and when the doctor from a neighboring town comes to your village, and whether Jane Brown is home from the hospital yet? Could the frigid buzz of a dial tone ever give you the comfortable feeling of neighborliness that comes when you give Central your number and she pauses to ask companionably: "And how's your mother feeling? Better, I hope."

Next, hats off to the mailman. He's the friendly genie who sweetens our day with magazines, advertising circulars from nearby towns and an occasional letter. We won't hold our RFD man responsible for the bills he has to bring; we are just grateful to the guy who plows through snow and sleet over unspeakable roads to deliver that precious stuff, yet always has time for a wave to eager little faces pressed against the window.

And now, my thank-you to the county librarian—a friend whom not enough farm people have yet discovered. My own particular angel-in-a-bookmobile goes all out in getting the books I ask for. If the county library doesn't have them, she writes to the state library; once she even went so far as to besiege the Library of Congress itself in my behalf, returning triumphantly with the book I needed badly.

If you need books—for a talk to your woman's club, or to steer you right in decorating or sewing, or just for fun-type reading—ask your librarian. She will help you.

So let's hear it for these friends of farm people. God bless them!

EDNA BEILER

The last to know

A while back our dairy farmer friend Del had a hand torn off while cutting silage. His wife, Kathy, rushed him to the hospital and not a soul in the neighborhood learned about his accident for days.

A couple of teen-agers and a hired man kept the work going. What gets me is this: Why didn't Kathy instinctively turn to us neighbors for help and moral support? Has neighborliness vanished from the American farm scene?

I can remember when neighbors got together as a matter of course— for fun and for mutual help, not just in a crisis. During the depression, when we were all poor, one farmer had an old-fashioned threshing machine and all the neighbors used it. The women would get together where the crop was being harvested and cook for the crew. Then everyone—cooks, kids and crew—moved on to the next farm.

Swapping work usually isn't necessary or even feasible in today's farming. But, *neighborliness* is feasible, and more necessary than we sometimes realize. How long since you and your neighbors got together, just for enjoyment?

DALE DeRUWE

Neighbors . . . community of interests

WE DON'T NECESSARILY BELIEVE THAT "GOOD FENCES MAKE GOOD NEIGHBORS." PROBLEMS ARE INEVITABLE AMONG PEOPLE IN A COMMUNITY—WE MUST LEARN TO COPE WITH THEM

The New Power Line

The tall black poles the line crew set this week
Along the lazy road that hides itself
Among the woods and dark swamps to the south
Look, somehow, out of place. They mar the sweep
Of smoke-blue distance that we call our own,
The far horizon that we built our house
To overlook from this long wind-swept hill
That we have always loved. But now they're there
We'll look above them some way, and around;
For Kovacs and his good wife will be spared
The toil of pumping water. We are glad
For Auntie Larrabee, whose lonely light
Will shine more brightly through the winter dark
Across the bleak mile from her little house.
I think we'll soon forget the poles are there.

LEONA AMES HILL

What scares Teacher away?

How can a community be sure of getting and keeping good teachers? Higher salaries elsewhere aren't the only thing that tempts away a teacher, although money is important of course. I feel that we fail dismally to recognize and praise good teaching. We lack respect for professional skill, and that alone can discourage a dedicated teacher.

Ridiculous things often happen in our small town. Cigarette-puffing mothers criticize a teacher for "setting a bad example" when she smokes in the teachers' rest room. The school authorities once reprimanded a teacher for riding in a car with a man of "questionable character." Actually, the teacher had accepted a ride home through a pouring rain—the ride having been offered by an uncle of one of her pupils.

Teachers, being people (and often parents, too) would respond to friendliness and appreciation as much as to good pay, I firmly believe. It goes without saying that if we do appreciate Teacher, we will see that she is adequately reimbursed for her services.

ARLEY CLARK

Pollution, circa 1958

I could write a book about rural garbage disposal, or lack of it.

Not far from our house there is a garbage dump that's an eyesore. On the night our baby was four weeks old the stench and smoke from the dump took over our farmhouse. None of us had ever spent such a horrible night, although in summer we have to close our windows if there is a wind from the northeast.

We went to the county commissioners. After three weeks they sent a bulldozer to clean up the dump. Three weeks later they had to clean it again. Now the situation is the same or worse.

We have haunted the commissioners and the health department. The former say it costs too much to keep our dump cleaned up. A state health official is trying to convince the county that something must be done, but he makes no visible progress. Everyone has garbage, but no one seems willing to pay taxes for sanitary disposal of it. Those of us whose farms are near this public nuisance are the victimized minority.

CAROL BARE

Good ideas that never hatch

How many women have good impulses and, like me, go about their daily tasks while the constructive thought develops no further?

For example, I've noted that a movie theater nearby has been showing only pictures that are suitable for family viewing. The manager should be commended for placing morality over profits. I was going to write him a note. But I haven't gotten around to it.

I've noticed the number of trashy books and magazines displayed in a drugstore and complained to a friend, "Something should be done about this!" And then I've walked on without letting the owner know I disapproved. Yet if more of us took our business elsewhere we would be amazed at our influence.

And, I wonder how many of us have been aware of a bill before Congress or the State Legislature and said, "I hope this doesn't pass— it's unfair." Or, perhaps said the opposite: "Now that makes sense— I hope it goes through." But we never get around to giving legislators our views.

I'm going to set aside 30 minutes a week to write letters that count. Three squares a day and clean clothes matter, but ideas do, too— *especially* these days.

Conformity versus values

One day this spring, about 20 of our high school students skipped school. The faculty suspended the offenders for three days and lowered their grades.

Parents were upset, but most of the students felt that the punishment was fair. Our son's diminished grades meant that he could not graduate, and that hurt.

Three of the students and their mothers called on me the day after the suspension notices. They were confident that I would join in their plan to have the principal ousted.

These dissenters had decided to operate on the idea that the kids all hated the principal and had skipped school to demonstrate their dislike. My son and others say otherwise: It was simply a beautiful day and, because there were so many in the group, they thought they could get by with skipping classes.

I was disgusted as I heard three teen-agers plan how to get their principal fired. One mother, prominent in the community, said: "I do hate to see this happen. But our youngsters are experiencing a wonderful example of democracy at work."

That's democracy? To disobey the rules and then contrive to oust the one responsible for enforcing them?

Our principal still has his job, but I wonder if he would have if my son hadn't written a letter to the school board admitting he was wrong. Or if I had joined the other mothers.

Fear of seeming odd or nonconformist sometimes causes us to forsake our values. Is it possible that most of the parents felt as I did, but were afraid of making enemies?

Farm-city swap

Back when our three children were in grade school, Will and I began hearing complaints: *Never anybody to play with out here. . . .*

At the same time, my town friend Charlotte and her husband moaned that their neighborhood swarmed with "too many" children.

One evening when we two couples were together, I burst out, "Let's trade homes for a year. You folks want to try country life, and I bet we'd enjoy a go at the city."

Charlotte thought I was out of my mind. But after we had pow-wowed the idea, it took us only a week to make the trade!

Such an exchange wouldn't be practical in all cases. But our husbands could easily drive to and from their jobs; mine had long kept a farm office in town, near our new "home away from home."

Our town friends loved the country. Even before our 12-month swap was completed, they started building the house they now occupy in the country.

Living so close to Will's business turned out to be a convenience to us. We finally decided to rent out our farmhouse through each school year. And we have been moving to town for the past few winters.

However, our youngest son, Jamie, is now campaigning for us to stay on our farm year-round. His 4-H animals, and the big dog he loves, don't lend themselves well to life in an upstairs apartment!

JUNE ERWIN

Inevitable

Our children have the measles;
The neighbors' kids have mumps,
Which situation warns me
Our kids will soon have lumps
Discarded by the friendly tots
Who will, in turn, be wearing spots!

VINEY WILDER

Gift of the city

It simply isn't true that farm folks have a corner on the virtues! To hear us sound off at times, you'd think people of the soil are automatically friendlier, more devoted to the Golden Rule. . . .

But let me start at the beginning. In February my husband, Bailey, and I sent an ad to a Philadelphia paper:

Let's trade vacation hospitality. Our 3-rm. lake cottage on a Minn. farm for accommodations Phila. or vic. Any time May 20-Oct. 10. We are five, youngest 12. References.

In no time at all we had several eager letters. We especially took to a family with children the ages of ours, and made this arrangement: They'd vacation in our lake cottage while we would take over their city home.

Risky? No more so than a rental arrangement, we decided. But then our new friends had a crisis—illness of a cherished relative—and had to abandon their plan for a trip. And you know what? They moved out of their house anyway (to the shore nearby) so we could use their home as agreed.

Which of us farm families would give up our home to another family—strangers at that—so they would not be disappointed? I wish our city friends would let me tell who they are, but they prefer to remain anonymous. I only hope we can repay their generosity next year.

MARJORIE BLAIR

Coping with town folks

National Farm-City Week, held yearly, is a fine time to become better friends with town people and non-farming neighbors. But this isn't always easy. Ask any group of farmers and they'll say, in effect:

"Town friends and relatives 'love to visit the farm,' expect to go home laden with fryers and eggs. They forget that we *work* for these things." . . . "City people out driving stop in to buy our products—and haggle over the price." . . . "Only a mean dog can protect fruit and nut trees from some people's help-yourself tactics, or woods from their picnic litter." . . . "Our new city-bred neighbors don't farm. Because we 'have machinery,' they expect us to come over and mow the field next to them. *And* look after their children— 'just let them play in that big barn.' "

But then some tiller of the soil will observe that the non-farmers may harbor counter-complaints. Perhaps better communication is the answer—which is what Farm-City Week is about.

Neighbors . . . brother's keeper

AM I MY BROTHER'S KEEPER? THAT QUESTION, FIRST POSED BY A SON OF ADAM, STILL CONCERNS HUMANKIND. ANSWERS ARE MORE OFTEN SEEN THAN HEARD.

I speak from experience, as editor of a rural paper, and as one who'll never again underestimate the heart—and the talents—contained in a typical farming community. When the doctors discovered that I had an advanced case of tuberculosis and ordered prolonged bed-rest, it was anybody's guess what would become of *The Treynor Record*. Anybody's guess, that is, who didn't know the people of this area.

What happened is unique in the history of newspapers. A self-appointed committee, made up largely of farmers and their wives, took over the paper and ran it. They were untrained—didn't know a pica from a kicker-line;·but they learned fast, and they knew what they liked to read!

My publisher friends shook their heads, said no newspaper could be operated successfully by amateurs. Nonetheless *The Record* kept right on coming out; got better and better, with no loss of circulation.

What do you say when you discover that your backyard is covered with diamonds? Words are my business; but I have no words now that are adequate to express my admiration and gratitude.

EMMETT Z. BUTLER

We'll start again

When tornados hit our state, farmers were left without livestock, machinery, or barns. Cows were wild and would not produce milk; chickens had to be sold to soup companies because they wouldn't lay eggs—poultry houses had been swept away. Some hogs survived, but their shelters were gone. One of our neighbors died of a heart attack on seeing the devastation of his farm.

Now we're rebuilding and starting again! We will always be thankful for the kindness from people near and far.

More food has been given to tornado victims than we can eat in months; more clothing is available than homeless people can use. Over 2,000 volunteers came in bus loads to clear the fields of debris so farmers could farm the land again. Carpenters, electricians and plumbers provided their services free of charge. Yes, people are good.

RUTH HAAG

Who "Secret Pal" is

Chris, our 12-year-old son, is a hemophiliac and unable to attend school. His days, without other children, are long and lonesome.

Last February, he received by mail a large homemade valentine—a plump, saucy kitten drawn on red cardboard, with the message "You Are The Cat's Meow." It was signed "Secret Pal."

This was the beginning of many surprises from Secret Pal. Chris was mystified, and so were we! Six months went by. Chris was remembered on St. Patrick's Day, May Day, Halloween. . . .

And then, one afternoon, I went to ask Mrs. Barton across the road if she would bake cinnamon rolls for our Grange breakfast. As we talked, she busily cut crossword puzzles from papers. I thought little of this until Chris received a gift that gave him many afternoons of pleasure—a handmade book of crossword puzzles.

So that was what our neighbor, Mrs. Georgia Barton, spry and 82, had been doing during my visit! Chris still doesn't know the identity of Secret Pal, the friend who has made a lonely small boy starry-eyed and no longer lonely.

LAURA SHANNON

Warmth in the blizzard

Recently my husband Mervin and I were driving through Kansas when suddenly we were in a terrible blizzard. The night was dark, the snow blinding. My husband was at the wheel, but we both peered anxiously out the car windows, fearful that he would drive off the road.

At last we reached a village—Winona. There, like a miracle, stood a small motel with its office lighted. Upon entering, we found the place deserted, but the owner had hung a sign: *To any travelers caught in the storm: Sign the register, take any key. We'll settle up in the morning.*

You can be sure that is what we did! Two weary pilgrims retired in warmth and comfort, glad to be out of the storm and happy to live in a world where thoughtfulness and trust still abide.

AUDREY S. DUDLEY

A tragedy of ignorance

Our church group had finished a study of world poverty, but none of us realized there were people in need in our own thriving community. However, my eyes were opened when I decided to follow up the study by driving down several country roads.

In one small house lacking conveniences and sanitary facilities, I found a family of 15, including an aged woman crippled by arthritis. Other farm families subsisting only on uncertain day labor were in dire need (once they had been sharecroppers). As the fathers lived with the families, the only aid the government provided was some food—surplus commodities.

With the help of others I obtained clothing and an unused wheel chair for the invalid. How heartwarming it was to see the children now nicely dressed and that elderly woman's smiling face!

So often we sit in our comfortable homes surrounded by blessings, not knowing or caring about poverty in our own neighborhood. The real tragedy of our ignorance is that such situations might be changed with effort on our part.

ADELYNE FOWLER

Memorable happening

Some very special children visited our farm one day last summer—a class of trainable retarded (IQ 20 to 50) from a public school.

Most had never been on a farm. What a thrill when it's your first time to hold a warm, freshly-laid egg or to tiptoe between endless rows of conversational hens.

On to the dairy barn. What fascination the swirling white depths of a big milk tank. How dry and dusty is cow grain sifting through one's fingers! But the biggest treat was to pet the soft coats of two newborn frisky calves.

A short hayride topped the tour. Children who could scarcely speak words squealed with excitement as we jounced over a bumpy field road. The tractor's noise and power had the youngsters bug-eyed.

Taste treat in the kitchen: hard-cooked eggs, cold milk, homemade cookies. As the bus rolled away I looked at my husband, who was holding our very young baby. Our prayer of thankfulness was for a healthy and whole child, and for this day when we had brought brief joy to children less fortunate.

JANET MILLER

Yesterday
and Today

*Time, even just two decades of it, brings
some astonishing developments. Pausing to
survey a stretch of road we've traveled
—and the mile we're on now—we view a
kaleidoscope pattern: the expendable old,
the often-controversial new—and now and
then a value that doesn't change.*

Yesterday and Today

Yesterday ... backward look

THE GOOD OLD DAYS

THE other day my husband brought down a 1936 mail-order catalog from the attic. We paged through it and were amazed at the changes that have taken place.

In 1936 there were no TVs, no freezers, no dryers or ironers, no dishwashers or garbage disposers. The catalog contained no radio-phonographs (let alone stereo sets!— Editor), no tape recorders, no nylons or nylon articles, no fluorescent lighting.

In the old book were five pages of harness—two of horse collars alone. And the prices! The best gingham was 19¢ a yard, "80 square" percale 16¢. Cotton dresses sold for 39¢ to $1.98, and they were pretty! People must have worked for just about nothing in those days.

Now we wonder what changes the next 20 years will bring. We have put the 1936 catalog back in the attic and eventually we'll place this year's beside it. In 1976 we'll drag them both out for another comparison. It should be fascinating.

L. K. CONNER

Were times really so tough?

We raised a family and tried to pay debts during the depression. Now some of our grandchildren are married and trying to get a start.

My husband and I have told our children and their children how rough things were when we began farming. Recently I ran across a diary I kept during those times. I passed it on to the grandkids, expecting them to get a laugh from the stories about their parents as children.

The grands were impressed by something entirely different. One said, "I thought things were tough in those days, but you folks had a ball. Picnics ... and all the books you read ... those band instruments and jazz sessions. How did you manage?"

I said we never really had a vacation. The books were from a lending library. We grew our own food. The band instruments and music lessons did cost money, but something else was sacrificed for them. Of course we had no utility bills—we had no utilities!

I was surprised myself to notice that money wasn't mentioned much in the diary, though I was never a Pollyanna.

I won't talk anymore about how tough times were. My children and theirs have so much we didn't have; but each generation believes "times were really rugged," and loves to boast to its young ones about "hardships you'll never know."

MALO M. WILLIAMS

Dream come true

High on the hill above our house is a spring that never goes dry. For years we planned on piping it down to the house—sometime. But as I wearily pumped water for cooking, laundry, thirsty chickens, shrilly peeping poults, and steers in the fattening pen, I wondered if it would ever happen.

Always there was something—poor crops, new roof for the house, new machinery, new siding on the house, surgical operations—until I was afraid running water in the house would never be anything but a wistful dream.

Then there came a year—plentiful rains in the early spring to get the grain off to a good beginning. Days and days of sunshine. The grain grew and grew. But the water in the well sank lower and lower. The creek water dwindled to mere pools in the later afternoon.

I dipped water for chickens and poults who daily grew bigger and bigger and needed more and more water. The spring on the hill flowed steadily on but sank into the parched earth before it reached the creek.

Slowly the grain turned. I held my breath at every cloud peeping over the hill. If lightning struck that grain! I watched every car on the road. A carelessly-thrown match or cigarette!

At last the combines sent a golden stream of grain into the trucks, and the trucks carried my hopes away to the elevator.

Then came bulldozers, ditch-diggers, cement blocks, pipe, crates of bathroom fixtures, the sink, water heater, built-ins. At last, after weeks of dust and dirt, I had water. Lots and lots of water. Never will I forget the thrill. Sometimes I think that one moment was worth all the weary back-breaking years of pumping.

NELLIE BAUNE

Worth the sacrifice

A year ago we went in debt to buy a set of encyclopedias for our three school-age children. One more payment, and they will be ours!

No doubt many people would say that we're foolish to buy books on the installment plan. But we have never regretted our choice. Instead, we feel repaid every time we hear one of our youngsters say: "Let's look it up." They have at their command a treasure-house of knowledge which can never be measured in money.

We don't yet have TV, an electric range, or the new car we need; but we feel that we have made an investment in the future which will pay dividends through this generation and the next.

MAXINE GIDEON

Bless those appliances

What a world of difference mechanical housekeeping equipment has made in the lives of us farm women! I can be a real partner to my husband since I have a freezer, dishwasher, automatic range, washer and dryer. Now my routine housekeeping takes short hours rather than overfull days. I can even attend meetings of our state cattle club with my husband. And when he was asked to accept the job of secretary, he said yes—because he knew I'd have time to do the correspondence for him.

Part of his cattle club job is to edit the organization's Jersey Journal. Deadlines invariably fall during some major farming operation— sugaring in the spring, haying in summer and so on. So for the most part I am the magazine's editor—that has given me a new and absorbing hobby.

I have time now for church work, time to attend Home Demonstration Club occasionally, time to entertain. Best of all, I can have such satisfying doings with my family!

Even if I still boiled clothes in a copper boiler, I guess I'd find *some* time to swim with the youngsters in the farm pond, ride horseback with them and go skating or coasting. But my good equipment makes it possible to have more good times together, with less catching-up-with-the-work afterwards.

EMILY FISHER

Prophecy from the fifties

High school boys and girls these days jump off the school bus, grab a sandwich in one hand, change clothes with the other, rush out to take care of their 4-H and FFA animals, help with chores, gulp down supper, change clothes again and rush off.

Tonight is band practice, tomorrow night FFA and FHA, the next night 4-H. Next day comes Sunday School and church services, church youth, play practice. Today's youngsters—worked harder by coach, teachers, bandmaster and church advisers, have little time or energy left for home life, study, contemplation or fun-type reading.

We are pushing our young people too far and too fast, and I predict in time a rebel generation.

TIME MARCHES ON . . . AND SURROUNDS US WITH AN EVER-GROWING COMPLEX OF ISSUES THAT MOLD AND DIRECT OUR LIVES

Issue . . . prejudice

OUT here in peaceful rural America, it's hard to imagine the violence that is going on across the country. When I hear of racial riots, I wonder where all this will lead.

In our Junior Women's club collect are the words, "May we put away all pretense and meet each other face to face." It could also read, "And may we put away all prejudice and always meet each other as one human being to another."

Whether we are black, white, a Catholic or protestant, it doesn't make sense to let prejudice overshadow our similarities. Don't all people strive for the same basic goals—security, peace and a better world for our children? Yet too many of us aim selfishly for these goals —without due regard for people who are "different."

Perhaps it is impossible to like each person equally, or even to treat each person equally. But I believe it *is* possible to give each person an equal chance to prove himself as an individual. The way to begin is an honest look inside ourselves.

SHARON JENNINGS

Issue . . . crisis

What to do in time of crisis

We live near an Air Force community where there is always some tension because of the continual preparedness for any eventuality. During the well-remembered Cuban crisis, for example, some people panicked.

A friend called me on the phone and asked what I was doing. "I'm ironing," I told her. She was shocked. "How can you stand there ironing when we might be attacked at any moment?"

I told her that I didn't know of any better way to "sit it out." I feel this way about the hazards of life. Catastrophe will have to catch me at the ironing board. I have crossed too many "it might happen" bridges, yet here I am.

I reminded my friend that every generation has had crises. Our forefathers (and foremothers) kept right on living, although they were in constant danger of being scalped. At one time a crow could fly over Georgia and not find enough food to survive; but people didn't pause in their rebuilding.

The future comes only one day at a time. If today is good, let us enjoy it and make the most of its benefits.

ANN DICKINSON

Issue . . . four-day weekends

Let's keep traditional holidays

It seems that no matter how long a vacation we have, most of us wish we could prolong it.

I like long weekends too, but I object to a recent proposal which would change our national holidays for the purpose of lengthening more weekends.

We know from past experience that whenever a long weekend comes along, our highways become scenes of slaughter. Why should we make a move which increases traffic deaths?

Also, our national holidays had special meaning when they were set aside originally. How much of the old significance can remain for what we once called "holy days" if we begin to see them simply as convenient excuses for more three- or four-day weekends?

MILDRED GRIFFIN

Issue . . . censorship

Let them read anything?

As a teacher and parent, I hear a great many discussions as to whether reading materials should be censored for children, especially teenagers. Many teachers and parents are horrified that my husband and I allow our son to read any book or magazine he chooses.

I am just as horrified by women who favor censorship, yet never read a book themselves and don't keep good magazines around the house. What do they expect their children to read?

Our son has brought home several magazines that should never have been printed, but neither his father nor I have shown any surprise or shock. We have allowed him to read any book or magazine so long as he will read a variety. And we make it a point to provide our home with good magazines and books.

Now our son is a senior in high school and we are pleased with his reading choices. It is gratifying to hear him say, "There is so much to read that's of interest, I can't understand why anyone wastes time with trash."

ANN DICKINSON

Like parents, like children?

So many parents worry because their children watch cigarette and beer commercials and shoot-'em-up westerns on TV. Maybe we ought to give the kids credit for having some judgment and common sense.

After all, most of us parents watch commercials which we don't take seriously. I've yet to whirl out to the clothesline and dance around hugging my clean wash. Maybe my husband and I are abnormal, but we never sing to each other about whether we'd have good grammar or good taste. Nor does my family sit at the breakfast table shouting praises of our favorite cereal.

Do I stand by smirking (like the mother in the commercial) while kids roller-skate on my newly waxed floor? No!

So relax. Kids probably take advertising with a grain of salt, as we grownups do.

LEAH VAN DER MARK

RAPPORT BETWEEN THE GENERATIONS CAN BEGIN WITH A SMALL BOY, HIS DAD AND A BOWL OF CORN HOT FROM THE POPPER. THE GAP MAY NOT BE A CHASM IN FAMILIES THAT WORK TO-GETHER, PLAY TOGETHER AND PLAN TOGETHER

A conversation I overheard, between a man and his teen-age son, gave me a flash of insight apropo of the generation gap.

They were debating the questionable worth and mortality of our fighting in Vietnam. The son presented a thoughtful and logical argument. Pop heard not one word. He was so busy rampaging about draft-card burning, drugs and irresponsible youth that he never got around to considering any point his son brought up. His own clincher was, "Believe me, I'm older than you—I am your father and know the score."

Most young people, I feel, urgently wish to share their views. But I doubt whether this son will ever again try to discuss anything with his father.

CAROL BEECHER

Do as I do?

I have a theory for what is wrong with the world today. The trouble begins at home—in the relationship between parents and children.

We see our youth in rebellion and riot and we wonder why. Aren't they trying to tell us something? Do they see us as hypocrites?

We give them rules and profess ideals that we abuse. We tell them they must not lie or cheat. But they are not so blind—they know that "excuse" we gave for not helping with a community or church project was nothing but a whitewashed lie. They know when a claim we turned in or a tax statement we filled out was not as we bragged about to neighbor Jones.

Our children judge us by our actions. If we treated each situation as if we would be put on trial for it by our children, wouldn't we think twice before we acted?

DOROTHY HINTZ

Generation gap insurance

My husband, Wayne, puts in long hours at work. But, as a farmer he has an advantage—he can take our young son Mark with him.

After breakfast, Mark hurries to get his clothes. Dad helps him dress; then, off they go to feed the stock and milk the family cow. Together they check on baby lambs or a new litter of pigs. As Dad scoops corn to feed the calves, Mark works alongside with his own little shovel. When Dad uses the tractor, Mark is eager to jump off to open and close gates.

Wayne lets Mark go with him as often as possible. This is a learning experience for Mark, and such times of companionship are a real joy to both father and son.

While they share the everyday life on our farm, they're becoming close friends. We hope that this bond insures us against a possible communication gap in later years.

ARLEEN HERRING

Adult homework

We parents' after-supper hours until bedtime stretched long on winter evenings, because TV is taboo while our children do their homework. Now we have joined our eager-beaver students in their quest for knowledge. My husband enrolled in a math course by correspondence; I, not to be outdone, and to renew an almost forgotten interest in good reading, enrolled by mail in English literature.

This return to school beside our own fireside has proved so satisfactory that we intend to enroll in more correspondence courses this fall. Studying makes more sense to children when they see their parents poring over books and shelling out money for the privilege.

TEX ANN ALDRIEDGE

Loser

When I was growing up, I had to listen to my parents. Now that I am a parent, I have to listen to my children. I must belong to a lost generation. Who listens to me?

ANNE D. NEUBIG

Issue . . . retardation

Purest love

Probably many people feel as I once did, that the greatest tragedy that could befall parents would be to have a mentally retarded child.

Having been for 13 years a parent of a retarded child, I can assure you that our tragedy has been our blessing.

In loving and caring for a retarded child, one has the opportunity to develop within oneself the purest and highest form of earthly love. It is difficult if not impossible to love a normal child in this special, selfless way. The love we have for our normal children is inextricably tangled with our hopes for them, and with our satisfaction and pride in them when they demonstrate ability, intelligence or achievement. If they fail, we may be angry and hurt, feeling that they scarcely repay our love.

With a retarded child we can have no such self-centered expectations. If we love him at all, we must love him simply for being. We must love him unselfishly, because we can expect no "return" in the form of brilliance or accomplishment.

Yet the love lavished upon a retarded child can bring the greatest reward of all, for it is returned to us exactly as it is given—in the glory of pure unselfishness.

GEORGIA BECKER

Issue . . . privacy

Privacy—forgotten treasure?

When I observe today's youth, I wonder what has become of the art of dreaming and imagining.

Many a boy (whose counterpart of 20 years ago dreamed of flying to the moon or becoming a hometown hero) now can't walk out of his house without taking along a transistor radio or tape recorder. When does he dream his dreams of the future? Surely not while someone is screaming, "Yeh, yeh, baby"!

I'll never regret the time I spent looking at cloud formations—picking out the shapes of lambs, bears and castles in the sky. Or the sunny wrappers, milk and fruit cartons you throw away each month? Plastic packs often contain two tomatoes or a small bunch of grapes! You are paying for them, honey, and who needs them? The fancier the container, the more it costs.

Take soap, for instance. Why not pack several bars in one plain, clear sack? Oh, no. Each cake is encased in glazed paper or foil with protective cardboard and fancy wrappings. For what reason? Is soap perishable? Will it fade?

If the grocer placed potatoes, onions and fruit bare-faced and nude in your market basket, as he used to, you'd have no containers to fill the garbage can. Right? Time, money and energy saved!

KITTY THORNTON

Photographer, spare that deer

Recently I was dismayed to read in our local paper that 400 hoofed animals died needlessly last year in our national forests, parks and other recreational areas.

And not from illegal hunting! The animals committed involuntary suicide by eating scraps of the self-developing film used in our modern cameras.

Please—let's save our wildlife by *not* scattering film scraps, or any other litter!

SHIRLEY BOWLES

Issue . . . abortion

AS A WOMAN, I BELIEVE THAT TODAY'S FEMINISTS HAVE VOICED SOME VALID COMPLAINTS AND OBJECTIVES

LIKE their predecessors, the suffragists who won us women the vote, these women sometimes go to unattractive extremes. Maybe they have to be shrill and demanding in order to rate any attention.

If women can get abortion laws universally liberalized, they will have done a great thing for all womankind, and for our civilization. But I will not be involved in this movement; I am too busy with youth and community programs.

MARY KJERSTAD

Human inhumanity

The apparently prevailing trend to loosen all restrictions against abortion is to me shocking—as the wholesale destructions of war are shocking. Isn't it time that our costly educational courses included more emphasis on human values—for example, a reverence and respect for life on this planet?

MRS. GARDNER FEY

Kansas afternoons when I dug worms, picked up my fishing pole and headed for the creek.

The idea of needing other "entertainment" never occurred to me. Wind rustling through trees overhead and the slap, slap of water against the bank provided all the music I needed for dreaming and thinking. A bellowing vocalist would have been an unwelcome invasion of my privacy.

Today, I see too many youngsters half-hypnotized by blaring music and (to me) senseless lyrics. I hope that somewhere in the U.S. there is still a boy or girl who knows how to dig bait and make a fishing pole —one who values the solitude and privacy of an afternoon at the creek.

LENORE STUMPF

Issue . . . drug abuse

SATAN IS A DRUG PUSHER. HE WEARS BLUE JEANS AND A T-SHIRT, THE PREVAILING COSTUME AROUND OUR COLLEGES AND HIGH SCHOOLS

IN this garb he spoke to my son. He told Son that drugs were fun; that they make a guy wiser, help him know himself. He told him that marijuana is not habit-forming; that a person can stop smoking grass anytime, but that while he is high on grass his mind will expand and he'll feel secure in a world of uncertainty.

Because of the familiar costume, our son thought it was a friend speaking and that his friend told the truth. Because he did not suspect he was being deceived he smoked the marijuana, he swallowed the pills, he experimented with whatever drug was offered him.

And because he believed those lies, now our son lies too. He lies about where he goes, whom he is with and what he is doing.

At times his father and I do not recognize the son, his personality is so changed. He prefers to sit and stare rather than work or play. He no longer enjoys challenges to his mind; the boy who used to get A's on his schoolwork has dropped to D's, Failures and Incompletes. He seldom reads a magazine, never a book. At home his only diversion is listening to psychedelic noises, which he calls modern music, on stereo records and T.V. The words that go with the noises promote the lie: that drugs are wisdom, sex is life, and who needs parents?

This boy who once loved animals and wanted to be a veterinarian now neglects to feed and water his stock, forgets to look after the sick calf. He is preoccupied with himself and nothing else matters.

That deceiver in blue jeans and T-shirt is an insidious masquerader. He uses Peace as a password, and proclaims with two raised fingers that he is searching for peace. But where he leads, peace can never be found.

At first this invader deceived our son. Now he *is* our son. We can only pray that God will save our boy from himself, and save other young people from the lies he represents and speaks.

JAN VAN

Issue . . . brother's keeper?

A challenge a week

In today's fast-moving world, some lines from the Scriptures seem more appropriate than ever. Each week I select a different quotation and post it on my teen-agers' bulletin board, trying to find lines that apply to the problems they may be facing in their daily lives.

AM I MY BROTHER'S KEEPER? stared at our son recently, prompting him to make a wise decision. Later he confessed that mulling the question around in his mind convinced him he must tell his best friend's parents that their son had started smoking marijuana.

Fortunately the parents were able to stop their boy before he got into trouble—with the grass or with the law. I am certain that not all the biblical quotes I select will result in such decisive action; but I hope they will help condition our children to make right decisions throughout life.

MRS. R. A. MORAN

Issue . . . over-population

ENVIRONMENT, ALONG WITH ITS CONTROVERSIAL COMPANION INHERITANCE, USED TO SHAPE AN INDIVIDUAL'S GROWING-UP. NOW THE INDIVIDUAL'S ENVIRONMENT *IS* HIS INHERITANCE, AND MAY DETERMINE *WHETHER* HE GROWS UP

ONE of our most threatening forms of pollution is over-population. A recent projection, that our world population of over 3½ billion will double by the end of this century, is frightening and demands action.

Most of us are aware that—on a worldwide scale—it is the birth of a couple's third child, and those after it which causes population to increase with breakneck speed. We also know that rapidly increasing the number of human beings means multiplying all forms of pollution, diminishing our natural resources and reducing the earth's open spaces.

We farmers and farm wives can help get the population under control by accepting the responsibility to limit our families to two children per couple (one child to replace each parent). The U.S. has less than 6% of the world's population, yet, with the exception of foods, we consume more raw materials each year than any other country in the world. The question is no longer whether a couple can afford many children; our planet can't.

I grieve to see a housing project where my parents' farmhouse once stood. The grove where we young ones had our secret hideout has been replaced by a shopping center; freeways slice through the pasture; our once-blue sky is now gray with smog.

This kind of destruction is going on all over. What a price to pay for careless planning!

PAULA WANSA

Weekend farmers—everywhere

Farmhouses used to be inhabited by farm families, but now my neighbors consist of a school teacher, corporation employees, and a sh salesman.

These "weekend farmers" amaze me. They love doing chores tha consider boring. Feeding their six chickens is an event, and hoeing weeds in their backyard is a joy.

They leave comfortable city dwellings to rent or buy a ramsha farmhouse. Soon they restore glass to vacant windows, hide pe paint with new siding, change a weed patch into a green ocea grass. We like to see these improvements to the appearan our countryside.

But one thing bothers me. Where will farmers plant their when the land is covered with homes of city-workers?

KAREN

Issue . . . pollution

One woman's clean-up solution

American taxpayers spend millions every year to clean up ca tles and packages that all of us scatter around the countrysid containers, and even the destruction of them, add to on world's most menacing problems—the pollution of our plan

Here is one housewife's solution to the mess: Since abou the junk in the U.S. consists of used paper, we gals, along friends, could arm ourselves with old-time market baskets a en masse on the supermarkets and demand *naked* product the surprise!)

Have you ever counted the soft drink bottles, potato

Where a theory ends

My husband agrees with me that women who do the same work as men, or work that's equally valuable, should receive equal pay and equal fringe-benefits. He nods when I observe that too many women are discouraged from entering professions for which they seem especially qualified—medicine and law, for example.

But he draws the line where his wife is concerned. He believes I should be at home when the children come from school—and at meal-time!

He says he would vote for a woman for President if she seemed to be statesman material. He wouldn't vote for me, though, because it might mean that he'd have to eat alone!

WILMA BUHR

Women's Lib—roots on the farm

We farm wives are one group of women who always have been "liberated." And we willingly accept the responsibility that goes with our partnership.

I'd like to see some of these Women's Liberation advocates in the city come out and sow a cover crop or wade in the mud all day during harvest. If they want equal treatment, perhaps they should move to the farm!

HELEN BARAN

To each her own

Recently I attended a Creative Womanpower program sponsored by the Governor's Committee on the Status of Women.

One speaker, from the Women's Bureau, Department of Labor, observed that the Women's Liberation movement could become more violent than the "revolutions" of blacks or college protesters. Another said that women are in fact second-class citizens—from legal rights to employment and salaries. Also that, now women are being freed by the Pill and by the relaxing of abortion laws, they should be encouraged to seek more creative outlets.

Since I am not in the business world, perhaps I have been unaware of the inequalities. But the speakers antagonized me when they intimated that a woman can't be fulfilled by being "just a housewife." Home and family—and community—may present the greatest needs for her creativity and skills.

Women have a right to be brilliant and still be homemakers. (I resent those commercials that portray housewives preoccupied with whose wash is brighter by virtue of which detergent.)

But women also have a right to work outside the home. Individuals differ—in talents and in needs. Girls should be encouraged to pursue careers in medicine, law, math, science, or in whatever area they show promise.

The world needs brain power. What matters it whether that power resides in a male or female skull?

JOANNE BIEBER

Women in action

I must tell you about a group called Women for Agriculture—enthusiastic women who are doing an incredibly good job promoting agriculture's story. These women, wives of farmers and agribusiness men, put on exhibits, make speeches, take opinion polls, promote newspaper, radio and TV publicity on agriculture and its importance to the economy and environment.

They cooperate with other farm-related groups and make it their business to write intelligent, concerned letters to government leaders, legislators and city friends in behalf of farmers and farming.

Farmers are by tradition conservatives, and some are reluctant to let their wives in on the business side. They are passing up a wealth of talent. As the old saying goes, "Nothing beats a woman for getting things done."

VIRGINIA MORGAN

I've unliberated myself

Two years ago I decided that my time spent washing diapers, mopping the kitchen floor and cooking three meals a day was not meaningful work for a college graduate. (What would my professors say if they knew I spent more time with dust cloths than with books?) A woman squanders her intelligence by doing mundane tasks, I reasoned.

That's when I became a "liberated" mother and returned to teaching high school English. ("After all," I thought, "if I'm happier doing work I find significant, my family should benefit, too.")

The challenge of teaching this active, alert generation of teens excited me; coffee breaks and conversations with other teachers were inspiring. I often mused, "If we were rich, I'd teach for nothing." I thrived on it.

However, leading a dual life was frustrating. My schedule became grueling. I neglected house and family to prepare for class, but there was never time enough to research thoroughly. I left for school wishing I had looked up just one more point; I came home wishing I had time to plant day lilies at the side door. My homeroom needed help with the class party; the younger children needed help making valentines. And conversations with my husband were cut short by stacks of papers waiting to be graded.

No single incident sent me scurrying to resign. What happened in those two years was that I finished the maturing I should have completed before having my children. I hadn't been as prepared for wife-hood and motherhood as I'd thought.

Now, once again I'm "housewife" on our tax return and I'm happy. My basic nature hasn't changed: I'd still rather read *Paradise Lost* than Fannie Farmer, and housework will never thrill me; but my attitude has improved. I've learned to do tasks quickly so I will have time for what I discovered to be the most meaningful element in *my* life: people —my family, our community and myself.

FRAN SMITH

No welcome mat for women

Has anyone ever noticed the treatment women get from farm organi-zations? A woman on a farm board is rare. The men seem to have assumed that we'd rather watch a fashion show or have "girl talk" than listen in on meetings intended to improve our farming.

Most of the farm women I know are partners to their husbands. And they want to know more about *their* business. At our farm meet-ings, there are seminars for the men —and separate ones for the wo-men. There's no law that says we can't walk in— but it would be nice to feel welcome.

HELEN KARNES

An under-achiever strikes back

Women are constantly being bombarded with lectures and magazine articles designed to make the average wife and mother feel like a dowdy, no-good sponger. As one of the so-called "under-achievers," I am lodging a firm protest.

As a mother, I'd like to defend all of the unknown, unnamed, self-less women who will never be seen in newspapers and magazines. They have had the courage and maturity to give up the glamour of a glit-tering career to become mothers.

For many years, we have felt pride in our rural youngsters. While their city counterparts were in mischief up to their turtlenecked heads, our children were turning out to be honest, industrious and responsi-ble young adults. Do you know why? Probably because they had mothers who worked at the job of child rearing!

These are the women who wait at home for the children instead of vice versa. These are the women who have a kind word and a plate of cookies to heal the day's wounds.

As a mother, I feel I owe the world a settled family—a family in which I have acted as stabilizer. I owe the world children who will be strong enough to become men and women, not follow the crowd.

It would be easy for a mother to abandon her job and hide under the veneer of a constant do-gooder, but it would be far less noble. Instead of being so wrapped up in satisfying their own interests, your achievers should remember the most important people—their families.

NANCIJANE HITCHCOCK CRONE

Creature of many roles

Women should by all means be involved in the world's big issues. Let the husband do his share of family raising! In these years of higher education and early marriage, young folks tend to leave home early; hence more mothers have time to contribute their talents and knowledge to important matters outside the home.

But in the final analysis, the woman shines brightest as an effective mother, wife and homemaker.

ANN BEUSCHEL

Mixed feelings

Job opportunities in our nearby town are not equal for men and women. In fact, I lost a job as manager of a local Savings and Loan Association as soon as I had built it up to a large enough business so that it could afford to hire a man. The directors told me that my being a woman was the only reason they were replacing me.

KAY ELLIOTT

Issue . . . peace

IN A WORLD THAT LONGS FOR AN END TO CONFLICT, ONE CAN'T HELP WONDERING WHETHER PEACE ON THIS PLANET IS ACTUALLY POSSIBLE

I have been reading Robert Ardrey's controversial book *African Genesis*. The author's theory is that man is descended from a killer ape, and that fighting is instinctive with the human race.

It is true that such atrocities as the Nazis perpetrated during World War II (and how about the more recent ones in Africa and Vietnam?) shock us into the awareness that we humans actually do wear civilization as a very thin veneer.

Can the individual person do anything to promote the cause of peace? I don't know. But I've reread, in a meditation saved from Daily Word, that *every time we add to the joy of one person, we add to the joy of the world; every time we add to the peace of one person, we add to the peace of the world; every time we add to the faith of one person, we add to the faith of the world.*

Can I, by contributing my small share, help bring about worldwide harmony? Again, I don't know; but I'm resolved to try.

DOROTHY WILLARD

. . . Not have died in vain

This is my memory for that moment of silence this last November 11:

We were in Georgia. Jim was completing his pilot's training before going overseas, and I had taken our baby daughter down to be with him.

We had only two months to be together then. And I relive them slowly. The time Jim brought home a block of ice and put a fan beside it and we caught colds from those wonderful icy breezes. The nights we sat at the kitchen table talking of things nearest our hearts—our hopes and aims and God.

But now Jim is gone. I think of him sitting in his Flying Fortress, encouraging his crew as they bailed out. When the boys in his crew got back from prison camp they came to see me, one by one, and told me how Jim held the plane steady until the last man jumped. Then the burning wing exploded and the plane dived to earth. Jim was gone.

Twelve years later I pray that as we rejoice in peace, we also remember the cost, and hence hold peace dear.

KAY BOSWEL

Peace or else

We must forever guard against the attitude that peace is an idle dream that can never be achieved. God has promised peace; but it cannot come about until human hearts are conditioned for peace, and we must all work diligently toward that goal.

It is frightening to realize that, in this nuclear age, if men do not learn to live in harmony, they may destroy the world amid atomic chaos. We are voters; only we can select wise, peace-loving leaders. Far better to work out our problems as nations around the peace table than with bombs, bullets and flames.

MRS. MICHAEL B. LITTON

Definition

What is peace? It is difficult to describe this intangible, especially since our world has experienced peace so seldom. Philosophers and statesmen and poets have used flowery language and catchy phrases in attempts to pinpoint the meaning. But a seven-year-old school girl from New Delhi defined it simply and with accuracy: "Peace is when frogs sleep on water lilies."

VERA KOPPLER

Crucial questions

Yesterday, after church, my family drove 200 miles to visit a cousin wounded in Vietnam and returned recently to a nearby Naval hospital.

Walking up to his room, I asked myself what I would say to him.

To my surprise, I found that conversation was no problem. He did most of the talking ... told us he was fine, explained how he was wounded, described what doctors were doing.

There he lay—an arm broken, both legs broken (one in traction and not properly healing).

When he told us of the volunteer mission during which he was injured, there was no regret, no bitterness, only pride at having been part of something he considered worthwhile.

As we talked, I asked myself: Why? Why should such fine young men have to be crippled, suffer or die for something not their doing? Why can't people and nations resolve their differences without wars?

Each of us needs to ask himself if we take our freedom for granted, and whether we aren't misusing human life when we ask young men to sacrifice theirs and others' on the fields of war.

Farm Boy in Vietnam

All my living I have nurtured life,
Have fed small pigs, rubbed breath into wooly lambs,
Propped timorous newborn calves on wobbly legs.
I have stayed from dark to dawn
Waiting for a mare to drop her colt.
I have not wanted to waste
A drop of blood, a grain of earth.

I have dammed up gullies,
Contour-plowed my land,
Planted trees.

What am I doing here?
Laying waste to a countryside,
Spilling blood in wholesale lots ...
I, who tramped the snow in weather to feed a cow.
Can I be oriented, conditioned to this waste?
Can I be filled with hate until I can't remember
How a mockingbird split a prairie sky with song?
I who love life deal in death,
Stabbing, burning, killing
And, to complete the irony, may die.

H. M. VIRDEN

Wider World

*There is a world beyond these walls,
beginning with our own acres, our own
community. I have a stake in this
planet—its pleasures and problems,
its people with their ideals and
confusions, its material wealth and
inner riches to be shared.*

Wider World

PATRIOTISM, IN THE SENSE OF "MY COUNTRY, RIGHT OR WRONG," MUST GIVE WAY TO A NEW CONCEPT: "THE WORLD IS MY COUNTRY, AND ALL ITS PEOPLE, NEAR AND FAR, ARE MY FELLOW CITIZENS"

I knew very little about the United Nations until recently, when I joined a church group that went to New York for a UN seminar. There were 55 of us, men and women, and we spent three days finding out what's going on in the world.

We toured the famous UN Building, attended a General Assembly and listened in on the five-language earphones, bought lovely souvenirs in the gift shop. Best of all, we talked with people from different nations, including our South African girl guide.

Everyone on the UN scene appeared to be intelligent, optimistic, dedicated, and often surprisingly young. We learned about UNICEF and the work this UN agency does to help hungry and diseased children all over the world. (For the first time I heard of yaws, a disease of tropical countries.) We heard reports of improvement in world health through work done by WHO (World Health Organization). We also learned about UN's technical assistance to underdeveloped countries.

I could go on and on; but if you haven't visited the UN, why not make up a group and enjoy this wonderful experience. You'll come home with a new faith in the future of the world, despite gloomy headlines.

BETH PHILPS

Builders of friendship

Bouquets to the sponsors of TV programs about countries and peoples. With civilization in a crisis, we must learn to know and understand our neighbors in the world. As we watch good documentaries, we enjoy armchair travel; and we get a clearer view of the roles various countries play in the international news.

BERNICE M. ANDERSON

Profile of America

Our Farm Bureau Women's group made five scrapbooks on rural living and sent them to pen pals overseas to give them a picture of American farm and family life.

We made a list of the 60 overseas pen pals we had and put the list in the back of each scrapbook, with the request that the first recipient pass the book on to the next in line and so on. The books are still going the rounds.

We included stories about our families, homes, work, our programs in church and school. Many snapshots and newsclippings went into the books also.

Our scrapbooks are not only making new overseas friends for America, but they've also made us, the compilers, prouder than ever that we live here.

CAROL PAHL

No place like it

Two years ago my farmer husband was drafted into the Army, and we were sent to Germany.

We have seen so much and met so many fascinating people. We have had thrilling trips on giant passenger planes and luxury steamships. We've skied Alpine slopes, picnicked in Germany's fairytale Black Forest. We've seen exquisite tulip fields in Holland, explored an ancient Roman fort. We have made fine new friends, and we enjoy recreation here that just isn't possible back home.

It's funny though. On Sundays we always seem to steer our car to the farmlands, to see how the farmer and his patchwork fields are progressing.

Instead of photographing a distant castle, we more likely take pictures of women harvesting wild mustard by hand. Instead of going to the Officers' Club in the evening, we are pulled to our little drafting board to alter the farm and farmhouse of our own that we're building on paper.

If one of us is lucky enough to find an American farm magazine on a newsstand, we buy it as a gift for the other, knowing that it will be more appreciated than the quaintest bit of Europe that the shops have for sale.

This experience has made us realize that no matter how monotonous farm work may seem at times, no matter how limited the advantages in our nearest town, once a farmer—well, you just can't get it out of your blood!

JOCELYN HOLMES

Blessings on blabbermouths

Reading the Declaration of Independence and the Constitution of the United States to our small son, I was impressed once again with the beauty and perfection of those documents.

I had just recovered from town meeting, and was rather weary of certain local blabbermouths. But it suddenly came to me that our national documents were the products of just such meetings. As much as we would like to think that in 1776 things were carried out with dignity and intelligence always prevailing, it probably isn't true. There were committee meetings and discussions, tempers lost and names called. It is even likely that those beautiful phrases were formed because some old fool (even as you and I) just wouldn't shut up and sit down.

So I say, blessings on the blabbermouths. They are in there trying. The dullest town meeting is a reassurance: *For men together to be heard can never be herded together!*

ETHEL WALBRIDGE

What's the hurry?

Our vacations always seemed so full of hustle, hustle, hustle, mostly putting mileage behind us, that my husband and I decided to take a leisurely trip for once.

Rather than driving madly day after day, we took a slow sight-seeing tour of our state. As a starting place we chose the Eastern shore of Lake Michigan and made a rough itinerary of sights to see. But we refused to hurry; if we liked a spot we'd linger.

We didn't see everything; we simply refused to hurry that much. In lovely Hartwick Pines Park, we prepared our breakfast under a canopy of spicy pine boughs. Afterward we meandered down the many footpaths.

One evening we visited the big city docks on Lake Huron. The big boats and sounds of shipping were fascinating.

We ate all our meals beside lakes or on river banks. No restaurant can provide atmosphere like that!

From now on, we'll take all our vacations at a snail's pace. Naturally, we'll see less, but we'll see more with thoroughness, and with maximum enjoyment.

And we'll be really rested when we get back.

MAURINE OLNEY

Thanks to pen pals

Several months ago my children came dashing home from school with the news: "We've got pen pals!" Since that day they sit for hours at a time, writing letters to their friends in England. Our globe and atlas, which used to collect dust, are now in constant demand. When Daddy brought home a world map, the kids pounced on it like our puss cat pounces on a mouse!

If anyone could see my children poring over letters and maps, they'd think pen pals are a great thing for kids. And they'd be right.

NINA LUDWIG

Poor but not impoverished

We live in a farming community in Spain, surrounded by orchards, patches of wheat and vegetables. Our neighbors are poor—really poor. Many work land with only hand tools, cook over an open fire, draw water from a well, and wash their clothes on rocks at a stream.

Yet I cannot describe them as "poverty-stricken." They express their natural friendliness by giving: They keep us supplied with fruit. They always have a snack for our children. They receive our expressions of neighborliness with appreciation. But their interest is in giving rather than getting. And those who give are not poverty-stricken —though poor.

Neither can I describe these neighbors as "depressed." They create order and beauty all around them. The veranda of the poorest home is lined with potted plants in tin cans. The women are scrupulously neat and beautify their homes with handwork. Those who create beauty are not depressed.

Some would argue that their acceptance of things as they are hinders their progress. Yet I am grateful to my "poor" Spanish neighbors for this lesson in living.

MARJORIE PRESTON

New light on Vietnam

Our daughter Carol rooms in college this year with Dao, a girl from Vietnam. She is learning much about Southeast Asia. When I read war accounts of blood-thirsty "terrorists," I think of what they could become, remembering petite, brilliant Dao with her lovely manners.

DONNA BLAIN

Wanted: worriers

What this nation needs is more people who worry.

I worry! I worry about people who think a thing is right because everybody does it . . . fertile topsoil in a rushing creek . . . little wet mittens in a zero snow . . . television chain-viewing.

Unguarded swimming holes, school bus uproar . . . the children of teen-age parents . . . motions that pass unanimously.

And I worry about people who don't worry.

SUE GERARD

Fighter in Vietnam

Our son Michael, overseas with the Armed Forces, sent us his war-correspondent's view of an American fighting man:

"The average age of a combat soldier in many units in Vietnam is 18½. . . . A pink-cheeked, tousle-haired, tight-muscled fellow who under normal circumstances would be considered by society as half-man, half-boy. . . But here and now he is the beardless hope of free men.

"He is for the most part unmarried and without material possessions except for possibly an old car at home and a transistor radio here. He listens to rock and roll—and 105mm howitzers.

"He just got out of high school within the last year, received so-so grades, played a little football, and had a girl who broke up with him when he went overseas or who swears she is still faithful. . . . He has learned to like beer by now because it is cold and because it is "the thing to do." He smokes because he gets free cigarettes in his C rations package and it is also the thing to do. . . . He still has trouble spelling, and writing letters home is a painful process. But he can break down a rifle in 30 seconds and put it back together in 29. . . . He can also dig foxholes, apply professional first aid to a wounded companion, march until he is told to stop or stop until he is told to march. . . .

"He has seen more suffering than he should have in his short life. He has stood among hills of bodies and he has helped construct those hills. He has wept in private and in public . . . because his pals have fallen in battle and he has come close to joining them. . . .

"He will share his water with you if you thirst, break his rations in half if you hunger, split his ammunition if you are fighting for your life. He can do the work of two civilians, draw half the pay of one and find ironic humor in it all. . . . He can save a life, or most assuredly take one.

"Eighteen and a half years old. What a man he is!"

SYLVIA KREBEL

The article, written by Tom Tiede, is reproduced in part by permission of Newspaper Enterprise Association—Editor

Why money for India?

Nothing we had read hinted that we would love India so much—its sounds, its aromas, its crumbling walls, but most of all its people. Their delightful non-conformity, their relaxed way of being themselves, their eagerness to help, their warmth.

We sense Gandhi's spirit here—his ability to see the best in people and expect the best of them. We suspect this brings out the best in us, too.

Both men and women are surprised that we do all our own work, for people who own land here rely on servants. They can hardly believe that I pull weeds, can drive a car or run a tractor. Some of the women feel of my hands and remark with surprise that they are "as hard as an Indian worker's hands."

We had chances to observe how American technicians are helping India improve her agriculture. The government is trying to develop the country for the good of all. But it can't possibly succeed by itself any more than the U.S. did in its infant days. During the time our democracy was first developing, England and other European countries invested in the U.S. large sums of money, some of which was made off of exploitation of India and other colonial territories. Shouldn't this be reason enough for the U.S. to invest large sums to insure that India is successful in her great experiment with democracy?

What a lot we could all learn through an understanding friendship with youthful, ancient India.

VERNEVA SALISBURY

Vistas visualized for her newborn child

My dear Faiza: The first day I felt you move within my womb, I heard the warning air raid siren. Lights were switched off and curtains drawn. Anti-aircraft guns were resounding. I asked myself, "How will I ever protect my little one from the wrath of men?"

The 18-day war with India (in 1965) ended as unexpectedly as it began. The United Nations had called for a cease-fire. There was no victor nor vanquished; the dispute remained suspended like a bomb in mid-air. I recount this to help you realize the futility of war.

You are well fed, well housed, well clothed. You shall have all the facilities of education and recreation your father and I can offer.

Please never lose sight of the sad fact that we are a privileged few in a country where the people, especially women, are largely illiterate. If you look beyond our home, you will see crude structures called homes—one small room housing many persons, with a roof that vanishes with wind and rain. Disease is common; poverty is a way of life. Food is limited.

In the fields around little villages, women work, plowing and harvesting along with the men. Women pluck tea leaves and cotton, care for cattle and sheep. They weave and embroider, care for homes, husbands and babies, and their labors often remain unrecognized.

Our government is geared toward development: more food, more clothing, schools, electricity, industries and farming equipment are the goals. Friendly nations are helping. Yet governments alone cannot conquer poverty and all the ills of society.

You and I have a duty to society. The disease next door does affect us; the poverty around us bears upon our family.

For years now, I have worked voluntarily with the All Pakistan Women's Association. As I look back, I am sure that I have helped and been helped. Laws have been reformed, women are on the road to emancipation; schools, colleges, hospitals have been set up by APWA. There is much yet to do.

We must awaken the women in rural areas. We must give them education and self-confidence and lead them to the realization of their worth. When you are old enough, do join this campaign and carry on where I have to leave off.

My blessings to you for a happy marriage with healthy children— a few. Marriage can be the most beautiful part of a woman's life, but it is only a part. I also want you to train for a profession. The talents and intellect of women go far beyond homemaking. By the time you are old enough to join the working world, I hope that my generation will have torn down the walls of prejudice against women.

Today you are too small to understand what I have written, but do read this letter over the years.

I hope you, too, will join with the many women in this and other nations who strive for a world of peace, a world that is without want and is free from disease, a world where women are equal in all walks of life and a world in which all can soar to heights of fulfillment and love for humanity.

YOUR AMMIJAN
(Your loving mother)

The letter adapted above, written by Begum Rashida Patel of Pakistan, won top award in a contest sponsored by the Associated Country Women of the World—Editor.

Let's give credit where due

Recently I have read some vicious attacks on the United Nations. These attacks show that many of us Americans know very little about the UN, even though its headquarters are in our backyard.

Since the UN was formed, it has contended with trouble in Iran, Greece, Berlin, Indonesia, Israel, Kashmir, Cyprus, Suez and (will we ever forget?) Korea. In all of these troubled areas the UN was instrumental in ending hostilities or warding off head-on collision.

I believe the UN Charter is the greatest single statement of human purpose developed in this century. That explains why new nations immediately seek membership.

The UN is like an iceberg—we see only a small part of it. Only 20% of its budget deals with political matters; 80% of its money and manpower goes to help people of the world survive to live a fuller life. In 15 years, 800 million people have been freed from malaria through their own national efforts, aided by the UN's World Health Organization and Children's Fund; 150 million have been vaccinated in a tuberculosis control program.

In 15 years the Food and Agriculture Organization has helped

273

double rice production in the United Arab Republic; has improved the nutrition of Syria, Haiti and Thailand by the introduction of fish-farming; has helped the Philippines establish a ship building industry.

We must remember that the UN is not a legislative body—it discusses, recommends. It depends on nations to carry out its recommendations and nations depend on the support of the people to act.

As a close observer of the UN for 15 years, I feel that U.S. tax money contributed to our international organization is well spent.

ELEANOR S. ROBERTS

Stranger than fiction

We have a new "daughter," a dark-eyed university graduate from Indonesia.

Back in 1958 I read of a project to send American magazines to people in developing nations. My 4-H members decided to join this movement, and the magazines we sent brought us many pen pals—among them, Frieda.

Then a high school senior, Frieda wanted to know all about 4-H. She became our long-distance member, soon enrolled her boarding-school friends in Indonesia's first 4-H club. They in turn started clubs in their home communities.

Our family's mail-order friendship with Frieda ripened. We sent her seeds, fabrics, kitchen utensils for her clubs; she sent us native gifts, delicately crafted.

She wanted to visit us here in America. Several times over the years a long visit was arranged; then unexplainable red tape would prevent her departure. It was a great day when my husband and I could at last meet her plane.

In American skirt and sweater, Frieda looks like a teen-ager. In her handmade sarongs, she resembles an exquisite doll. Her reactions to our way of life intrigue us. (The way self-service stores trust customers—amazing! Our TV commercials—hilarious!)

We are grateful for our new daughter and we hope she can stay with us a long, long time.

LENA F. REED

From a friend in England

I have American pen friends—one a farmer's wife in Iowa. These letters tell me about America.

First, I find to my delight that Americans are more interested in religion than you'd guess from seeing American films. Your home ideas show that your furniture and decoration have a more direct application to family living than ours. A room is planned around its uses.

Girls and women do more dressmaking than I realized. Over here, America is famous for inexpensive mass-produced clothes. If it's American, it's chic and slick. We're surprised to know that you sew at home.

American hospitality is famous around the world; so the visitor to

America is certain of a warm welcome and wonderful memories of time spent in the States. But the American away from home seems to be different.

From my American friends and magazines, I know that not all Americans are rich. But it is difficult to argue otherwise when they whiz past in expensive cars, whirring movie cameras.

And now I am going to mention one thing that gives us a bad impression of Americans. It's a problem that must be faced by your service men and by parents of your young soldiers.

The USAF uniform stands out in a crowd, and people judge your nation by the behavior of men in uniform. These boys are lonely and homesick. Instead of taking it out in dance hall brawls, and with girls who aren't very good representatives of *their* country, wouldn't it be better to enter into our community activities, and know people more like folks back home?

I've heard America's national character torn to shreds by people who have witnessed the irresponsible actions of American fellows in uniform.

I love America, and know how heroic her men can be. To me your Statue of Liberty, your wide farmlands, your busy industrial plants, schools, and churches are an outward symbol of your aspirations. The world looks to you. Don't let us down.

MARGARET WHITE

Moss on my brain

Yesterday our second son, who has just graduated from college, announced that he has been accepted to train as a Peace Corps volunteer for Afghanistan. I'd hardly known there *was* an Afghanistan.

Suddenly I realized that not only are my three sons a foot taller than I am physically, they are also yards taller mentally. With my middle-aged spread I may be broader than they, but intellectually they are as broad as the world.

For too long I have let my interests reach only to the boundaries of our farm. When our college-trained sons are talking, I often fall silent simply because I don't read much besides our weekly paper and the Sunday School lesson.

What do I plan to do about this? This morning I went to the library and got books about Afghanistan and history. From now on, dust may gather under my beds while I read, but moss won't gather on my brain.

NAOMI WRIGHT

A habit to break

Headlines, editorials, people you meet—they often have one thing in common. Everyone has his own particular gripe. I have one too. I'm fed up with gripes!

High taxes are a favorite topic for farmers to moan about. Instead of beefing, let's try to remedy injustices and be grateful that we live in a land where individuals are allowed to get an education, choose their occupations and own property. The taxes we pay maintain a government that insures our grandchildren similar opportunities.

But gripe subjects seem to be limitless! If the PTA plans a party for the children, inevitably someone will challenge the menu.

Teens, individuals or groups, are another target for the dissenters. Is this fair? I saw crews of teen-agers pitch in and save a large portion of a nearby city during a recent flood. They worked willingly and tirelessly when we needed them.

Now, I am by no means implying that if someone steps on your foot you should grin and bear it. There's a vast difference between standing up for your rights and merely griping because you've happened to form the habit.

No sir—or ma'am! You can't convince me that griping solves anything. Now if you'll kindly remove your foot from mine . . . .

PHYLLIS McLARNAN

Wider World . . . for mama

WHEN I WAS A LITTLE GIRL, I WANTED TO GROW UP AND BE A MAMA. NOW THAT I HAVE ACCOMPLISHED THAT, I WANT TO "GROW UP" AND BE A PERSON —IN WAYS THAT EXTEND MYSELF, AND MY WORLD, AND MY ROLE IN THE WORLD

BY day I cheerfully grapple with chores common to mothers and farm wives. By night I am an insatiable bookworm, wriggling my way through pages of printed treasures.

Lost in a make-believe world, I poke about in an ancient, musty castle, sit at a king's table and listen in on royal intrigue. I may join a band of mountain climbers and, attaining the top, reach out to touch a star. Or I'll stow away on a creaking old ship that heaves about like driftwood on an angry sea. (We reach port, despite pirates.)

Biographies grip me; I love to relive the life of some famous and no-doubt doomed person. Last night I was Marie Antoinette fleeing the mob, when—mercy!—our clock bonged the hour of three.

As I joined· my softly snoring husband, I added to my bedtime prayer: "And thank You for people who write."

FRANCES OLSON

Wanted: word power

I began to keep a vocabulary list a few years ago. Whenever I'd see a new word, I'd write it down in a notebook.

This notebook still stays on a shelf by the kitchen sink; as I do dishes I rehearse my words. I am amazed at how long the list has become!

Tending our three children has cut down my reading hours to the daily paper, a few magazines and a book or two a year. Nevertheless, I've added 1,000 words to my vocabulary—and forgot dishpan drudgery while I did it.

MARGIE KAUFMAN

False alarm, good lesson

One day as I answered the doorbell, I thought for an instant that the visitor was an old flame of mine—and I looking like the wreck of the Hesperus! My blue jeans were wet, baggy and faded (so what if it was wash day?). Lipstick I wore not, and as for my blouse, it was a dodo— a past number. Certainly I was no figure of romance, so I was relieved when the caller turned out to be merely a salesman.

Afterward, I started wondering why it should have been less awful for a beau out of my past to see me at my worst than for my husband seldom to see me any other way! Yet he is the one I chose over all others.

Needless to add, I got myself gussied up for the homecoming of the man I love—and looking nice has been my practice ever since.

CAROLYN THORNTON

Never too late

With our three sons in university and our college daughter about to begin VISTA training, I found my role of mother less time-consuming and less creative. So I took up the matter of my own long-postponed higher education.

I started with an evening course the day before I became 41. Now I am a senior at our nearest state college, majoring in History and taking courses in Behavioral Science. I've even made—and stayed on— the President's Honor Roll.

I still help my husband and our 15-year-old Karyl with the dairy chores (he milked tonight, because I had Geology Lab). It's a 10-mile drive to the college. To pay for tuition and books I raise bull calves— five a semester.

The college experience is more than worth the cost. I enjoy the students, and feel that they gladly accept me. My own young adult children say, "Instead of worrying herself over us, Mom concentrates on keeping those young professors in line." And, though I am at an age when friends are likely to say "It's her age, you know," I've not had the least bit of time to feel menopausal!

MILDRED DOSSEY

How much is your time worth?

I wonder how often farm women underrate their worth. Just for fun, I began to jot down the jobs I do and what I thought each was worth. My husband and I were amazed at how much I accomplished and how much it would cost to hire all this work done.

It's impossible to put a value on some chores (for instance, I'm the farm errand girl). Other jobs, such as freezing vegetables or sewing, are easy to estimate.

By paying myself (on paper, at least), I realize what I accomplish, and how to organize my time so as to "earn" more with less effort. My family now thinks of me as a wage earner, not just a housewife!

ISABEL WILSON

Late learner

I was one of the last of the non-driving farm women. We lived over a mile from the nearest neighbor, and five miles from town; so when my husband died, I knew I had either to be tied to the apron strings of my grown-and-married children, or take myself by the back of the neck and sit in the driver's seat.

Well, this is my second year of driving, and I'm still around! Getting my driver's license was one of the most wonderful things that ever happened to me—partly because my husband used to say that I just couldn't operate anything mechanical.

While learning, I did all the funny things the cartoons show women drivers doing: I pushed out the back of the garage, scarred a post while turning in at the drive, took a corner too fast and plowed into a corn crop. But, by jiminy, I finally did earn my license—thanks to daughter Bea, my teacher.

How I preened the first time friends asked me to pick them up for choir practice. Now I reflect that I could have been a better partner to my husband, if I had learned to drive years ago. I recommend that if there is another non-driving farm woman in the world, she learn this skill. If this unmechanical mouse could do it, so can you.

GRACE CUBLER

Plans, not wishes

When I first married, I found myself carrying a wishbone in my hand. "I wish I had time to take a sewing course, or join a bowling league. . . . I wish I could speak Spanish."

My husband suggested I choose one interest and follow it for a season. I did, and ever since I have selected one a year—always something to fit my time and energy.

One year—that year an illness kept me housebound—I took a correspondence course in contemporary literature. Another year I joined a Toastmistress Club and enjoyed public speaking. Recently I took a course in buffet cooking.

One "selfish interest" a year stimulates me—and in turn my family.

WILMA GARTEN

Solo vacation

I didn't contrive my vacation alone on purpose. Going by myself just seemed the only way to manage a visit with my parents, in Arizona.

We found that going by plane would cost very little more than buying a Pullman ticket plus train meals enroute; and flying would save us four extra days of "hired milking."

A sister-in-law helped me iron and pack; she also drove the four children to the nearest city, where a cousin would keep them in exchange for a farm vacation for her children later on.

Well, Mama boarded the plane for her first flight. Only it wasn't "Mama," for suddenly I was a person; I was *me*! I had not anticipated such magic, but here, for the first time in 10 hard-working years, I had a gift of time—which gift I instantly dedicated to being myself.

High in the clouds, whence the people below could not be seen and the earth was an abstract form, I found myself thinking objectively: Milking cows and diapering babies have their time and place, but they should not be allowed to absorb all of a mother's time and energy.

During my six-day visit, my parents and I did a hundred fascinating things together. We explored parts of the Arizona desert—a world different from my green Ohio. We visited missions built by conquesting Spaniards; we discovered art and curio shops. On Saturday my mother treated me to a hair-do, and Sunday we went to church.

Enriched and refreshed, I started home. Above the clouds again, I thought of the words from Ecclesiastes: *There is a time for everything* . . . to which I added, "A time to stay at home and a time to go away." I also wrote down some conclusions:

A home should be the center of a family, but not the boundary. . . . The scope of a child's thinking is seldom greater than that of the parents who shape it. . . , The desire to give is good, but one's methods should be re-evaluated and varied as a family's needs change.

As I embraced my family again, I felt that now I had something extra to give the people I love.

ANN MUNCARA

Good medicine

Am I foolish, as my husband thinks? Our only child is married and doesn't live near; so last winter I took my first full-time job. I'm so glad I did!

First, It's great to have my own paychecks. Also, I've lost 27 pounds and wear a size 14 dress. But best of all, keeping busy prevents me from brooding over my family, and over every little ache and pain of my own. In fact, since I've been employed I've felt better—and I sleep better, too.

My job isn't easy; I work in a state mental hospital caring for the emotionally disturbed. But it's very rewarding work, and I've found that by helping others I help myself too.

GOLDIE WEAVER

Reading on the road

Unlike some farm wives, I didn't enjoy trips to town. I preferred to stay home and catch up on my reading. But occasional trips were unavoidable, so I combined business and pleasure.

As we'd ride to town, I began reading aloud to my husband. We enjoy both sharing books and discussing them. Reading on the road makes this sharing possible.

For nature lovers who are aghast at my burying my nose in a book as the scenery slips by, I'll say that after driving back and forth over the same 30 miles of parched, flat country, usually concealed behind Johnson grass growing in bar ditches, Mother Nature has few charms for me.

To the health worriers who argue that this reading en route is bad for my eyes, I'll say that the pleasure more than compensates for the risk I'm running. How else can a busy farm wife and her husband find time to read?

JEAN CALLAHAN

Cure for tomorrow's boredom

For months my married daughter had wanted to take art lessons. "There's gorgeous scenery all over this farm just crying to be painted," she told us repeatedly.

She had every encouragement from her husband, her young son, and me. But as days slipped by, she ceased to mention the idea and so did we. One morning, she read an article that startled her into action.

The article dealt with the plight of elderly women who were lonely and bored. They had failed to fortify themselves against the emptiness of old age by learning a skill or taking up an interest that would give them enjoyment through the years.

As she finished the story, my daughter exclaimed, "This is not going to happen to me!" She stepped to the telephone and arranged to start art lessons that very afternoon.

ANN NUNN

Lady landowners band together

In our county half the farm owners are women. They are widows of farmers or of professional men who invested in farms, or single women who bought or inherited land.

We women found it difficult to make decisions, what with the fast changes in agriculture, so four years ago we organized the Lady Landowners' Association of Christian County. We have about eight meetings a year. At an all-day workshop we may knuckle down to study government farm programs, weed control, rental agreements and leases.

Our county farm adviser, Kermit O. Roe, helps us line up experts for our programs; we've had the farm manager from a local bank, college economists, S.C.S. technicians and so on.

We find that we are not as timid about asking questions as we would be in larger sessions with the men. At our meetings you hear questions like these: Which is better—to put on nitrogen in the spring or in the fall? About how much does it cost per acre to put in tiling?

Our Lady Landowners are now incorporated and we have elected officers. We charge no dues. Our membership is about 125.

Because of this organization I am able to deal more intelligently with my tenants, hence I'm money ahead.

JUNE E. CALLOWAY

A month for Mother

For the past few years I have tried to make February "my month." I cut housework to a minimum and do the things I want most to do.

I didn't mention my plan the first year I tried it. Later I told my husband and he thought this was a good idea. No one has suffered, because the family is fed and clothed as usual.

One year during "my" month I wrote children's stories (I sold two). Last year I spent six wonderful days in San Francisco, visting a friend. This year during my month I plan to refinish two antique chairs, read at least three books and give a Valentine dinner.

MARY BAGLEY

Wider world . . . adventuring from home

IN MY MORE OR LESS UNTRAVELED LIFE I HAVE DEMONSTRATED THAT YOU CAN DELIGHT IN THE WORLD, AND SHARE IT, WITHOUT BENEFIT OF GLOBE-TROTTING

WHEN Marian Anderson came to the city nearest us, my husband and I went to hear her. Tickets cost $5 each—and even today $10 will buy quite a little sack of groceries! My husband didn't complain, but I felt a little guilty.

The concert was sponsored by a Negro congregation and held at a new Jewish temple. It was almost like being in some strange foreign city. The couple in front of us spoke with strong French accents; the people behind us were just as obviously Irish. To our right sat a middle-aged Negro couple; beyond them, the conductor of the city symphony and his wife. Across the aisle, a man kissed a woman's hand—his natural way to greet a lady. The governor of the state was there, the director of the city museum, the editor of our leading newspaper, our younger daughter's music teacher.

I had studied the program and guessed that the familiar songs and spirituals which came after the intermission would be the part I'd like best. For a while I thought I was wrong; I had never heard anything more beautiful than the songs of Handel and Schubert that opened the concert. But when Miss Anderson sang "My Lord, What a Morning" and "Roll, Jordan, Roll," and finally, "He's Got the Whole World in His Hands," tears came to my eyes and I forgot everything else in the beauty of those moments.

Now years have passed, but we were forever enriched—with music and with an awareness that human brotherhood isn't just possible—it exists. Deep inside us echoes that magnificent reassurance: *He's got the whole world in His hands.*

HELEN T. OLSON

Fishing companions

Many a farm wife cares little about fishing, but has a husband who is mad for it. This can be a dilemma. Some stay at home; others grab something to read and go along for the ride, but are unhappy anyway.

I licked this problem by getting a hobby that requires that I be out of doors. I became an amateur rock hound, and have seldom had more fun. The thrill my man experiences on landing a four-pound bass pales when compared to my rapture when I find the specimen I need to complete a classification.

If you don't go for rocks, there are other interesting outdoor hobbies—painting, collecting butterflies, bird watching. One friend of mine collects and classifies wildflowers. She never misses one of her husband's fishing trips, although she hasn't had a rod in her hand for years.

And what such wifely hobbies do for husbands! Now the guy can say "How about going fishing?" without a single guilty pang.

MILDRED HAWKINS

Cure for loneliness

Have you heard the expression "Live alone and like it"? I do live alone and, believe it or not, this past winter was the happiest in my lifetime. I wrote all the letters and cards I wanted to send. I read books and magazines. I exercised, and practiced piano selections. Bird watching became another interest, and identifying the footprints of small game in the snow. I even partially trained two dogs.

There was time to sew, to cook appetizing meals and enjoy them by candlelight with soft music. Occasionally I built a fire in the fireplace, turned out all the lights and watched the shadows form pictures on the walls.

On cold clear nights I looked at the sky with her bouquets of stars and listened for quiet sounds in the dark. To some this may be loneliness, but I found it a season for self-improvement and enrichment.

EDITH TATE

What's your adventure?

One day I opened my Bible to familiar lines: *I will lift up mine eyes unto the hills . . .*

Our ranch lies in a beautiful valley circled by high mountains. Inspired by the Psalm, I gazed upward with new eyes. The urge came, and grew, to climb those hills—to probe their mystery.

As always, I found John, my husband, a willing partner. How many things we've done together: built the cabin we live in, gone gypsying in the Northwest to work in the fruit and vegetable crops . . . .

Now mountain scaling! We practiced in the foothills, finally tackled Castle Rock, a bare, craggy peak with its head in the clouds. We started at daybreak, and it was late afternoon when we reached the summit. (I literally crawled the last lap, my husband walking protectively on the abyss side.)

What a view! Range upon majestic range—peaks snow-covered, glowing sunset pink. Clouds reflecting a golden radiance . . . .

Since then we have roved rather regularly among the heights. We have encountered deer, curious and hazel-eyed, but never a human being up there. The last inhabitants have long since departed, but their spirits seem to linger on. We find their artifacts—arrowheads, boring awls, knives—all made of stone.

Just about every couple should tackle one glorious, improbable challenge. For us it is mountain climbing. There's a particular elation about toiling toward, and finally attaining, a pinnacle goal.

JESSIE DUNCAN

Shared heritage

Our county's Pioneer Crafts Day was planned as just that—a small-scale fair to honor our first settlers and display the skills of their time. Bonus: a warm new upsurge of friendliness between town and country folks.

This is the second year our county historical society and Farm Bureau women organized the event. About 1300 of us—men, women and children from town and farms—spent a day together.

We watched quilting, knitting, candle dipping, soap and cider making, rug braiding and weaving on looms—all demonstrated by local men and women dressed in early-day costumes. You should have seen the children's amazement as they watched a spinning wheel at work, and the fun they had carding wool! Another treat for all of us was watching an artist make and use natural dyes from plants.

We're lucky to have an authentic setting for our Crafts Day. It's an ancient farm site with the original cabin of logs still containing its original furniture. There is an old barn, too, full of antique farm implements.

These permanent museum exhibits added more than just atmosphere to our day. They brought back memories and invited laughable comparisons with modern practices.

Donated items—old-time foods, corn husk dolls, bittersweet gourds—were sold at the General Store. Sales netted enough to finance the day.

I know I am not alone in looking forward to our next Pioneer Crafts Day. I have new-made friendships (some town ones) I want to renew then, if not before.

BEVERLY EVERETT

Living with history

Several years ago, one of the teachers in our school had the idea of taking her classes on "field trips" to visit at Grandma Wolfe's home so our children could learn how their pioneer ancestors lived. For Grandma Wolfe still weaves and spins. She demonstrates these arts to the children so that appreciation of such things won't be lost.

After these visits each child has a vision of how differently people lived in earlier days. They learn something about the fabrics Grandma Wolfe weaves, see how a design is developed. They watch her spinning wheel which came West on a covered wagon, and on a map they trace the overland route the wagon followed.

Not only do the children briefly touch the past, but this experience stimulates their interest in such a way that it is a push-off toward learning other things. For example, tracing the route of the covered wagon is a geography lesson; history lessons on the pioneer era follow. The thank-you notes each youngster writes to Grandma Wolfe after the trip are lessons in composition, spelling and letter writing.

It is hard to say how many children have visited Mrs. Wolfe over the years—but at least hundreds.

GLADYS B. PRICE

Autumn adventure

If I'm stewing over a problem, I whistle for Vodi, my dog, to come take a ramble with me. His eager curiosity about the out-of-doors takes me out of myself completely, and makes me notice bits of color-ful forest life I'd miss if he weren't along.

Yesterday Vodi and I started out on a prowl in the bright autumn sunshine. Prancing ahead to investigate a tree, he first led me to polished mahogany buckeye nuts, bursting from their creamy-lined hulls. I picked up a few—just to enjoy their smooth "feel."

The buckeyes hinted that there might be fruits on the paw-paw trees by the brook. So we went to find the pendant clusters, growing like pale green bananas among the strange leaves.

I hated to see the brook so low from lack of rain, but I loved Vodi's dignified wading while schools of minnows scurried from his path in the clear brown water.

Next Vodi dashed into a wild grapevine thicket. There we found a fallen log, and another souvenir: beautiful brown lichens in the crumbling wood.

When we came home, I was refreshed and Vodi exhausted. While Vodi dozed, I made an interesting arrangement of lichens on the porch table. The paw-paws were dessert for supper, and our whole afternoon together was something good for me to talk about.

MARY ANN BECKETT

Learning about laws

When my husband died, I found I could not do as I pleased about my land—there were laws regulating the way it should be operated.

I wanted to know more about this, so I obtained work with the state legislature. I found the lawmakers eager to answer questions.

Then, since I was citizenship chairman of our Home Demonstration Club, I often got some of these legislators to come to our club and explain laws to us. We also study pending legislation and constitutional amendments, and our club members are more interested in voting.

Every citizen should visit his state legislature as often as he can, and write to his representatives.

ROBERTA FARRIS

Hearts of stone

Once while I was searching for agates, I found some smooth-worn stones shaped like hearts. Collecting these unusual rocks became my inexpensive hobby. Their beauty endures, and they come to us from a faraway past.

Whenever I happen to be walking along country roads or in parks, I keep my eyes open. It takes some experience to spot a heart partly covered by other stones and dust. My treasures are black and white.

Some stone hearts are very beautiful. I have one that has a flower design on one side; one has a face pictured on it; another a cross. When you find a rock that intrigues you, you know that you have an exclusive. No two are alike; they were not formed by human hands.

MARIE NORRIS

Sounds of the seasons

One drab day last winter, I replayed a tape made in summer. As I had shelled peas that warm day, and sung by an open window, some wrens outside had joined in, singing their hearts out. Cheerful music for cold days to come!

For another tape, I had turned the volume up high and slipped the mike out through the window to record prairie chickens as they fed on a patch of newly-planted alfalfa. Played back, their "bum-bumboo," or (pardon the expression) "you-damn-fool," comes through loud and clear.

Sometimes I listen to night noises while I'm watching television. I set my recorder on "monitor," hang the mike out the window and use the ear plug. Along with the regular TV program, I get fringe benefits —the screech of a night bird, the hoot of an owl, the yip-yip of a coyote or the sound of shifting leaves as some light-footed animal goes by.

Next spring, I'll tape a frog melody for my sound collection.

FERN HRABE

Creative exchange

After eight years of marriage, my husband and I felt the need to get away and spend some time alone together. Since my sister and her family live in a nearby town, I sent this letter to them.

Dear Mr. and Mrs. Reding:

I represent the Weaver Travel Agency and have been authorized to offer you and your family a quiet weekend in the country, all expenses paid. You would be guests in a lovely house with modern conveniences. The house overlooks two beautiful ponds. Nearby woods offer restful strolls. Small fish can be caught sometimes in Caney Creek, which winds through the property.

Your only obligation would be to keep an eye on two small children, ages seven and four, and see that the pets do not go hungry. Pets include one shepherd pup, one cat, three kittens, two rabbits, seven ducks and two horses.

The reason for this offer is that the owners would like to take a second honeymoon. I hope to hear from you soon to arrange a tentative date for your visit.

Respectfully yours,
(Mrs. R. M. Weaver)

The Redings were delighted with the letter. They had a country outing, and my husband and I spent a wonderful weekend in Hot Springs.

HAZEL WEAVER

Homemaker and public servant

In 1969 I served on our county's grand jury. The experience was one of the most informative and satisfying of my life.

We were rather new to this area and I couldn't have been more ignorant about our county government. When you've lived all around the country for 22 years as a Navy wife, you don't get involved in local concerns. I didn't even know what a grand jury does.

I learned that its function varies in different areas, but in general it acts as a watchdog over county government—a snooping committee to probe for facts when wrongdoing or laxity is suspected. Another of its jobs is to bring indictments; that is, bring a suspect to trial if the evidence warrants.

In this county one is named for the grand jury list by the judges of the superior court. Of the 30 or so listed, 19 are picked for duty, the others remain in reserve. We were seven women and 12 men. Our foreman was a successful farmer, who worked long hours and probably neglected his own work in favor of this public service.

At the end of the year, the jurors and their mates had an informal party. We celebrated a year of hard work, achieved with a minimum of controversy and a maximum of good humor.

MARIE ROBERTS

More than we paid for

My husband and I did some grumbling a year or so ago when our state began charging admission to its state parks. We live near one of the most popular ones, and visit it with our children several times each summer.

Gradually it dawned on us that, once we'd bought a "state park car sticker," we could visit any or *all* our state parks. We're bound to get our money's worth! So we've forsaken aimless Sunday wandering in favor of planned trips to "see Wisconsin."

Every state in this nation has a wealth of historic and scenic treasures. The nominal price is little enough to pay toward the development and upkeep of such landmarks.

DORIS BRECKA

Backyard nature walk

"Hey, look at these monsters fight!" our 8-year-old son called from the yard. The "monsters" were miniature—two chameleon lizards, probably males fighting over territory. Suddenly one chameleon wrenched free and scurried away. Now the victor, eyes closed, basks in the sun or laps dew off a leaf.

One day in the vegetable garden, we saw a bird fly from under a sweet potato vine. Under the vine was a nest with *two* kinds of eggs. One egg was speckled, the other marbleized; next day there was another of each. Now the nesting bird—a spotted sandpiper, we think—sits on six eggs, three of her own and three belonging to that intruding cowbird.

A nature walk in your backyard yields wonders worth learning about. We use reference books: The Animal Kingdom (Macmillan, 866 Third Ave., New York, N.Y. 10022) and Birds of America (Doubleday, Garden City, N.Y. 11530). We've also read other nature books suggested by our librarian.

MARGILEE ROZELL

Enrichment without pressure

When we were first married, my husband, Bob, knew nothing about music or art, read little and had no interest in sports. We couldn't afford a TV set then, so I brought mystery stories and westerns from the library, and he discovered the satisfactions of reading.

Listening to my record player, Bob developed a taste for jazz and for folk singing. Recently he surprised the boys and me with a new stereo set.

Sometimes I order art prints from our state library. At first my husband paid no attention to the prints; but when we sent them back, he missed them.

My father-in-law has retired from farming and has nothing to do. (Wouldn't think of gardening – that's women's work. Not interested in bowling.) His whole life has been farming, and he doesn't know how to develop other interests.

I hope my husband will be better prepared for ultimate retirement. And when it's time for our four sons to be on their own, I hope they'll be as broad – minded and well-informed as their dad is.

To welcome a new citizen

I wonder how many people realize what a moving drama a naturalization ceremony is. I have been thrilled to watch people of all races and nationalities take the oath of allegiance to our country in the presence of their friends and family.

The ceremony, conducted by a Federal judge, symbolizes all that the poem at the base of our Statue of Liberty commemorates: *Give me your tired, your poor, your huddled masses yearning to breathe free . . .*

The Extension clubs in our state join with other groups to make this day a more personal and memorable one for the newly-naturalized. If the new citizens have small children, our club members baby-sit during the ceremony. We are on hand to greet the new citizens. Some Clubs present a flag and a copy of the Declaration of Independence.

This is a grand and fulfilling occasion for the new citizens. But it's also an inspiration to the civic groups, high school and college students who fill the courtroom beyond capacity. Because the interest is so great, our club members may participate only once, in order to give others a turn.

To see these well-groomed, radiant-looking people from other lands take the oath of citizenship deepens our own appreciation and pride as Americans.

NANNIE B. PRITCHETT